YO U YO

You Should Have Been with Me When I Was Alone

C.W. YOUNG

PublishAmerica
Baltimore

Second printing

PublishAmerica has allowed this work to remain exactly as the author intended, verbatim, without editorial input.

Jacket, designed, with the assistance of Kim Walters

Hardcover 9781456066949
Softcover 9781456066956
eBook 9781627727198
PUBLISHED BY PUBLISHAMERICA, LLLP
www.publishamerica.com
Baltimore

Printed in the United States of America

An ancient Chineese proverb states, that, "a picture is worth a thousand words"

If so, the cover illustration of this book cleverly encompasses several thousand words, as the artist has captured a myriad of several different pictures, all with a nuance of meanings.

That doesn't mean that you can refrain from looking inside, beyond the cover.

Words, simple but profound, are used to weave thoughts, actions and opinions by one individual, the author, while inviting the reader to *place their self* within the context of what the pages contain.

Are we the same, or, are we different? Do we share one creator, or, were we born by *happenchance*?

Does our pasts, our ambitions our accomplishments and finally, our demise, really vary much?

Or, is it our friends, our families and our faith, that comprise our real worth?

Is it by luck or divine intervention that determines our successes and our failures?

This is a book that other persons having similar circumstances may have written, but did not. All that was needed aside from procrastination was a good memory and seventy plus years of living, the remainder, is history.

You are invited to relax, reminisce and apply a smidgen of leisurely mental participation. Avoid getting too *hung-up* on what seems *too* weird or *too* wondrous.

This book was written *with the purpose* of helping you feel good about life, to put behind any *not-so-happy* incidents of the past by concentrating on and applying what is most important, to live the remainder of your life, in the present, the ***now** of the moment*, adhering to unquestionably confidence that *the future* and *the hereafter, as intangible and indefinable as they may appear*, will ultimately take care of you, me, and everything else.

cwyoung

Acknowledgement

To my birth parents, to all my fathers and mothers that came before, to my brothers and sisters, my extended family, my friends far and near, to my home community of Branch LaHave and to all the neighbouring communities that helped mould my thoughts, actions, character and life, and to all others that I have had the opportunity to meet, work, play, socialize, or be associated with in any way, I say "thanks".

Wanting to see, to know, to seek and find new worlds, while not straying far from one's roots wasn't all that difficult for me. I found them all in the nucleus of the local neighbourhoods. During the years of my youth, *they, and that,* was my universe.

While not fitting the roll of scholar, *in the academic sense,* by acquiring any compliment of *letters,* tangible awards or certificates, I, like most of my family, friends and peers of my era, still managed to do "okay".

I have attained knowledge through books and magazines, of *what others did* and *knew.* I have travelled *in fact,* and I have travelled *in fantasy.* I have laboured hard and played seriously, I have failed and I have had success, I have seen grief and I have enjoyed happy moments.

As the generations that passed before used rudimentary tools and survival skills to change their lives and landscape, I too, not unlike them, feel just as competent and comfortable using a power-saw as I do a pen or a typewriter - my *tools,* to change *my* life and *my* vision of *my* world.

The struggles of my ancestors while seemingly long ago and far away, are not completely lost, forgotten or abandoned. Because *of their being, their will, their spirit, their determination and collective memories* of family lineage history, I discovered that we are not *so far* removed from our ancestors, as many would believe.

My family tree is large and deep-rooted. It remains, growing ever stronger and *Younger,* standing firm, continuing to aspire, providing new vision, positive expectations, inbred determination, maintaining a strong and ever-lasting faith, one that the ravages and winds of time cannot deter the objectives of our birthright, where, even today, in 2010, I and my entire family remain proud to be an integral part of that tree.

To all *of you, past and present*, again I say "Thanks"
CWY

Recognition

What this book is about.

This book contains a mixture of realism and mentalism, of tangibles and memories, of action and spiritualism.

No part of this book should be construed as fiction.

While there may be errors in verbal usage, the intent and content of the message is readily recognizable.

This book may be found in bookstores in their *real life* section or amongst religious publications. **You Should Have Been There When I Was Alone** resides comfortably in either venue.

The author.

C.Wm. Young, once a simple country boy remains a simple *seventy four year old plus,* retired businessperson who *now* considers himself awfully lucky to be still around. I, *CW,* as my daughter **Margo** used to call me, have written scores of business related letters and documents but have never written *a published book* with the exception of a thirty-four page *fun* book on how to play a particular game of cards. I entitled my first rendition **Skunks are Double the Fun.** *It sold approximately fifty copies.* But, because of a string of almost unbelievable incidents in my life I began to wonder if others might enjoy reading *a true tale* about the life of an ordinary human being, *who, has above great odds, survived,* when survival *should not have been* the end situation.

Who do I thank?

Being born, raised and therefore *implicated to life in a rural setting* with all its' quirky language and bizarre characters did much to cast my mental state.

My present physical *well being* can be credited to an adequate diet of *actual working* and *a body filled with inheritance* of both *quality genes* and my mother's ability to pass on her *delightful and contagious* laugh. Thanks to my brother **Arthur** for helping me fill in some of the blanks of *forgotten* family activities and to my youngest sister **Marjorie** for her *candid* tale about two very diverse but enthralling experiences. A special kind of thanks is owed to *both* sisters **Marguerite** and Marjorie for their assistance in providing photos of the homestead and family, including several *originals* of *the tin-type* variety; and to brother **Rex** who provided fodder for *a memorable* article along with inspiration and lyrics for the song entitled Mom's Golden Wedding Band.

I also extend heartfelt thanks to the following members or the **Whynot** family, **Wayne, Doreen, Evelyn, Hazel** and **Wilbert Junior** who contributed openly and honestly, unpleasant memories of their family history.

Editor

Another person who shares *a lion sized piece* of credit, for moulding this book into a pleasure instead of a nightmare, to read, is the verbal **editor Eleanor DeLong.**

Eleanor is non-other than the wife of my good friend and contributor, **Reid**.

Being a retired schoolteacher, Eleanor made time to correct my almost countless grammatical errors, *many* of which made me blush and more that made me laugh aloud *while I was alone* correcting them. I can swear on something sacred that I believe that Eleanor could have written a more interesting and *easier to read* book than I, if only she had had the fortune or misfortune of experiencing my many **Incidents.**

Publisher

The last and perhaps the most important entity to thank are the publishers of **You Should Have Been With Me When I Was Alone**. As writers know or soon find out, publishers are very selective with content and saleability potential. Without a publisher I would still be wallowing in the *outer lim*its.

I thank them for giving me this opportunity, may we both live happily ever after.

CWY

Divine Law

If you would keep young and happy, be good; live a high moral life; practice the principals of *the brotherhood of man*; send out good thoughts to all, and think evil of no man. This is in obedience to the great natural law; to live otherwise is to break the great Divine law. Other things being equal, it is the cleanest, purest minds that live long and are happy. The man who is growing and developing intellectually does not grow old like the man who has stopped advancing, but when ambition, aspirations and ideals halt, old age begins. {Author unknown}

Preface

Simplicity is the opposite of complexity.

I suppose this one line compresses and composes much of what my life was and is all about.

Being born into a family that was honest, hard working and God fearing was not a matter of choice but of Grace. I was blessed from the moment I was born. There was never any want of food, clothing, warmth or shelter. No one in the family ever went hungry and there was always an abundant supply of dry hardwood for fuel.

If any relatives or friends dropped by, they were always welcomed to share in whatever was on the family table.

I was also blessed in having two brothers, two sisters, loving and caring parents and grandparents, all living together under the same roof.

Having money didn't seem so important back then; it was being together that counted most.

I was born, as were my two brothers and one sister, in the original wood framed farmhouse that still sits there on top of one of the highest hills in a community called Branch LaHave.

The Branch, as everyone called it, was a typical small, one road community, situated between the two main arteries of the beautiful LaHave River.

The waters of the LaHave flows approximately twenty miles easterly, going through the centre of the town of Bridgewater, on downward, passing by several other picturesque communities and miles of fertile river valley farmland before finally reaching the North Atlantic Ocean.

The Branch was home for dozens of families and folk with similar body statue, lifestyle and work habits, much the same as every other village in the county and province.

But as similar as the residence appeared physically, the social strength of the Branch came from the array and diversity of their character, both male and female.

All the residents that settled in the Branch and most that settled in neighbouring communities were of German origin. The influx of European immigrants occurred primarily between the years 1850 – 1860.

Although all the settlers came from a like background, many were as different character wise as you might expect to find in more heavily populated communities.

They brought to this their new homeland, hope, independence, pride, stubbornness, and a *committed will* to persevere, all they asked in return was opportunity, freedom, and an honest day's pay for an honest day's work.

Those simple but necessary attributes were the keys to their survival and success in this young and promising, but rugged land.

It was from the many colourful stories told and repeated down through the generations, about *their* dreams and struggles, that *I* drew many of the conscious, creative and defining conclusions about my own life, conclusions that I now wish, before it's too late, to share with others.

Chapter One

Local *differences - International sameness.*

The more we change the more we stay the same.

"It's six of one, one half dozen of the other". Elva Young, my grandmother.

For those who do not know - *we* are closer than you think.

Chances are good that you have never heard of the village of **Branch LaHave**, the village where I was born.

The total "land mass" of Branch LaHave is approximately 2 & ½ square miles

Population presently 150 {originally {est.} about 40}

First settled around 1853 by Europeans, mostly from Germany.

Families settling in *the Branch* have names *now pronounced;* Rhodenizer, Conrad, Crouse, Meisner, Bollivar, Whynot, Wentzell, Veinot, Joudrey, Oickle, Lowe, Mailman, Connell and Young.

The original ancestral names were spelled and pronounced differently but not *so* different that you would mistake what persons were spoken of.

First or Christian names were often Biblical, like Adam, {Adam Hebb} my great grandfather on my mothers side, and Isaac, {Isaac Meisner} the name of my great grandfather, father of Elva, {Elvin's wife} on my grandmother's side of the family. Joseph *Jung* was the name of my great, great grandfather and his son James Elias *Young* was my grandfather on my dad's side of the family.

Recent generations carried Royal names like Henry, my Father, William, my uncle, Arthur, the name of both my uncle and brother,

Harry, my wife's father's name and George is the name of his brother.

My brother Arthur has named his youngest son James Arthur Henry encompassing several royal names in one sibling.

The same name list goes on and on and most families carried on the same naming traditions.

If you pay attention to the names of children born to you and your friends since and around the year 2000 you will find names, especially male names, have gone full circle.

In my present family alone we have a William, a Sam, Liam Joseph, a Matthew and a great granddaughter named Zoë and my sister Marguerite has a grandson named Adam.

My eldest brother Arthur has a son named James and a grandson named Joshua.

The only names missing from several generations past are Isaac and Elias.

The first Youngs to settle on the land where I, and my siblings were born, was my great great grandfather, Joseph Jung {now Young, according to family records}

Joseph married Mary Magdalene Ernst {b} before 1836, that's exactly 100 years before my birth.

Maria Magdalena {original spelling} was born before 1817

Joseph Jung was born before 1817

Joseph purchased the land {not yet a farm} from Christian and Anna Seemon {now Seamone} from LaHave, Lunenburg County, on November 1st.1836.

Records show that he paid one hundred and fifty three pounds for the three hundred acre lot.

Joseph's and Anna had a son, James Elias Young, 1843–1908. He was my great grandfather. He married Eliza Crouse, 1841–1920.

He passed the land down to his son James Elias.

James Elias then divided the land into two sections and passed it on down to two of his three sons, one being my grandfather Elvin who married Elva, daughter of Isaac Meisner, while the remaining half section was willed to Elvin's brother James William Young.

James Elias's third son Henry was given ten dollars instead of a one third share of the farm. Henry left the original family behind and moved to the United States. Little is known about Henry's sojourn, either about his whereabouts or of any surviving family members?

I recall a story being handed down about my great grandfather James Elias dying at an early age of blood poisoning. According to the family grapevine his death was caused from blood poisoning precipitated from the spreading of fertilizer on the land while having an open sore on his hand.

According to his last will and testament James Elias, dated July 20th 1908, being signed by an X, his mark, the will was prepared only a short time before his death in 1908, meaning that the man knew he was going to die and made stipulation in the hastily designed document, providing for his widow {his wife Mary Elizabeth}, as well as the division of his property between his sons, James William, Elvin Harris and Henry.

James Elias Young's son, Elvin, my grandfather, was willed one half the original farms acreage, being one hundred and fifty acres {more or less}

After perusal and interpretation of the letter {the last will and testament} left behind, it appears that the one half of the land mass that was bequeathed to my grandfather, did not contain the original Young house, meaning that grandfather Elvin constructed the house that still stands on Young's hill. The original house was built on the parcel of land bequeathed to brother James William.

Elvin then passed his portion, approximately one hundred and fifty acres, now containing an enlarged house, a large barn and several out buildings, down to his son, my father Henry Wallace Young.

Henry then passed the land down once again to his eldest son, my brother, Arthur who now is the sole owner.

Arthur, now seventy-five years young, has, like our ancestors before, worked the soil and woodlands diligently for all of his life and as a result of his labour; the Young property still produces a generous bounty of hay and wood products.

The future of the old farm is now uncertain, as few, *if any*, heirs to the property have shown interest in continuing the tradition of farming, or of even in residing on the property, as it contains few if any of the modern conveniences and none of the luxuries that most people of today's social order have become accustomed.

Since mom has moved away from the once beautiful and vibrant property, it has lost most of its appeal. What still burns bright in Arthur's mind is an idea, illusive as it is, one that he is presently pursuing, through the legal system. Arthur would like to find a way to retain the property in perpetuity, thus allowing the children and subsequent heirs of the Young family to retain a land bank, one, that *he is sure*, will be vital to them sometime in the future.

It is a novel idea, but over time, where ageing and absence has its way of changing a heart and a great thought into a hard and harsh reality.

Other settlers in the adjacent communities are named Hebb, Zwicker, Wile, Getson, Lohnes, Slauenwhite, Naugler, Feener, Cook, Beck, Corkum, Smith, Heim and Langille

Several miles east of Branch LaHave the settlers there had names like Pentz, Miller, Nowe, Sperry, Romkey, Rafuse, Robar, Haughn and Creaser, while several miles West the names were predominantly DeLong, Mac Kay, Mader, Mosher, Ramey, Silver, Zinck, Wagner, Penney and Varner

Branch LaHave *is not located* in the Deep South *nor is in the far north* of the North American continent. It's sort of in the middle.

If you should take a close look at any map of North America *you will not find Branch LaHave* on it, as the Branch is only a tiny community situated within the rural interior of the South Western shore of the Province of Nova Scotia, Canada.

Even most Provincial maps exclude Branch LaHave.

The Province of Nova Scotia is attached to homeland Canada by a sliver of land linking N. S. to the neighbouring Province of New Brunswick.

On any map, Nova Scotia appears near the north eastern boundaries of the United States.

Nova Scotia can be reached in a few hours by either crossing from the town of Portland, Maine, by travelling over water, to the town of Yarmouth by way of a high speed Ferry called *the Cat*, or we can be reached by driving from the State of Maine, passing over into Canada through Calais into New Brunswick and again take a ferry from the city of Saint John over into the town of Digby N.S.

There is also a longer route by road.

Post note.

Since this was written, a newly elected Provincial government in Nova Scotia has decreed that *the Cat* is no longer affordable by the people of the Province {because of tax subsidization} and it will soon be discontinued. Until alternate water transportation is restored, any travel to and from the United States will have to take the other established routes.

My personal preference of travel is by road and automobile. I can leave my home in Bridgewater, after an early breakfast at home and enjoy having a late afternoon dinner in Calais, Maine. That's how close Branch LaHave and Bridgewater are to the United States.

Nova Scotia is one of ten Provinces that comprise the enormous country called Canada.

Nova Scotia is the second smallest of all the ten Provinces and Territories.

Beautiful and quaint Prince Edward Island has the distinction of being the smallest Province.

You will notice that the geographic shape of Nova Scotia is that of a lobster and that it is nearly surrounded by the North Atlantic Ocean.

Nova Scotia is also accessible by sky.

My home community of Branch LaHave is located a ten-minute drive away from the town of Bridgewater {pop. approximately 8000} and only a one hour's drive to the Stanfield International Airport which is located just outside the Province's largest city of Halifax.

The Stanfield International connects Nova Scotia to many of the world's major cities.

In my fifty years of travelling North America, mostly by car, truck, bus or plane, what I have perceived from those travels, is this. There are hundreds of villages {or there used to be} that have similar looking building configuration, comparable natural resources, land terrain, lakes, rivers and small streams, road and rail network, as that of my home Province of Nova Scotia.

During those travels I have also seen hundreds of small towns and countless small *rural* villages that are, or were, supporting an active lifestyle and social order, not unlike that of my own home village of Branch LaHave and surrounding neighbourhoods.

I have driven by hundreds of barns with roofs *bent by time* and neglect and *an even greater number* of the same vintage farmhouses, some that had roofs sagging, and others that had been given a *smattering* of repairs, providing a few additional years *or more* of usefulness. Most North Americans *can only imagine* the countless farms, barns and houses that have disappeared altogether from the stress of time and weather, never to be seen again except in some faded photograph.

The sameness of natural surroundings and lifestyle was uncanny.

Many of the *original* structures have been replaced by contemporary styled homes with modern storage barns, but a far greater number of centuries old, and older, farm buildings and farmland, have been demolished and rearranged to make space for modern highways, factories and subdivisions.

Whether that is good or bad is left to the memories and the experiences of the individuals who were born and grew up in those homes and on those farms.

Survivors can forgive the hardships, the sweat and tears of the past as acceptable ways of making a life and a living back then, but forget them, never.

The present generation wants little to do with hearing or talking about those times and absolutely nothing to do with actually experiencing similar working or living conditions as did their ancestors.

For a rapidly disappearing generation who still hold on to such diminishing visions, or who still hear the echoes of an earlier life ringing or singing in their ears, this may be the book for you.

It may serve as a tool for relighting dying embers in an *aged* mind, or it might possibly ignite a spark to a long forgotten memory of *times past,* when only old styled country homes, heated by wood fuelled fireplaces and large iron kitchen stoves necessitated high brick chimneys that silhouetted the landscape.

Memories alone may never warm the body but they might serve an even greater purpose, that of renewing the soul.

The contents of these pages may also serve as a gentle reminder to those that have and will, come after, of the trials, tribulations and hardships, endured and accepted by those that have gone before.

I first started by writing down some thoughts and ideas that, *I thought*, others might find interesting or exciting to read about, but as time and pages passed by, I soon found out that I was writing down more of what was *most meaningful* to me, like the memories of both usual and unusual events from *my* youth, the descriptions of my many colourful friends and siblings, the recollections about the old farmhouse home where my two brothers, one sister and I were bor*n*, the comforts, security and habits of being a member of *a large rural farm* family when *all about me* was rural, plus the interesting *if not unique* community of characters where I lived and destined to become a part of.

You may find my experiences, *my* incidents and events, very similar to those that you too have experienced on this wonderful journey called life.

Settle back; relax, read, and enjoy.

Chapter Two

YOU should have been with me when I was alone.

Preamble

Writing this book is a new adventure for me, as I am neither a writer of note nor am I a teller of stories. That is one very dubious beginning; isn't it?

I do have friends that are. It would be nice to be both, but I will settle for one.

If I have a *smidgen* of writing ability it is inherent, used for my personal satisfaction only. Approximately one year ago *I had* written a thirty-four-page book on how to play cards. I entitled it Skunks are Double the Fun. It was written and produced in only a few weeks. I attempted to distribute it by using only local outlets. It was popular for those who played auction 45's, but the volume in sales did not warranted the cost of production and the time I spent in distribution. But it was fun and an experience; I still have several dozen of the original two hundred copies that were created by using the local weekly newspaper services.

I do remember composing several *poems and songs* as a youth, and as I grew older {when time allowed} I continued to pen details about events that meant something special to me.

I intend to include a few pages of *my* poems and songs in this book.

I always thought that *if I had the time* to do so, I would like to try my hand at writing, for in the few opportunities that have *come my way*, I seemed to be able to put my thoughts down on paper *more descriptively* then when I spoke them. Perhaps *this text* will be my first *real* opportunity to prove my theory.

Many people can relate, with ease, long and interesting stories about themselves. Tales that would rival Robert Louis Stevenson's novel about Robinson Crusoe, about *their* personal *real life* experiences, all jazzed or coloured up with bits and pieces, some true, some fictional, of *facts* that have over the years grown or changed in stature *in their mind's* garden of memories. Memories fostered from years of either nurturing or neglect, whatever the case, but every story having a foundation *of truth.*

Other than a few acquaintances, that are presently or had once been employed by the local weekly newspaper, I have no friends who write professionally.

I do have one friend that has written a poem that in my mind should be published.

I am going to ask him for his consent to include it in this book when he returns home from wintering and golfing in Florida.

Hopefully, his writing, entitled, On the Shores of Jubilee, can make-up a fraction of the contents of this book, as I believe that you will enjoy reading it as much as I have.

My friend's name is Reid Delong. He was once a member of the RCAF {Royal Canadian Air force} He later became employed by the Michelin Tire Company, where *he earned and accepted* a management position at a rubber processing plant in the State of Georgia in the USA.

He has since retired.

Reid has accumulated many proud processions over the years. One of his most highly prized is a painting that was presented to him for *special achievement* during the period of time he was employed in the United States.

It is endorsed with the signature and with *personal comments* from the former President of the United States, Jimmy Carter.

Reid and I first met at a church service in our hometown of Bridgewater Nova Scotia where he introduced himself to me. Almost immediately he extended an invitation for me to join him and two of his relatives, his son Steven, and his uncle Garnet Burns, in travelling to the Canadian Province of Newfoundland for a fishing trip.

That meeting happened in 1989.

It was something new and entirely different from what I had previously thought of as a fishing trip, as all of my previous fishing *trips* had taken place *just around the corner* from my home, never too far from where I lived.

From that moment on, everything I ever thought about fishing, changed.

We have plans for another fishing trip, perhaps our last one, scheduled for early June 2009. He and I and two other friends, not always the same two, have spent the past nineteen years, about ten days on average, fishing and adventuring together in the wilds of Canada's youngest Province, Newfoundland.

On the Shores of Jubilee, is in *my mind,* the equal of the famous novel written by Robert Service, who in his timeless gem, penned the story *in poem form,* of the trials and tribulations that he experienced, in *first making* and *then keeping a promise he made* to his friend Sam McGee.

For those that haven't read this epic tale, it's about the friendship, death, cremation and subsequent disposal of the remains of McGee. The setting for his tale was in Alaska, the land of the midnight sun, not unlike the wilds of Newfoundland.

Postscript

My friend Reid and his good wife Eleanor have since returned home from wintering in Florida and upon my request, Reid has kindly given his permission, allowing me to include his poem in this book.

Reid's poem, using meaningful metaphors, akin to those from Albert Bigelow Paine's 1908 novel, The Tent Dwellers, speaks *in almost tangible phrases,* of the experiences that he and I and our two companions Roger Zinck and Barry Naugler shared, together, for several years.

Our friendship was forged from many hours of planning, travelling together by various transportation methods, to get there, then flying in to the lake on a tiny *Beaver* float-plane by a friendly and competent pilot by the name of Gene Ploughman, and ultimately *our goal, that of fishing* the wild and wonderful waters of Jubilee Lake.

Here is Reid's poem, read it slowly and methodically.

Let the message of the words serve as both *a melody to sooth your soul* and *a stimulus to excite* your most adventurous senses, as they have mine.

On the Shores of Jubilee by Reid DeLong

Come; shape your plans where the fire is bright,
　　And the shimmering glasses are-
When the woods are white in the winter's night,
　　Under the northern star.

And let us long for the days of spring,
　　While yet the north wind blows!
For half the joy of the trip my boy,
　　Is getting your gear to go.

Now the lakes that break and the streamlets wake
　　And the sap begins to flow,
And each green bud that stirs my blood
　　Is a summons, and I must go

Now the day is at hand, prepare, prepare-
　　Make ready the boots and creel,

And the rods so new and the fly-book too,
    The line and the singing reel.

Then away to the heart of the deep unknown.
    Where the trout and the black bear be-
Where the fires burn bright and the camp gleams bright
    On the shores of Jubliee.

Nearer the fire the shadows creep-
    The sticks burn deep and red-
While the pillow of sleep lies soft and deep
    Under a weary head.

Now, dawn her grey green mantle weaves
    To the lilt of a low refrain-
The drip, drip, drip of the lush green leaves
    After a night of rain.

Where the trail leads back from the waters edge-
    Tangled and overgrown-
Shoulder your load and strike the road
    Into the deep unknown.

The black rocks jut on the hidden pool
    And the waters are dim and deep
Oh, lightly tread – tis our bed,
    And Caroll lies deep asleep.

Where the path is thick and the branches twine
    I pray you, friend, beware!
For the noxious breath of a lurking vine
    May whither your gladness there.

By the lonely shore, mid thicket deep,
    The she moose comes to bear

Her sturdy young, and she doth keep
    It safely guarded there.

The lake is dull with the drifting mist,
    And the shores are dim and blind;
And where is the way ahead, today,
    And what is the path behind?

Now take the advice that I do not need-
    That I do not heed, always.
For there's many a fool can make a rule
    Which only the wise obey.

Oh, never a voice to answer here,
    And never a face to see –
Mid chill and damp Barry builds our camp,
    On the shores of Jubilee.

Tonight, tonight, the frost is white,
    Under the silver moon;
And lo, I lie, as the hours go by,
    Freezing to death in June.

Now snug, .the camp – the candle-lamp,
    Alighted stands between
And guided by Rog to the camp ahead
    We listen to yarns til three.

Oh, the pulses leap where my fall was steep
    And the rocks rise grim and dark,
Where the swirl and sweep of the rapids deep,
    And the joy of the racing bark.

There's nothing that's worse for sport, I guess,
    Then killing to throw away;

And there's nothing that's better for recklessness
    Then having a price to pay.

Then, scan your map, and search your plans,
    And ponder the fisherman's guess –
While the silver track of the brook leads back
    Into the wilderness.

You may slip away from Caroll and Reid
    And thrive for an hour or two,
But you'd better be fair and you'd better be square,
    Or something will happen to you.

Oh, it's well to live high as you can my boy,
    Wherever you happen to roam.
But it's better to have enough bacon and beans
    To take us fishermen home.

Oh, it's up and down, the Jubilee way,
    Through islands, rocks and waves
With never a rest in our fevered quest,
    Hurry the fishermen brave.

When the utmost bound of the trail is found –
    The lost and loneliest lair –
The hordes of the fish shall gather round,
    To bid you a welcome there.

Caroll has tuned his lute again,
    And the pipes of Roger are near,
For the gods that fled from the groves of men
    Gather unheeded here.

You may pick your place – you may choose your hour –
    You may put on your choicest flies,

But never yet was it safe to bet
    That a single trout would rise.

Oh the waves they pitch and the waves they toss,
    And the waves they frighten us.
And if ever we get our boats across
    We'll have stories to discuss.

It is better to let the wild beast run,
    And to let the wild birds fly.
Each harbour's best in his native nest,
    Even as you and I.

Then breathe a sigh and a long good-bye
    To the wilderness today,
For back again to the trails of men
    Gene flies us on our way.

Once more, tonight, the woods are white
    That lie so dim and far
Where the wild trout hide and the moose abide
    Under the northern star.

Starting from Scratch

Perhaps this poem was the seed that germinated within me, my attempt to do the *impossible;* to relate on paper a life filled with adrenalin and adventure, from the mundane to the unbelievable, a tale that readers of *real life experiences* might enjoy.

Are the events of my life any more remarkable than those of many other human beings on this planet? I believe that the sheer volume, the diverse variety, some being as strange as fiction, could never have happened to anybody else on this earth. That's a challenging statement and it will be up to the readers of this book to decide its merit.

First I had to re acquaint my memory with those events of years past. I then had to reassemble them in my mind and now I will *attempt* to articulate the *incidents* and experiences to others. First a word of caution, many of the events of my life will be difficult to believe, especially to those amongst you who are doubters.

There is also a section for readers *that retain doubts and questions* about *the reason for their own life* and *why* they exist.

I will attempt to connect with you, *the sceptics*, to put belief into you, *the unbelievers,* and in *some simple way,* convince you, that *your life* didn't just happens, it was pre planned.

Some say that we were born on planet earth, we will die on planet earth, and our friends will dispose of our remains, or whatever is left of us, as they see fit. Case closed.

There is nothing more than land, water and sky, that there is no such thing as heaven or hell, there is no higher power in the universe, there never was and there never will be.

Again the case is closed from the sceptic's point of reasoning.

Write this down, *there is a power in and above and around this universe*, and the very same power exists *within* every-one of us. It is a power so immense, so all encompassing, that *no words can be found to explain it.*

I have thought about Einstein's theory, $E=mc2$, quantifying that everything in the universe is energy and that energy cannot be created or destroyed; that *only its form* can be changed.

I believe Einstein.

My mind has wrestled with the infinitesimal size and life of microorganisms, to the infinite enormity of planets and space. The reality of radio signals, laser beams, and every other real and imaginable phenomenon, from, why does the core of the earth remains extremely hot, what is a black hole and how in the name of heaven, can planets much larger then earth just disappear, swallowed up, with never a trace to be found that they ever existed?

Now if you can get your mind around that, how about infinity or eternity?

How far is it to the ends of the universe? Is there an end?

Few people will dare say that there are thousands of other planets similar to earth existing *out there* in *deep* space. Perhaps one or two, maybe three or four, but what boundaries are there to limit *thousands of earths* from existing if infinity goes on *forever and ever?*

How about a thousand million earths?

Who put a limit on the number of planets that exist, and if there is a limit, how can that be? And, if there isn't a limit, how many do exist?

If space goes on forever, as it must, then there can be no giant bubble encasing the existing multiple of solar systems, right?

Just simple questions needing *profound* answers.

"Blessings" was the title I first intended to give this book. When all is said and done and after several, if not a dozen other titles, have been considered, I may in the final analysis discard the other titles and stay with Blessings.

Why would I entitle my first book "Blessings"?

Why not call it, "The Adventure of Living"? "The Unlikely Life of an Average Man", or just plain "YOU", as all three-*merit* consideration.

"Blessed", should have been the title, as no other word or combination of words can explain the *incidents* in my life better than, blessed

The following is a litany of my life's episodes, ranging all the way from mundane to the near impossible.

Was it luck or blessing that I was born of parents who cared for and loved me, or grandparents from both sides of my family, that shared those same values?

Was it by happenstance or blessing that I was born in a country free of tyranny and poverty?

Was it coincidence that so many *unusual* experiences came my way?

Was it providence that provided me with hundreds of wonderful friends?

Did fate provide me with a family who nourished and fulfilled my life's ambitions?

Was it just plain old *good luck* that saved me from the many life-threatening *accidents* that are detailed later on in this book?

Or was it *something else*; a higher power, a power that had selected me *long before the beginning of time*, to experience all of the elements of life, to live that lifetime to the max, including those times of toil and testing, to find out if *my faith, should I have any, would waver* or break?

Some may argue that I have failed that test but that's their problem.

Another book, the Bible, was first written on pieces of parchment before being translated and retranslated, many times over the years. It contains a passage that tells us, that, *I knew you before you were born, while you were still in your mothers womb.*

Who knew this?

Who could have ever, even in their wildest dreams imagine and expound such thinking?

It had to have come from another source, *but who, how, why, when and where?* Think about it.

It's an awesome statement especially *if you accept it* as truth, as I have.

YOU SHOULD HAVE BEEN WITH ME WHEN I WAS ALONE

"You should have been with me"..............

Humans have a penchant for getting involved in things and events, voluntarily or otherwise, all ending with a variety of results. For most people their actions have happy endings. Others, while experiencing similar events, end up having disastrous results.

Compare the results of Swissair Flight # 111 that crashed near my home, about thirty miles away, a few years ago, to that of the recent January 2009 incident of American Airways Flight #1549 out of Boston, now referred to as the Miracle on the Hudson.

Regardless of the end results, the number of tales emitting from both catastrophes ranged from *total despair* for the families of one flight, to only those of *hope and heroism,* from the survivors of the other flight.

While very *different* tales emit from both incidents, numbering in the tens of thousands, *all* have one *similarity*. The individual relating the story needs to tell it to someone else, to anyone and everyone who will take time to listen. It is just plain old human nature to share both good and bad stories with others.

But which story to believe.

The simple fact is, that when there are two or more persons involved in the *same incident* there are always two or more interpretations of what happened, and often there are two, or more, *very different* versions of the *same* event.

Individuals, not involved, but only hearing or reading about such events, have an option, which story or person to believe, and unless there is first hand undisputed evidence supporting the teller's claim, some choose not to believe, even though the event was true.

When notable events happen to one solitary person, the listener or reader has no option but to believe or disbelieve *the one and only version* of what happened.

So what are others, not involved, expected to believe when *incidents* take place where there are no witnesses, *not one solitary witness,* to confirm that the *incident* really happened?

That is what much of this book is about, of having to convince you the readers on its merits, its truthfulness, not about just one, but of several, near death experiences, that I have had, *while being alone.*

This is *my* story.

Why the Title?
"You should have been with me when I was alone" were words mouthed by Basil Conrad to Granville Grace, both friends of mine. Basil moved away from the Branch a number of years ago.

Basil was excitedly telling Granville about an experience that he had while driving his car at a high rate of speed. Whatever happened during that wild ride was *for Basil,* something he had to tell another person about. It was *something* that was true and real, *it did happen to him* but to anyone who wasn't privy to the event, it sounded almost unbelievable. W*ho* would believe his story unless they had been there first hand and experienced it for themselves?

"How could I be with you if you were alone"? Was the question that Granville then asked Basil?

Today, Granville and I laugh often about Basil's statement and up until recently I never took it seriously. Then I got to thinking, maybe its not so crazy after-all. Thousands of people everyday swear that they; either see, feel, smell, are touched by or are visited by *something or someone*, usually attributed to recently deceased family members.

Personally speaking, no matter how hard, or long, or how many times I've searched, and tried to find evidence of an after life visitation experience, I have yet to experience this phenomenon. My friends say that I'm not a good receptor of such visits, perhaps they are right.

Ghosts

"Imagination is more important than knowledge". Albert Einstein

Some years ago when my youngest daughter Pam was assigned a school project *on ghosts,* I quickly volunteered to help her out.

I had heard, and there was solid local, *verbal documentation,* that a man by the name of Wilburt Crouse was haunting the Main building of the South Shore Exhibition Grounds in Bridgewater. Several people had seen Wiburt on different occasions. *During the sightings he was usually* seen walking around inside the main building. These sightings continued for many years *after* his death. Some of the witnesses may still be around today.

And so, Pam and I spent one full night inside this old building, The Big Building, as some called it, sitting up or lying down, all through the *long* dark night. We heard every creak and squeak that old building could muster, all the while listening intently for footsteps, for a voice, or for any sound that might be termed unearthly, waiting, waiting, to see or hear *something, anything* that sounded out of the usual.

We were also anxious for morning to arrive. But we still wanted to know, to find out first hand for ourselves, was it true, did the past Secretary of the Exhibition's Board of Directors really haunt this building?

While several locals were willing to swear on a Bible that they had seen Wilburt long after he had died, we both came away doubting, tired, no better informed, convinced, or any wiser for our ghost hunting endeavour.

Perhaps Wilburt was away that night.

I am sure that there are others out there that can share more positive endings to their *ghostly* stories than Pam and I.

I did see the Devil once.

I was only young, maybe seven or eight years old.

My grandmother had warned me *lots of times*, that if I didn't behave, the Devil was sure to get me; I never really believed her.

But sure enough, there he was, a man with an animal's head, two pointed horns and a long narrow tail, just the same as Grammy had said he looked.

He was standing out in our barnyard nearer to the barn. He was about sixty feet from my visual point inside our house. I was looking out from the kitchen window

Man was I frantic!

My dad, along with the help of others, had a difficult time to restrain me and I was only a kid weighing about sixty pounds. They said I had unusual strength for a boy so small

I was shouting and kicking at them like crazy. Maybe the devil was really after me?

Did I forget to tell you that I had been sick for several days prior and had a fever with very high temperature?

"Hallucinations or *delirium were caused by the fever*," the Doctor said.

After all, I wasn't that bad, *was I?*

The one time I did see something quite *tangible* and out of the ordinary, was some twenty -five years later. It happened early one summer evening while I stood facing Southeast, looking directly towards Gerald Hebb's farm, which was and still is, located on a hill directly across from my, then, place of business.

A fireball the size of a full moon came into my view, and within a second or two it disappeared over the horizon in an arch like trajectory.

Look! I shouted to the person that I was with, but before he could turn his head *and look* towards the hill, the fireball had disappeared from view.

Other people had seen the same fireball as I had that evening and the newspapers reported the following day that it was a phenomenon caused by swamp gas and the sightings of swamp gas in the form of fireballs, was *nothing special.* It happens all the time, the paper reported.

All I can say to that statement is this. My family and I and hundreds of others *have* lived our whole lives on hills high enough to allow us a great view for many miles around in all directions and not one of us has ever seen swamp gas that looked like *what I and others had seen that evening.*

Dreams and Premonitions

"Always do what you are afraid to do". Ralph Waldo Emerson

Two dreams in particular.

As dreams are not something most men speak about; I have never spoken much about them either, but these two dreams *or visions,* seemed *so very real,* and they kept reoccurring.

One dream was about me falling. Not like falling down and hurting your knee or elbow, but of a continuous falling, falling, falling. It was a frightening experience, as I never stopped falling, until what seemed forever, and suddenly, without hitting bottom, I would wake up.

As terrible as the falling sensation was, I never wanted to land, for to have the dream stop by me hitting bottom, I was convinced that I would die upon impact.

Could that really happen?

The few people that I did entrust in telling them about my *falling* dreams gradually provided me with *some insight* into dreams of falling.

It was quite evident that I was not alone in having such dreams, about falling, as it seemed "from my conversations" that many people experience them. The general consensus was, that if you ever hit bottom *you certainly would die.* A sobering thought, but as the dreams continued it finally came to *decision time.*

Either consciously or unconsciously this falling dream must stop, but would I die on impact *once I decided* to let myself *hit* bottom?

To tell you how I dealt with and finally overcame this falling dream might help others who also struggle with finding a solution to similar dreams.

After finally coming *to my wits end,* I garnered enough courage to end either *my* life or the *life of my dream.*

In my last *falling dream* I was again falling, falling, falling, but this time there was going to be a different ending.

I had convinced my mind, my subconscious mind, that enough was enough, it was either the dream ends, *or I die.*

Obviously I never died from the *mind-conceived* impact, but curiously, I never had the falling dream again.

My *courage to overcome my* personal *insecurities* was the answer.

It is a subtle but important lesson that I have carried with me throughout my life, a few times to my near destruction.

The second dream was not so much a dream as it was a *premonition.*

Many nights I would awake from sleep after one of these *half completed* dreams, wondering what might have been the conclusion had the dream been completed to the end.

It was about me, alone, and I was travelling on a major highway with lots of big semi trucks rolling past on both sides of me.

But why was this conscious or subconscious thought, this dream or this vision, always incomplete? What was the dream trying to tell me? Did I or was I about to have an accident? Or was it only a nuisance dream? What was about to happen? Did I die in an accident or did I survive and why in my dream, are all those eighteen-wheelers all around me and why does this dream keep reoccurring?

It was clear that {in my dream} *I had had an accident* and it had happened on a busy highway where many big trucks travelled at high speed. This same vision came to me a dozen times or more over the course of several years. I even mentioned the dream to other people.

It was not until I had one of my near death *incidents* {that I will detail later in this book} did I realize the magnitude of what I had seen in my dreams or visions so many times before.

All I will tell you now is this. After an accident on highway 401 in Ontario, one of the busiest highways in Canada did the dream cease, *never* to return.

Are there times, when through a dream, we really do see a vision of the future?

Procrastination

"Never put off till tomorrow what can be done today". Author unknown

I came home from the funeral home last night. I went there to pay my respects to the family of an old friend that died a few days ago. His name was Fred Arenburg.

In our younger days, Fred and I had played broomball together, first as opponents and then as teammates. That was some twenty-five or thirty years ago. *Freddy* as he was known was a defenseman, big and strong but kind and gentle. He was good at his roll as a defenseman. He was only 57 years old. That's 15 years younger then I am. He died with his boots on, sitting on the seat of some huge earth-moving machine that he was operating for his employer. He had just spoken to two of his co employees and said the following. "I will follow out behind you guy's in just a few minutes". That's when he died.

That's pretty sudden. And that's when it struck me.

I am now seventy-two years and three months old, if I wait much longer to write my book, to tell my story, I may just wait too long.

Today is always the best time to start a project, as we cannot start yesterday and we can never be sure of tomorrow.

I believe my *physical* body is in reasonably good condition and being in *sound mental* health, by my estimation, I still retain a sufficient number of active brain cells to think and write coherently. Having a measure of *common sense* reminds me that I must find ample time, working in sequence with my internal motivators to get *my show* on the road, or at least on paper.

It's a statistical factor that at my present age, the law of averages assures me that I have only a few of life's chapters left in me, so, that being the case, if I have anything worth offering others, that might be of some benefit, I had better get on with it.

I truly believe that you will find this book interesting, intriguing, sincere, inspiring and filled with faith and hope, plus some genuine personal motivational qualities, expressed with *down-home* honesty and simplicity.

At least, that is my objective.

So, with so many bizarre and blessed moments to tell you about, let's get started

The best is yet to be.

I am now and have always been a believer; that *the bar* is still low, for *greater* achievements, in the setting of new records, for speed, {human and otherwise} for the building of faster cars, boats, planes, ships and trains, for higher and greater achievements in the arts and sciences, for *more inspiring* songs, poems and movies, and I am totally convinced that greater speeches and books have yet to be written.

That for countless ages humanity has been rallied, inspired, recharged, uplifted, informed, emotionalized and have been changed and moulded by historical events and entities from the past. We are continually challenged to do better than our predecessors.

That being true, should we then expect anything less from this present age and not hold even greater expectations for future generations?

I think not.

The best is yet *to come, and be,* in everything, and behold these things of which I speak are continuing to happen "as they must" even as I write, and you read this line.

Never put off for tomorrow

Nature never ceases in its journey to continually renew itself, *not even for an instant*, for as soon as you cut, damage or remove a blade of grass, a twig, a flower, or a tree, nature doesn't miss a beat, it just goes on doing what it was designed to do, to *reproduce continually.*

Human life is much the same.

Life, lifestyle and lifetimes are as varied as the elements that make up this universe. No two people are exactly the same and yet, no two are totally unlike. From their human composition at birth to that moment when life ends, we all are a part or particle of the same elements that compose life's greatest mystery, a mystery that has yet to be understood and until recently wasn't even imagined.

It is what happens in *the brief time and space that spans our lives*, "that *time* that exist between our birth and our dying", "my moment-your moment" and everyone *that has been born* has or had their moment, and no matter the duration, it is a moment worth telling others about.

This is my moment.

"The more things change the more they are the same" Alphonse Karr 1808-1890.

You might call this my disclaimer should one be necessary

"To be fore-told is to be fore-warned" so expect very little, in this book, that differs a great deal from the *incidents* of my life when compared to the *incidents* in other lives you may have heard or read about.

Chances are that some amazing, astounding, or almost unbelievable "things" happened to *you* in your lifetime. Has it, and if so, have you told others, and if you did tell others did anyone believe you?

Most humans on planet earth experience only one, maybe two, or perhaps three, *incidents* in their lifetime. I live to tell you about an even dozen.

That is several more near death experiences than the proverbial cat.

These unplanned, unscripted and totally spontaneous *incidents* in this book have happened "almost unbelievably" to just one person, in one lifetime; *me.*

At home on the farm we were told that *cats have nine lives* and we believed it, as we actually tossed cats up in the air just to see them "turn around in air" and land on their feet; which they did, *every* time.

The same scenario applies to a lot of humans, who, no matter *their dire circumstances*, land on their feet or pick them-selves up, dust them-selves off, and continue on with their lives with hardly a break in their step.

I may be one of those *cat type* persons, as I have been tossed around more than my fair share of times and while not always landing on my feet, I am still around to talk and even laugh about some very *unfunny* incidents.

Oxymoron

You should have been with me when I was alone.
The earlier statement "you should have been with me when I was alone" first sounded to me as an oxymoron. The dictionary describes oxymoron as "where a contradiction of words, are placed together".

Earlier on I described oxymoron as "a contradiction of diction and the misuse of verbs" But once I thought the statement through it now has become to me a statement of hope, faith and wisdom, in *the knowing* that *there are profound moments in our lives that we experience alone "or we think we are alone" when in truth we were never more surrounded by the universal powers of love and light.* Some say that we are surrounded with angels, other say it is our loved ones, friends or family members that once shared our lives physically and having "past on" are still wanting or needing to be near us through their spirit.

Some call it the work of the Saints.
*Some call it **God***

In any event there are many personal experiences, some good, some otherwise, that take place when there isn't another earthly soul around to bear witness to the truth.

I am speaking of spontaneous events, not events that are pre planned or practiced for and then performed before large or small audiences, in public or on a stage.

Most unusual events happen only once in a lifetime and they rarely happen before crowds, most times occurring without having another *solitary soul* around.

Those people {the survivors} of such events, live and work among us and share our lives daily. They are the persons who are the *living victims* of *near* disasters, *survivors* of personal and social tragedies, of "near misses" on both land and sea or in the sky, and for *the many*, who experience such traumatic life altering events, do so alone.

But, being a survivor means we must tell someone, anyone, who will listen to our exclusive "once in a life-time" event.

I am one of those persons, and I too have a need to tell somebody, anybody who will stop, look, read and listen to not only one story, but to my several stories of the "once in a lifetime" events that happened to me *many times* during my life.

But before I tell you about those "near life ending" events I should first tell you about how my life began and about the mini events that had *previously* impacted and moulded that life.

In the beginning

I was born at home, as were my two brothers and my eldest sister, in the *original* Young farmhouse on September 25th 1936; the second son of Henry Wallace Young and Lois Katheleen Hebb in the *small* rural community called Branch LaHave.

The *Branch* is located on the west branch of the LaHave River, six miles from Bridgewater, the largest town in a county called Lunenburg {population presently is approximately seven thousand} in the province of Nova Scotia, Canada.

My birth certificate records me as being *Miss Carol* William Young, an onerous beginning, a mistake in the recording of my birth-date, that only came to light some fifty years later when I needed to contact the Provincial Records Office to acquire a passport for travel outside of Canada.

Upon seeing that I was quite obviously a male they {the attending clerks} immediately changed the records from Miss to Mr, but they {the clerks in charge} would not change the spelling from the female C-a-r-o-l that had been recorded on the birth certificate by the local Lutheran Minister, to the *male* spelling C-a-r-o-l-l.

It was not a life altering error but after finding out about this information or misinformation I thereafter signed my name as CW instead of Caroll W.

The question of my gender gaffe comes up in conversation from time to time, always in good humour.

To correct mistakes like this one would be the metaphor for my life.

My grandfather Elvin Harris Young, born on April 8th 1884, inherited his portion of the land on July 29th 1908. As the original home was on the half that was willed to his older brother, Elvin must have built the old styled farmhouse that we knew and lived in.

The house appears to have been built in stages, the kitchen and porch being constructed first with the larger portion of the house being added later.

The original house where James Elias and his family lived appears to have been built by Joseph {Jung} Young, his father, my great great grandfather sometime after he first purchased the original three hundred acres back in 1836.

There is documented proof that Young's have owned the land continually for some one hundred and seventy four years.

This being true, my immediate family and heirs lived on the hill from 1908 until Mom moved away in June of 2009, 101 years.

Verbal, but not documented, has it, that my great grandfather, James Elias, died from *blood poisoning* from having an open sore on his hand while spreading fertilizer in the year 1908 at the age of sixty five

The land was to become home for Elvin, his wife Elva, their son, my father Henry, his wife, our mother Lois and *their* five children.

Elvin and Elva had two other children, a daughter, Beulah, who married Edgar Bolivar and move away from the hill to live in her mother Elva's, home-place, and a younger brother Clarence, died at home as a young man from physical and mental defects that he was born with.

The remaining Young family siblings consist of me, my elder brother Arthur Henry, younger brother, Rex Oscar and sisters Marguerite Alice and Marjorie Adelia.

What's in a name?

Most children or that era were named after someone in the family who had the same name and who were well liked by the parents. It was a way of showing honour for, and affection *towards,* them.

Brother Arthur was named after our mom's brother Arthur and his second name is that of our dad Henry.

My name, Caroll, was the name of my grandfather Carl Archibald Hebb. My middle name is William after that of my grandfather's brother Willie, who lived on the next farm down over the hill from ours.

There is another story associated with my first name that is a bit bizarre. It seems that on the day that I was born a man by the name of Caroll Wentzell was visiting the Young farm. As Caroll and his wife had no children of their own, nor did any of his several brothers, Mr Wentzell asked my parents if *he was to give them* two dollars, would they name "that boy" {being me} after him. Now two dollars was a good sum of money back then and as good a reason as any to name a child after someone. So the truth of my name may not be *so much* after my grandfather Carl Hebb as it was after Caroll Wentzell, the *childless* man with the two dollars

Brother Rex was named after a friend and his middle name Oscar was also the name of a family relative.

Sister Marguerite's middle name, Alice, was the name of our grandmother's sister, and our youngest sister Marjorie's middle name, Adelia, was the name of one of Mom's much loved relatives Adelia Wile.

Century Farm

Around about 1967 the Federal Government decided to honour rural residents by providing wooden signs embossed with the words "Century Farm" for Canadian citizens who lived on farms that were at least one hundred years old.

Joseph Young, my great grandfather was the initiating force behind the building of the original barn and house on Young's hill. They both still stand with only minor alterations. Soon after the recognition programme was announced my mother applied for, and the family farm received the simple but prestigious sign engraved with Century Farm. It is a bit weathered and worn, having withstood over forty years of sun, wind, rain and snow berating it. It still exists where it was first erected, hanging from the side of a, then small, now much larger, ash tree. It tells all who visit there, that 100 years of country pride still exist.

The sixty-foot barn had two large lofts located above the main floor. They were used for the storage of hay. A smaller loft was built in the middle section of the barn and was used for the storage of straw. The lofts were only accessible by way of a wooden ladder. The barn provided shelter in the winter not only for the animal foodstuff and farm machinery, but had two rows of stalls for the cows, calves, oxen and a horse. All the pigs {hogs} lived down underneath the first floor of the stables until sometime in the late 1940's when a twelve-foot shed was built on one end of the barn. The new section was to be used to house feedstuffs on the top floor, with the lower space to be available for another three breeding pens for {litter} pigs.

The hogs {we called them pigs} were useful not only for providing winter pork for the family but also for keeping the bedding {the straw, shavings and the manure from all the other animals} "chopped up" by tramping through it. This chopping up and mixing motion by the pigs aided the removal of the mixture *known as dung or manure.*

The manure was then spread physically, {by hand; using iron pronged forks} onto the hay fields and cultivated land. This tedious work had to be done either in the fall {autumn} or in the springtime of the year.

The manure was removed from the *dung cellar* every year and was a vital ingredient for the enrichment of the soil to produce productive gardens and sufficient hay crops year after year.

Machinery has since taken over doing this *backbreaking* work in most farms

The Omen

"Life can only be understood backwards; but must be lived forwards" Soren Kierkegaard 1813-1855.

The omen of my mishaps began early in my life.

I nearly fell off the barn roof one day. It happened while *the men* were replacing the roof's weather worn shingles.

As the roof of all barns of that vintage were built with a steep sloping design in order to let the rain water and snow remove itself rapidly, wooden supports and planks had to be nailed to the roof to enable the work to be completed safely. I was only about eight years old and should have never been up there in the first place, but I was. And for some reason, I wandered off to an area where the men were not working, an area, where there were no roof supports. All of a sudden the soles of my shoes began to slip and slide out from under me!

There were no rubber-soled sneakers back then.

I was sliding downwards towards the roof's edge, with a long drop to the ground below awaiting me. Unable to stop my momentum, I, in a final act of survival, flopped myself down on my backside and low and behold my body slowed and finally stopped sliding as the friction of my bum against the rough roof saved me from going over the edge.

I never told anyone about this, as nobody would have paid much attention to me anyways.

It was almost as bad as if I had been up on that roof alone, as I couldn't tell anyone without someone suffering some kind of reprimand *from my grandmother* about why in the world was I allowed to be up there in the first place.

Sometimes it's better to remain silent.

Home on the hill

Our homestead was, *and still is*, located on one of the many high and rolling hills *known as drumlins* that comprise the county's landscape. With an unlimited supply of clean air and lots of sunshine, it was the greatest and healthiest place to live on earth, in the spring summer and autumn, but God-awful during the winters.

Most mid to late nineteenth century homes were built on the highest hill available. Those locations were needed more for communications than for any other reason. Communication with your neighbours had to be visual, as back then there were no telephones available in most rural communities.

If there was a home that was fortunate enough to afford telephone service, it was rare and should you have need of it, it usually meant travelling several miles to access it.

In the case of family emergencies a black sheet or blanket was hung on the outside wash-line. This was done to enable the neighbours who were living on adjacent hills to see the black sheet and then respond by going to their aid.

No phones or e-mail back then, but it worked for the most part, and no one ever reported *blanket* overload.

Like every other rural family in those days, we had no running water, not even a hand pump, no electricity and no ploughed roads in the winter.

A water tank was attached as a part of the stove. It was located on the end opposite the firebox, of our old Enterprise woodstove. The volume of water from the tank was limited to only a few gallons and was used mainly for the washing of grimy hands and dishes, and this luxury was only available when the stove was being used for heating, cooking or baking. When the tank was cool or empty, in its stead, a large hot water kettle was always a fixture on the stove.

When there was a need for a large amount of water, like, for washing clothes, a large metal tank called a boiler, was filled and heated on top of the stove.

In the winter the horse was hitched to a V shaped hand made wooden plough and with the additional weight of several extra bodies sitting or standing on top of the V plough to hold it down, away we would go down the hill and around the hairpin curve at the bottom and out the road, clearing away the snow *off the hill* and the additional one half mile that comprised the length of Young's road, ending when we reached the main village road.

Sometimes the snow was so deep that the horse couldn't pull the plough through; then the road had to be shovelled out *by hand*. If hard work never kills you, then everyone in the country should have lived forever.

For interior heat the house had two wood stoves, one in the kitchen that was used for cooking, baking and heating water. The second stove, located in the dining room was used for heating only.

A fireplace was included in the original house design but the frontal area was covered over and never used during my lifetime.

The house would get very cold on a long dark winters night, so cold in fact that sometimes you had to put your head under the covers and use your breath to keep your body warm.

When morning came and time to get out of bed, your feet would sometimes stick to the floor from the moisture of your warm feet touching an ice-cold floor. If you didn't sleep with your socks on, as we often did, you had better be quick about getting those home-knit *heavy woollen*s on.

There was never any shortage of warm socks or mittens for all as Grammy spent most of her time knitting; using wool from the several sheep we had. She than refined the wool into yarn by using our *home owned and hand operated* spinning wheel.

We kids got plenty of outside air and exercise, especially in the winter, just by keeping the wood-box full of kindling and dry hard wood. The men {dad and papa} always made sure there was more than enough "good" wood, *cut and dried the year before* to last through extra long winters.

In the acquiring and preparation of the firewood, the men would first cut and pile it and then let it dry out. We kids would then help to load the wood on the wagon, sometimes in longer lengths; but most times it was sawed by hand, using a Swede saw, into stove lengths of 18 inches.

A single horse or a team of steers was then used to haul the wagon or sleigh to the farmyard where we piled it into the woodhouse.

M younger brother Rex told me recently that he had helped put firewood in *that old woodhouse* over sixty years ago and that it is only now being used, and the sticks of wood are still in excellent condition.

The box that contained the stove wood was located in a porch that was attached to, and an integral part of the main house; it was never a long carry to keep the stove box *continually* filled, as the porch was only about thirty feet from the wood house.

Outhouses

The wood house or wood shed *as we called it* also contained the family toilet or outhouse.

Only in recent years did indoor {*inside the farmhouse*} plumbing arrive on Young's hill.

The outhouse toilet section was built on the lower side of the woodshed. It only had one access door, one window and three different sized *user* holes. The smallest hole was for the kids, the one average size hole was to suit the women and the children's growth pattern, and the one large size hole was to accommodate the adult men of the family.

To my recollection, even though lime was used periodically to keep any obnoxious odours under control, I cannot remember the outhouse ever being used by more than one person at a time. I wonder why?

We used the *out of season* Simpson and Eaton's catalogues for wiping paper. Man was that paper stiff and slippery-especially those coloured pages.

Once in a while there was some newspaper available; that was much better.

Toilet time usage was never wasted *on just going to the toilet*. It was a time for contemplating life, for planning for the future and for catching up on neglected reading, as we kids scanned, studied, and remembered every page of those catalogues for the things that we dreamed about someday owning.

Snow and Cold

"Sunshine is penicillin for the soul" CWY

Speaking of long hard winters, I remember more than one winter when so much snow fell during a storm, that *with some help from a strong north wind*, the snowdrifts became high enough to allow us kids to slide or coast off of the garage roof.

We could access the roof by climbing up on a pile of lumber that was *conveniently* stacked near the rear of the garage.

There were also times when that same North wind created drifts large enough to enable us kids to "construct" long and winding tunnels through them. Talk about fun!

Keeping the farm animals fed, watered and bedded down during the winter months was *seemingly* never ending work. It meant carrying water in eight to 12 quart pails, twice a day, from a well located about two hundred feet in back of the barn.

This tedious and muscle building work was the responsibility of the older or bigger boys, that meant my older brother Arthur or me. The cows drank most of the water that we delivered and we usually had three or four milk cows, along with several large oxen, a few pairs of steers plus one horse.

Boy oh boy, how I hated those thirsty Jerseys.

Farm Food Crops

All farm families planted large amounts of potatoes, turnips, mangles, *barn* corn, dry beans and peas. We needed to, as these crops were the year's *main stay* of food for both animals and humans. A garden was always located close to the house for the women to easily access. *It* contained the household vegetables, including *edible* corn, green and yellow beans, beets, cucumbers, radish and carrots.

Pumpkins or squash were usually planted amongst the potatoes.

Planting the seeds was okay but weeding and thinning the young plants as they grew larger wasn't much fun.

The most enjoyable times in harvesting the crops was when we dug the potatoes, the fun part was just to see how many and how big they were.

My mother has always insisted that potatoes were the dominant food staple for our family and other and that potatoes should have reigned over wheat as *the staff of life.*

Maple Syrup Time

With the arrival of February, it meant the cold hold of winter was about to relinquish, into sunny days and cold, but not too cold, nights, and that meant that the maple trees would soon be flowing with sap, sweet tasting maple sap.

The sugar maple trees on Young's farm were located an eighth of a mile away, for the closest tree, and up to a third of a mile away from the house for the furthermost trees. That meant, if we were going to have maple sap to boil down into thick flowing sweet tasting syrup we had to boil it longer and still *further down,* into sugar. For this we needed to get the raw sap out from the trees and into the fire pot. The fireplace was located between the house and the outhouse. In earlier days the horse pulled the raw sap out from the woods in a large metal container fastened onto the bed of a heavy iron clad sled. That method of gathering stopped because of too much work for too little return. Now, it was either carry it out in pails, by hand, or else there would be no maple syrup or cakes.

I can remember carrying two large pails that we normally used for watering the animals, that when filled with sap, was more than I could carry physically from the distance between the woods and the fireplace.

I spilled more sap than I wanted too or should have, but I hated to leave any maple with a can, that had sap in it, without emptying it in my large pails, even though I was overloading my physical prowess to carry it all out in one trip.

I was a firm believer back then, that it was quicker and easier to make one trip than two, even though I did lose some along the way.

The picking up of the sap was done in the morning before going to school and again in the late afternoon when arriving home from school, a distance of about one mile each way, totalling about four miles per day.

Around the age of thirteen, I had been troubled with the occasional attack of appendicitis.

One spring during maple sugar time, I had an unrelenting attack. Doubled over in pain I was carted off to see our doctor, Dr. Sam Marcus, who after seeing my dilemma, proceeded to thrust both of his hands, folded together with pointed fingers, into my lower abdomen with such force that it brought me springing upright with a loud screech. He decided then and there that I did indeed have an attack of appendicitis and immediately sent me off to the hospital for an emergency operation.

There were complications. The appendix had been ruptured and the poison from the appendix had secreted into other regions of my body.

Carrying the heavy pails of maple sap got the blame for precipitating the attack

I loved maple syrup but I hated Dr Marcus.

Bringing in the sheaves.

Grain was also a farm animal necessity. The fields had to be first mown with a scythe, *by hand to* prevent any damage to the grain-head that might be caused by machine mowing, and also, to make sure the mown stalks all fell in the *same* direction. The fallen grain lay in what was known as swaths. This style of hand mowing was deemed necessary to prevent any future loss of the *now* dry grain-head, before it was to be removed later, for storage, by a thrasher. A thrasher was a machine designed to *beat off* the grain head from the plants stem. The finished product was called oats.

Most thrashers were powered by water being released from a storage dam. The released water would then turn a large wheel on the thrashing mill.

The water that supplied the power to run the mill came from the community brooks. It had slowly accumulated behind a dam, over a period of weeks or even months, prior to the anticipated time for harvesting the grain. The nearest thrasher to our farm was located in the adjoining community of New Canada. It was located about five miles west of our home in Branch LaHave. The fully loaded, heaped up wagon of dry grain was then pulled *to, and from* the thrasher by a horse or ox-team.

We boys just loved those trips to the thrasher, sitting high on top of the world in that wagon full of golden coloured pleasant smelling grain.

There was also a Gristmill located behind and adjacent to our farm, in the village of Midville Branch. It was used to grind wheat or barley into more palatable food for the livestock. I cannot recall our family ever using that service. I only remember the large grinding wheels, hewn from solid granite by hand; lying scattered around the area of the mill site years after the mill's usefulness was no longer required.

Many farms {as did ours} had an acre or two of orchard land providing apples for both man and beast, for most of the year.

Back then the trees were very large and produced a variety of apples from Russets, Bish-a-Pippins and Gravenstiens along with *August* apples, and another variety we called Pumpkin apples because of their large size. To harvest the apples from the trees the limbs were shaken by using a pole {while standing on the ground} to loosen the apples from the tree, and once the apples had fallen to the sod below they were then picked up, with the best ones being stored in the cellar of the house while the small and inferior ones were stored in the barn to be fed, mostly, to the pigs.

While most of the apples were consumed while they were fresh and whole, a small quantity of apples were cut, bagged and stored in the attic *for drying. They* came in handy during the winter *or the following spring and early summer* for making pies and sauces when the fresh apples had been used up, and before the new crop was mature enough to harvest.

The orchard created many long lasting memories, first for being a smorgasbord of different tasting apples, then the challenge of climbing up amongst the limbs of the biggest and highest trees, or, watching the robins gather mud and twigs to build their nests, then to lay four beautiful blue eggs and later still, to see the young robins *hatched and nurtured* by their parents and finally came time to vacate the nest. We always left the robins vacated nest in the trees where they had built them, hoping that they would return again next year. They usually returned but they never used the same nest.

Sometimes the adult robins had to fight off the blue jays when the jays would try and rob the nest of their eggs.

When we kids were around during a jay's attack we assisted the robins in saving their eggs by chasing away the jays.

Some times our best intentions and efforts went for nought as the jays were smart and would attack the robin's nest when we were absent. That hurt.

Sort of sounds much like our own human *social society,* where there is always someone trying to live off the hard work and bounty earned by others, doesn't it?

Attire

"Clothes make the man" Author unknown

Most of the clothes we boys wore were either *handmade* or *"hand me downs,"* descending down from one brother to the next youngest. While this seemed normal for us boys I cannot recall the girls sharing the same fate.

In school I can remember wearing a dark blue shirt {the shirt colours were always dark blue or dark brown to cover the brand name of the flour manufacturer} with the name Robin Hood still visible through the blue dye.

It did not seem embarrassing, *or even out of place*, to wear *hand made* clothes as many of the children in our one room school wore much the same attire.

Mom bought us some Sunday "go to meeting" clothes. They were the very best "boughten" clothes we owned and to make sure they stayed looking like new, we only wore them on special occasions. The one outfit I remember having and liking best was a navy outfit. It was not just the navy colour, for my suit had real naval styled pants, a white shirt with special cuffs, a blue collar, a matching blue jacket with a row of shiny brass buttons on the front and on the sleeves. It was the finest suit in the land. I wore it with great pride, as you can tell.

As we grew older I was blessed with having a grey and maroon corduroy jacket and Arthur had an equally sharp looking maroon gabardine one; *boy, oh boy*, did the girls like those jackets. I never gave it a lot of thought at the time, but maybe it wasn't the jackets that they admired so much.

I cannot remember what Rex wore for a jacket. All I can remember, is, that *one time* while I was carrying it, I lost it. It happened on a Sunday, when he and I and dad were walking back through woods and over fields, heading over to the next village for a visit with our grandparents, Archie and Grammy Hebb, from mom's side of the family

I can still remember him crying out that the lost jacket was the only thing he planned on wearing that year. That made me feel awful but I didn't cry when dad scolded me *hard* for losing Rex's jacket. We later retraced our steps and found it lying by one of the closed gates of a fence *that we had climbed over* along the way.

"Some things you never forget".

Fishing the West Branch of the Beautiful LaHave River

"In the spring, a Young man's fancy turns to fishing" CWY

Tom Sawyer and Huck Finn never had any better times than my younger brother Rex and I had during the several summers of our youth that we spent together, fishing the waters of the west branch of the LaHave River. The LaHave was located in close proximity to our farm's property line and there was never a problem crossing other peoples land to reach it.

We two seemed to be the only ones that fished it as I cannot recall ever seeing another person {child or otherwise} fishing there.

Maybe it was because of the rough terrain or perhaps it was because of the lack of trout as both are deterrents, except to the most energized adventurer.

Whatever *we* were, we didn't seem to notice either.

With *a rod* {I once used an old car radio antenna as a fishing rod} or a wooden pole, a piece of fishing line {usually a piece of cod line that was readily available, as it was used for the making of lashes for the whips to control the oxen} and a good supply of worms, Rex and I would spend hours {daily} fishing away the time. Sometimes we would stay away for up to three or more hours.

We fished all the way from Josh Crouse's mill site to as far down river as the "big" falls at the lower end of Midville Branch, a distance of some two miles.

We never caught many fish but we never lost our desire to keep trying. We knew that those *big ones* were hiding from us some-where, perhaps beneath that fallen tree or that big old log *or* behind that big granite rock, *or*, just maybe, back there under the river's overhanging bank. *Or some place.*

Kids should never *ever* be denied the simple joys of trout fishing.

Jaybirds were never any freer than Rex and I, during those summers of our youth.

Lock Jaw

Lockjaw was a dreaded disease usually caused by a rusty nail piercing the skin and contaminating or poisoning the body's supply of blood. It was something that we kids were all warned about and for fear of not being able to open our jaws to eat or talk, we never ever wanted to get lockjaw.

It almost happened to me, not once, but *twice*.

The first time was when I was running and jumped onto a board with a rusty nail sticking out of it. The nail went up through the sole of my rubber boot and into my foot.

The second time was when one of my brothers was following behind me too closely, while pushing a barn fork along ahead of him. He accidentally ran one of the tongs of the fork up and into the bottom of my bare foot.

Needless to say I survived getting lockjaw {both times} by mom quickly binding salted herring {full length} to the bottoms of my feet. This was necessary, to draw out the poison.

When the herring were *large ones* and your feet were small, you had to have good body balance as I remember walking with a rocking "back and forth" motion.

Besides salt herring another popular home remedy was the mustard poultice.

This was used primarily for congestion or colds that had situated down in the chest {lung} area. The poultice was made up of milk, flour, mustard and whatever else was available.

It was then placed onto the front of the chest and secured firmly by wrapping the upper torso with a torn-up bed sheet. The mustard poultices always worked and were successful in saving me, as well as others of the family, countless times, from prolonged cases of *the croup*.

World War Two

"To see what is right and not do it is want of courage" Confucius

As kids we knew that *war was bad* and that people {including children} died in wars, and when they, the bad guys, had aeroplanes, they could possibly hurt or kill us even though we lived a long ways away from where the ground war was being fought.

As our home was located on a high hill it was easy {we thought} for the pilots of enemy planes to see the light from our oil fuelled lamps shining out through the house windows at night, so everyone in the family was put on alert, always keeping the blinds pulled *fully down* to prevent the enemy from knowing where we were.

The government didn't do much to allay our fears as they distributed a gas mask to every kid in every school in the country; they said "just in case" of an attack.

Looking back it seems to me now that this action was a *laugher* and was complete overkill and that somebody or some Company, probably made *a bundle* of money, producing and selling those masks for our, *none use.*

We tried them on "just in case" we had to use them, but they not only steamed up *so bad*ly on the inside, from our breath, that you could not even see through them. But even more frustrating than not being able to see through them, was, we kids couldn't even breathe through them properly when we put the darn "things" on.

I sure would not want to be a soldier and have to fight a war wearing one of those *ghastly* masks.

Another memorable aspect of the war period was the times I lay on my back *on the cool green sod* on a warm summers day, with my hands placed under my head for support, just staring up into the bright blue sky, watching the planes flying over our farm.

It felt safe and it felt good to see the planes flying over me with their red white and blue circles painted on them, as I knew *that those were our planes.*

A few times a squadron of several large *fighter planes* flew so fast and low over our farm that the leaves on the apple trees fluttered and came loose from the turbulence of the plane's wake

Mom's brother Parker was a foot soldier in the Second World War of 1939-1945.

Parker along with a host of Lunenburg County boys were part of a fighting regiment known as the West Nova's, coming from the South Western part of the Province of Nova Scotia.

He like others from the Branch and from neighbouring communities had to go overseas *to England* to help and fight off those German Nazis. Our grandmother told us *"they* were trying to conquer the whole world". Ironic isn't it, that many of these boys that went to war against Hitler and the Germans had German ancestry.

But not one of them betrayed the land of their parents and grandparents, their "Home and Native land, Canada". They left home and family to travel to foreign shores, to put their lives on the line doing their duty when their country called them.

Parker would return home "on leave" only on rare occasions, and one of those times he shot a deer. It wasn't so much that he shot the deer but it was the incredible distance that he shot at it and hit it.

Parker said to others who were watching, "See that deer over there on yonder hill" and with that he up with his army rifle {I believe that the army edition was a 303 calibre Enfield} and standing up without the aid of any rifle support, he took aim at the deer, which was standing in a ploughed field about two hundred yards away. Those watching could barely see the deer, but with one shot from his rifle, a cloud of dust was seen rising up in the field, caused by the deer falling dead.

With soldiers like Parker no wonder we beat those Nazis.

As happy and carefree children back then, we had no idea just what an enormous debt we would come to owe *every one of those young men* we called "our" soldiers.

Freedom was great; it still is.

In Town Tonight

Saturday was the red-letter day of the week.

That was the day the men {dad and papa} came home from the woods.

Better still, Saturday night meant "going to town night" for many families living in the communities of New Canada, Branch LaHave and Lower Branch. I was about ten or eleven years old back then and along with my brother Arthur, who was about a year older, we would walk out Young's road, a distance of one half mile and wait to be "picked up" by Calvin Snyder's truck. Calvin had a large International log truck that he converted once a week into a people carrier. He did this by installing a large wooden box with high sides, adding several long benches with only a canvas "flapping in the wind" top.

There was little to keep you from falling off the back of the truck so you either had to stand up and hang on to the side boards or sit down on one of the several long benches that Calvin provided There were no Provincial regulations for the protection of citizens being transported in this manner but if my memory serves me correctly no one ever fell off of Calvin's truck.

On clear nights the canvas top was removed and we could lean out over the sides and take in the scenery.

Together with approximately twenty to thirty other "like minded" citizens from the several communities along the route we were all off to Bridgewater for a period of about five hours. We were then returned home again to the same roadside location from where we had boarded the truck earlier. The return trip cost twenty- five cents each.

As a child of eleven or twelve years old it was natural to want to go to Bridgewater, as there is where the action was. It was exciting just to mingle with the large crowds that filled the town's one narrow King Street sidewalk, or to have enough money {15 cents} to buy a hotdog "or two" at Mrs Simmons hot dog stand also located on King Street.

I swear to God she made the best tasting steamed hot dogs I have ever tasted.

Then it was time to purchase an action packed comic book {usually the Two Gun Kid, Captain Marvel, Superman, Batman and Robin, The Lone Ranger or Wonder Woman} to read later on in the week, with just enough time to take in a two hour movie at the old Capitol Theatre. To know years later that *if* I had saved all *or even a portion* of those *iconic* ten-cent comic books I could have sold them and retired at fifty.

What a night; what an experience, what a trip, for a grand total cost of seventy-five cents. But for a kid my age, to have seventy-five cents back then was almost a King's ransom.

I could manage on sixty-five cents, as that was enough to pay my travel fare, get into a movie and buy a hot dog *or* a comic book. Sometimes I had as much as ninety-five cents, which meant that I could buy *some caps* for my toy pistol and another comic book.

This money was *not just given* to me I had to work and earn it. I did this by doing chores around the home like getting-in the firewood, carrying water, helping out around the barn and *for behaving*. To earn any *extra* money I had to wax the kitchen and dining room floors. I know that the family invented the need for excessive waxing of those floors just to give me the money I needed, because the wax on that old worn out oilcloth in the kitchen was so thick you could scrape it off with a shovel. It could have gone for months without waxing but why should I complain, for the extra cash I gladly waxed it nearly every week. The women justified the excessive waxing by pointing out that the men never removed their shoes or boots when they came into the house unless they were going to lay down and rest and found that keeping them on was too uncomfortable or cumbersome. I guess that my fresh thick weekly waxing kept those worn out floor covering respectable and longer lasting under such extreme conditions.

A born Salesman

Much of my adolescent life was supported by sales.
All of my adult life has been supported by sales.

First off, I provided my community neighbours {mostly women} with their *much-needed* household necessities such as needles, thread and sewing necessities. Then I progressed all the way up to fulfilling their greeting and sympathy card needs, like Christmas, Valentines and Easter cards, before moving on to the more serious selling of magazines. I sold the Liberty, an informative 1940-50 era contemporary monthly.

My selling evolution continued with the inclusion of hairbrushes, floor mops, cleaning supplies and perfumes, all *quality* products *from the world renowned* {at least in Nova Scotia} Fuller Brush Company.

For the next several years I sold new and used cars. Then it was on to selling life insurance for "The Rock" the Prudential. Next up was *selling* mobile homes {then they were called trailer homes} before settling into my own business of *selling* mobile {manufactured homes} and modular homes, contracting and building homes from scratch and finally on to the business that I am in today, that of *selling* and servicing Recreational Vehicles.

Selling seemed to *come easy* to me, as I was reasonably successful at every sales opportunity that came my way. My apparent ease of selling and ensuing success in business, was honed years earlier at home on the farm, where as a youth of twelve, I spent a lot of time {as I related earlier} on the road, selling and meeting people. First it was those needles and thread and household necessities, next came Easter and Christmas and Valentine cards; slip in the sale of several magazines, before I finally became old enough to get a regular job.

I bet those ladies in the Branch were glad to see the last of me.

Funny thing is that when I look back I can scarcely recall a home where I was not welcomed. Most families had little money but what they did have, they found a reason to share it with me by purchasing some of my *necessities*.

All of those friendly customers I had *as a child and youth,* have since left this earth but I haven't forgotten *even one of them* for being so kind and generous when I was *that* child.

There is an old saying that goes like this; to be successful at selling, you need "the gift of gab". I cannot remember having *that trait* but I did have a pretty successful line that I used. It went something like this. After knocking and being greeted at the door, usually by the lady of the house, I would immediately say "*My name* is Caroll Young, *you know*, Henry Young's son, from over on, or from up on the hill". I was proud of using the Young's name and learned the familiarity and respect that it carried.

That very same opening line, worked well for me for all of my *selling* life.

Dogs

"*When a dog bites a man that is not news, but when a man bites a dog, that is news*" Charles Anderson Dana 1819-1897

I learned from personal experience never to show fear of dogs, *around dogs.*

I had to crank up my "show no fear of dogs" confidence level every morning as many of my customers owned dogs and I needed to get into their homes.

I first learned something essential about dogs "*especially* essential *to me*" being a house-to house sales person. After coming into contact with most varieties I found that they all have one similarity, they too have fear levels. I learned to *never* carry anything in my hands *that might appear to them* as a weapon or anything that might threaten them in any way, but, more importantly, I also learned that I must never show my fear {as if I had any} of them, as dogs seem to be able to sense your fears and their inbred instincts can often induce them to take advantage of you.

Many dogs will push you to the limits in protecting their turf, but when bluff comes to bluff {like humans} most will back down.

I will relate one hair-raising situation where I tested *my lack of fear theory* of dogs, to the limit.

This incident occurred, not out in the country, but down town Bridgewater right on our dealership's car lot.

My job at the time was selling automobiles and in order to get to the particular car that a customer wanted *to try out,* another customer's car was parked in a position that was blocking the removal of the car I needed.

Inside the customer's car was a large brown dog and as soon as I {or anyone} neared the car, the dog would snarl and bite viciously at the car's side windows, leaving large amounts of saliva running down the sides of the closed windows.

It was a scary scene.

The owner seemed to be missing *without a trace,* as a search for him *or her,* turned up no one.

Vital moments were passing, and if I was going to make a sale to my waiting customer, I needed to remove the car with this "mad" dog in it, and so it came time to test my theory.

I had bluffed several dogs successfully before, but never one as big and as mean looking, sounding, and acting, as this one.

I sucked in some extra oxygen and strolled briskly up to the side of the car, grabbed the handle of the driver's side door and stepped in.

I recall saying something to the dog, something about *keeping its mouth shut,* as I proceeded to start the car {the driver had left the keys in the ignition} and began removing it from its *blocking* position as quickly as possible.

I can vividly remember feeling the dog's *wet nose pressed firmly against the back of my neck,* but the dog never opened its mouth to bark, snarl, or bite. I had taken it completely by surprise.

No sooner had I removed myself from the car and closed the door behind me, when again the dog went back to its berserk barking and snarling actions. Either my theory worked *to the letter* or the dog was stunned, baffled at this *unbelievable opportunity* of having so stupid a person right under his nose {and mouth} and not attacking me.

I, not being a dog, will never know for sure what the dog thought and I have never tried that trick since.

Would I believe you *if you were alone*, and you told me *this* story? Would you expect me to believe you? Hardly, but in spite of what you think, every word of the story *is* true and to this day, most dogs I meet seem to like me, *sensing* that I also *like* them, and also sensing *that I do not fear* them.

"I wonder what a dog psychologist would say to my theory". I think I know what a psychiatrist on human behaviour might say about it, and it may not be printable.

Bingo

There was one time that I was annoyed as hell over something that happened to our family dog, Bingo.

We only owned a few dogs during my growing up years and the two that I can remember best were Bingo and Sandy.

Sandy was a beautiful friendly little blond coloured shaggy haired dog who was immediately claimed by younger brother Rex *as his dog*. Rex built a pleasant looking doghouse for Sandy and put Sandy's name right above the door. That doghouse with Sandy's name emblazoned above the entry door, still sits where Rex had built it, out in front of the old house. It remains a part of the landscape. The weather has taken its toll on the paint used to print the name Sandy, but if you look closely enough you can still make it out.

The incident that happened to Bingo should have never happened.

Bingo was a kind and dependable farm dog that had one habit of doing what most faithful farm dogs do; he followed the wagons *and car* as they trekked around the farm and sometimes around the community.

This fateful evening he made the mistake following dad as he left home with the family owned 1941 Ford car. Dad drove up through the Branch until he arrived at his destination, being the home of Garfield and Hazel Oickle.

"I see your dog has followed you", Garfield *probably* said to dad. "Yes he always wants to follow me wherever I go" would have been the usual reply.

"I can cure him from that habit" said Garfield. "Can you" "and how do you do that?" would have been dad's reply.

With that dad followed Garfield's instruction. The cure was to hold Bingo fast in a firm and in an accessible position exposing his anus, while Garfield dosed Bingo's rectum with turpentine.

To have this happen to a human, as ghastly as it is, would be mild compared to having a dog experience it, as humans we do have arms and hands to reach that area of our bodies and hence able to wash or rinse the area clean of the burning caused by a substance like turpentine. Dogs have no way of reaching their anus except by using their nose and tongue and that would prove to be very ineffective against the stinging of the turpentine that had been poured *deep* inside Bingo's body.

The pain would have been so intense that any such cleansing would have been ineffective and the only easement to the pain would have been to run as fast as he could to the salvation of the brook or milldam and hope that the water would reduce the agony.

That is what Bingo did.

Now we *Young* kids were playing around *the yard* that evening when Bingo suddenly appeared, panting and soaking wet and his coat all dishevelled.

He rushed past, paying no attention to us kids and on into the house, smashing through the screen door of the porch, leaving a gaping rip in the screen behind him. He emerges a few seconds later, still frantic, back into the yard, where he, in desperation, dragged his backside along and against the ground and gravel that formed the foundation of a pathway between our house and barn, with enough downward pressure to cause dust and gravel to fly from his frantic zig-zazing motional behaviour.

Before reaching our house and bursting through the screen door of the porch Bingo had travelled over two miles. Two miles of frenzy, confusion and never relenting pain, and the harder and faster he ran, the more intense the pain must have became, as the turpentine continued to leach deep into his anus.

Bingo's soaking wet body came first from his running and then from swimming through the brook or the millpond above the dam in search for some relief. He was sweating; he was frantic, he was out of his mind with pain.

Bingo probably wondered what he did so wrong to deserve this sort of treatment and why his master would ever do such a terrible, *terrible thing,* to him.

I have asked that same question of myself; *why do such a terrible thing to your family dog.*

Certainly what Bingo did by following after the family car did not deserve such archaic treatment procedures, did it?

I think that dad must have also felt some measure of guilt and betrayal, as I heard him say afterwards, "I guess I should never have done that" meaning that he and Garfield did a bad thing to Bingo.

I cannot remember if that *awful* treatment cured Bingo from following after the car or not. Mom reminds me that it did.

I was too young and too small to defend or help Bingo back then; I am sorry.

After the Bingo incident, I grew a strong and lasting dislike for Garfield.

Imagination

Radio was our only contemporary means of hearing the news and getting other worldly information, as the Free Press only came once a month.

The mail carrier {Elea Weagle} delivered the mail to the community Post Office by a single horse pulling a four wheeled buggy, three times each week. The Post Office was at *the home* of Fred and Etta Veinot. We kids would wait *after school*, on the Veinot's large swing, until the mail arrived. We then gathered in the kitchen and waited until Etta sorted and then handed out the mail.

It was exciting to anticipate, and better yet, to actually receive something from the mail.

At home we had a Marconi radio with a smooth plastic body. It was about 14 inches long and eight inches high, had two buttons, and a large dial consisting of two beautiful blue directional hands. One button controlled the *on and off* power and the volume, while the second button controlled the station location.

A battery about twice the size of the radio powered the Marconi, and it, being so large and heavy that it had to be stored in a strong wooden cabinet, located *one drawer* down below the Marconi. Batteries were expensive and lasted for about six months.

Replacement of the battery took some advanced planning because of the high cost of replacement. I cannot remember the Young's ever having a second radio in the house and the Marconi always remained in the kitchen, sitting in the exact same location.

In the late afternoon, between three and five o-clock the family, *mostly the women,* would listen faithfully to Ma Perkins and the Gillian's. The Gillian's was a continuous daily story relating the life and activity of a rural farm family who lived in a small community somewhere; I thought to be, in Nova Scotia

I always had this idea that Sunny Brook Farm was located in a farming community called Sunny brae located in Colchester County, about one hundred miles from home. I was *probably* wrong.

Why was this programme so memorable and so popular?

One simple reason being, the members and actors on this *satirical programme* experienced *many similar joys and problems as ours, on Young's hill*. It was a well *thought out* programme; even we kids would listen once in a while.

The Marconi also provided the *local and National* news.

I can remember listening as the radio delivered the *war news* from a *broadcaster* named Gabriel Heater. I believe he was from the BBC {British Broadcasting} He would always begin his nightly news programme with these words "friend, *there's war tonight*"

In the early evenings on five days of the week, we children, mostly the boys, listened to back-to-back to back action stories. They were called Superman, Batman and Robin and Captain Midnight. The Lone Ranger came on later in the evening. These programmes lasted for thirty minutes each, with only one brief break during the programmes for advertising.

I remember *the hero* Captain Midnight struggling with his *archrival* Ivan Shark in a *warlike* scenario.

In the western epic, *The Lone Ranger*, it was Tonto, *his* faithful Indian companion, along with a *great* white stallion named Silver that combined to thrill us with their amazing feats of overcoming hate and injustice, by defeating the bad guys, the outlaws.

Several of these super heroes are still around thrilling and enthralling kids today.

As each programme played out for us on our Marconi, we had to listen intently to envision the *radio sounds*, the *tones* of the voices, *the physique, and demeanour* of the people {actors} and the scenes in our imaginations. We had to "make up" the events, portraying them to be *what we wanted them to be*, to be as alike or as different as we the individual listeners wished to make them.

With imaginations being as varied as were the number of listeners, etching the many sound, scenes and events into our mind's memory bank, made for varied conversations afterwards.

With the advent of the visual media of TV there is little need of having to use our imaginations. I believe that the world has lost a great resource *unintentionally,* by *systematically eliminating* the need of using imagination.
"What a loss"

Inventions

I suppose that many of you, like myself, yearned, during the days of your youth, to become famous by inventing something worthwhile, to benefit both mankind as well as yourself.

These, I *want-to-be* an inventor, ideas, did not come to me as a youth, but as a man.

How many of you have lost hundreds of dollars worth of fishing spinners, lures, spoons, lines, rods, nets and hundreds of other *valuables,* overboard, into never to be found again, deep dark water of your favourite lake?

It happened to me often enough that I thought, there must be a way that I might stop this exercise in futility of searching a, look a like, lake surface, and give me at least a chance, to recover them.

The idea fermented after one fishing trip where I lost my friend's prized net.

This wasn't just any old net, it had a collapsible handle and he had fished the waters of Canada both coasts, a keeper of a net if there ever was one.

The invention was designed like this.

A hollow plastic floater containing a length of fishing line with a lead weight attached to one end of the line was rapped around a spool inside the float. The line should have been the length of the deepest part of the lake waters where you were fishing.

The float was large and colourful enough that it could be seen floating, bobbing up and down with the breeze, on the water of the lake, from a good distance away.

Immediately upon loosing your prized lure or other valuables you would throw the colourful bobber into the water where the lead weighted line would immediately sink to the bottom of the lake, like an anchor, leaving the float in a location exactly where you could return immediately or the next day with an opportunity to make a retrieval of whatever you lost overboard or that may still be attached to the end of your fishing line.

Even though I think it was an excellent idea and a marketable device, I never did expand my thoughts beyond the initial draft design of how the device should look and be constructed.

The second *could-be* invention was a perpetual motion engine.

I and three friends, one a refrigeration expert and one a lawyer, had an idea how a wheel might be able to turn continuously without any outside energy created by wind, water or fossil fuel. "Sounds interesting so far, doesn't it"?

The idea was first conceived after watching a toy, a plastic duck, ducking its head up and down into a small pool of water only to resurrect itself and then continue the process endlessly.

The secret was what was inside the long plastic handle that made up the duck's neck and body. It contained a liquid that changed from a solid into a vapour, a gas, immediately upon having its temperature changed by the water. A simple but effective way, we thought, of making a perpetual movement without outside forces.

After the investment of several thousand dollars in the construction of the device, establishing a simple but effective trade mark record, establishing a company called Nova Reactionary Engine, we lost interest in pursuing the idea any further. The device still sits in my basement. A great conversation piece for anyone that eyeballs it and asks me "What's that"?

I like to refer to it as Caroll's folly; just one of several I have had in my lifetime.

School Days

"Education may not make you any smarter but the time spent acquiring it does help to smarten one up, especially about the lack of common sense employed by many teachers"

Case in point. A friend of mine, not named, to protect the guilty, while attending his very first week in school, in *the Branch*'s one room schoolhouse {at the age of seven} was asked by his teacher if he had his ABC's done. He answered "yes". With that his teacher took a closer look at his work page and found that he had missed a letter or two in the *correct* completion of the alphabet and *without warning* gave him a hard smack with her hand over the side of his head. He had given *what he thought to be* an appropriate answer to her question and was feeling quite proud of having his assignment, what he thought, completed accurately. The smack coming from the blind side of his head, surprised *or shocked him* so traumatically, that he was unable to bring himself around to going back to school for the remainder of the year. Consequently, he never did very well in school thereafter, and all his life he wondered why.

He has worked *hard* physically for most of his adult years and mentally he found that he was mathematically *quicker* and smarter, than most people he dealt with. He became a successful businessman and retired before the age of fifty.

I include this story of *physical and mental abuse,* only one of many, *as an example* of the inappropriate actions of scores of teachers that took place in many of the small country schools *during the teaching times* of me and my peers, actions that *by today's standards* would not be tolerated.

Most schoolhouses of my era were constructed with one large teaching room and two smaller halls. One front hall was for entering, removing your boots, with a row of hooks on the walls for hanging your clothes. The back hall contained a white; *two-foot high,* water cooler a large wood storage box and an entry by ladder to the upstairs where *seasonal items* like the Christmas decorations etc. were stored.

The front wall of the school was *taken up* by the installation of an enormous blackboard. All teaching was directed by examples written {by the teacher} by hand, on the blackboard with a white chalk stick and if the lesson was meant for you, you had better get the message written down in *scribbler* quickly, as the board might soon be erased for other *ongoing* teaching procedures.

Lead pencils were the only mode we had for *recording teaching subjects* in my early years, as ballpoint pens were not yet available to us, because of the high costs and *ink pens* were even more costly and troublesome.

The availability of lead pencils, with attached erasers, was a major step forward in the evolvement of *schooling*, as back a previous generation, in my mom and dad's learning years, school children had only *a slate* to record teaching messages The white chalk could be easily erased *when necessary*, but also, *just a easily*, it could be erased, sometimes *accidentally*.

This was before *"the dog ate my homework"* excuse, became popular.

I can recall one *unusually funny* incident where our teacher asked if one of the boys would climb up the ladder in the back hall and retrieve some items from the schools attic, for use in an upcoming Christmas concert.

Pete Mailman was the biggest and gangliest boy in school. He volunteered to do the job.

The next thing I remember is hearing a crash and looking quickly up from my seat, I saw one of Pete's *long* legs, hanging down through the schoolroom ceiling.

Apparently the school attic had no *boarded in* floor covering over the schoolroom ceiling and Pete had only the ceiling joists, which were constructed eighteen inches apart, to support him from falling down through the ceiling panels.

Peter's foot must have slipped off a joist, as I cannot believe that he would have *done that* on purpose.

Pete's gone to a higher place now but we who remain behind remember him well and continue to have a good laugh, at his incident, whenever we get together to reminisce about school, about teachers and learning and about accidents.

Then again, "Pete just may have done it on purpose".

The exterior colour for most country schools was red; ours was painted yellow.

The toilet was located *separate* from the schoolhouse and was located about fifty feet to the rear of the school. It had two separate entry doors and *a board divider* segregating the boys from the girls. It worked well for the most part.

One memorable incident was the time when several of *the older boys* were discovered removing the boards from the rear of the toilet and were caught looking up at the girls bottoms from behind and below.

I remember being part of this exploring group but I guess I was too young to know what I was looking for, as several of the boys got the strap; I did not.

The strap, while not the only method of teacher control, was the most intimidating.

It was either made from a complete beaver's tail or from a piece of mill belt.

Those naughty boys that felt its wrath said *it really stung*, especially if the teacher was strong or really mad.

I can only speak from the tales of others as I guess that I was spared the teacher's wrath {and strap} by being, too young, too innocent or *very* lucky.

Our school held thirty or more children representing up to ten different grades and we never had more than one teacher. Many of our teachers were young women. One I remember, a Miss Zinck. She taught us as a permissive teacher, as she had not yet graduated as a licensed teacher. She was teaching, or making an attempt to teach us, while having only a temporary license. It was not a happy or successful year for either our teacher or us kids.

As teachers were not considered important, in the country scheme of education, they consequently were never paid very much, but as community schools were soon deemed a necessity, by government decree, a teacher with qualifications, however minimal, had to be retained by every rural community's to educate the children.

Assessing the community residents to pay the teacher's salary through a local tax rate system was the simplest and fairest method of raising money, but the local residents having barely enough money to live on, hated any extra taxes that went to paying for *the luxury* of employing a community teacher.

Some things, including a lot of negative things, take a long time to change.

As time passed, teachers and schools soon became accepted *as necessary*, even by the *most cynical thinking* citizens, and most parents were soon convinced that in order for their children to get away from the, not much future, Branch, their kids would have to have a school taught education.

I can remember having two excellent teachers, one was a Mrs Mrytle Norwood and the other, the one and only male teacher I ever had, a Mr Basil Arenburg. Basil stayed with us as our teacher for three full years, quite a feat back in those days.

The strange thing was that both Myrtle and Basil were very strict; so, we had to obey them or else. We listened and we learned. Not too hard to figure out why, when you think about it, is it?

I never liked going to school very much *in those early grades* and by the time I started to enjoy it, *it* was time to quit. I graded, *not passed,* back then, into grade eleven from grade ten as that was as far as the teacher could teach.

I never made any plans to enhance my education beyond grade ten, by attending town-school in Bridgewater, as the extra cost would have been more than our family could afford

The one good thing about not having much schooling is that you always know you still had a lot to learn.

Perhaps that's the reason I cannot stop reading just about *everything that is available* or that I can lay my hands on. I prefer *good* books, true to life stories and autobiographies. I also have a passion for listening to local and world news at every opportunity.

It has been said that, *the older we get the more there is to learn.*

It is only after living almost a full lifetime that I now realize that I still know very little *about anything* and that, in contrast to a few people I have met, I cannot possibly live long enough *to know it all.*

Growing up fast

My older brother Arthur completed grade seven and was considered smart enough to quit school. He was also big for his age, which would be helpful in finding a paying job.

So at the tender age of fourteen, Arthur got to quit school and go to work. The whole family was happy for him, how fortunate he was that he could start earning money so quickly.

Arthur had no problem finding work, as he was willing and able to do *a mixed bag* of things, from working in the logging woods to assist in repairing roads and railroad, do bridge repairs, peel pit props, to cutting and tying Christmas trees.

He once took a job driving a truck on a government job. It lasted a few weeks until it was found out that *our family's* political *leanings* were not acceptable to those of the governing power *at the time* and as a result, his truck driving days ended abruptly.

Arthur had a trait that was foreign to me; he saved most of his money and always drove nice cars.

Arthur was forced to be a man long before his natural time. By leaving school early and immediately going into the workforce, he had to grow up fast.

Work was abundant but only in the physical realm.

Long before Arthur ever reached *the ultimate grade* of *eight* he left school and was entrusted with training young oxen {called steers} to do farm related chores. He delighted in cutting *alder* bushes and *wire-birch* trees down, from within a small fenced enclosure close to the barn, called *the pound*. He then loaded the cut wood on to a small pair of sleighs or a wagon and then delivered his load {by using his newly trained pair of steers} back to the farm yard

The wood was later sawed up in stove length pieces to be used in the house stoves.

I tagged along to help when and where I could, mainly to stand in front of the steers when he stopped to load the wagon or sleigh.

Arthur was and still is one of the foremost ox teamsters to come out of Nova Scotia. I for one have never doubted where he got his early training.

Arthur was a man {or a boy} of action, as I remember once that he had to use the full length of his extended arm to reach down the throat of one of his steers in order to retrieve some *lambkill* that I saw one of the steers eat. I do not know to this day if lambkill really does kill animals, but Arthur wasn't taking any chances.

His knowledge and love for oxen has not waned in over sixty-five years.

Doing man's work took him to Sallie Napthal's pit prop yard in Bridgewater. A pit-prop yard was a place where eight foot hemlock logs were debarked, left to dry and then taken away by train or ship to be used in coal mines {mostly to England} to prop up the mines roof.

Peeling pit props has to be one of the most labour intensive jobs that anyone could imagine but Arthur was young and strong and the pay was good.

Both Arthur and I had a suspicion that convicted criminals who had been sent away to prison, supposedly to do *hard time* labour as retribution for their crimes never worked nearly as hard as did my brother. Some-how that never seemed right.

Arthur has never stopped working for either himself or others; because of his ambition and honesty, he has been elected as a local municipal councillor for nigh on to thirty years and has recently been recognized recently by the Province for his outstanding community work.

Strong Men

"How like us is the ape, most powerful of beasts" Ennius 235-169BC

Every country community had plenty of strong men and some very strong women.

The men "in our neck of the woods" were all strong; they had to be to survive.

All work demanded plenty of muscle, from farming to woods-work, and that's about all there was to do.

I listened as my grandfather spoke about several of the men from Branch LaHave who lifted heavy objects that only a trained weightlifter of today could lift.

A popular past time was to see which man could lift an iron rimmed wagon by grasping it by the centre of the "long-wit" {that's a pole about 16 feet long} that connects the front portion of the wagon to the back section.

Along with four large wooden "hub-ed" wheels, circled with iron bindings, the wagon had a pulling pole {where the oxen or horses were hitched to} that was attached to the front section that added to the difficulty of the lift.

The entire wagon weighed several hundred pounds.

Balance was critical for a successful lift as the wagon had to be lifted off the ground and then swung end to end, before dropping it down in the same but reverse position as it was found.

In recent years a young man from Lunenburg County was acclaimed the world's strongest man. He did this for two consecutive years by making *two* very *different* and *extremely difficult* lifts.

On his first record-breaking attempt Gregg Ernst successfully lifted two fully-grown oxen plus their two teamsters {men} for a combined weight of nearly four thousand pounds. He made this record breaking lift on a Friday evening at the South Shore Exhibition before ten thousand witnesses.

One year later in his second record-breaking challenge he attempted *an almost impossible lift* at the same South Shore Exhibition grounds {The Big Ex}. Gregg lifted two new Ford cars including their two drivers at one time.

The combined weight of cars and drivers was almost five thousand pounds.

This event was also witnessed by thousands of spectators.

To my knowledge neither feat has ever been duplicated.

I know first hand about the car lift as I was one of the drivers and in the ox lift my brother Arthur was one of the teamsters.

Gregg Ernst, {the man who successfully made both lift} gives all of the credit for his great strength to his consumption of sauerkraut, a chopped up and fermented food made from cabbage, and to drinking gallons of whole milk; straight from the cow.

His diet is not unlike that of many Lunenburg County families, who have consumed sauerkraut dishes *consistently* for generations.

"A strong back and a weak mind" was a common saying back then. Most strong men *in modesty* said that about themselves when asked about the reason why they had such physical power. If the truth be known it was not a fair assessment, as many farmers and men with abnormal strength also had a great capacity for mental strength. They were and still are among the most intelligent {most cerebral} residents of the country and you can include many lawyers and most politicians amongst that mix.

Siblings

"To love playthings as a child, to lead an adventurous and honourable youth, and to settle when the time arrives, into a green and smiling age, is to be a good artist in life and deserves well of yourself and your neighbour". Robert Louis Stevenson.

My younger brother, Rex, was the first child in the Young family to attend the *new* Rural High School in New Germany, about twenty miles away by bus. He went there from September to December before he suddenly quit and joined the Royal Canadian Air Force.

I believe that Rex had been enrolled and studying in the eleventh grade when he renounced school.

Rex said he gave up school because he was forced by the teachers to study French as an essential subject, so he, being a man of independent thinking, quit school and joined the Air Force.

Rex has kicked his own ass ever since for being so dumb.

I once shot Rex in the buttocks with my brand new Daisy pump action "BB" air rifle.

I can remember that he was quite a distance away {approximately 100 feet} from where I was standing and I never thought it possible that the Daisy had enough power to hurt him.

He was standing with his back towards me. I took sight, pulled the trigger.

I hit him in the buttocks and the small copper BB stung him hard enough that he cried.

I felt like the stupid fool that I was.

I quickly learned to respect the power and dangers of guns, even *air powered* BB guns.

I got a *good* reprimand and I never tried that stunt on anyone else ever again.

Rex became a long distance runner, *a good one*. He ran in dozens {maybe hundreds} of local and provincial road races. He also ran in the Boston marathon. He never won the Boston race and he never thought that he would, but he still has several cabinets filled with trophies *to confirm to others* and *to remind himself* of his "glorious" running days.

He still runs in competitive races but mostly to keep old friendships alive and for the exercise.

Like the rest of the boys in the family Rex is a great fan of the Montreal Canadians hockey team. He even purchased *a section of a seat* that was removed and *auctioned off* from the old forum in Montreal as it was being demolished some years ago.

Arthur

Arthur enrolled in a Diesel mechanics course that he first saw advertised in a magazine

A company representing the Chicago Vocational Training School placed the ad there.

The school not only taught you top-notch mechanical know-how {by correspondence} but upon successfully completing the course, they {the school} promised to get you a job.

It sounded *so good* that I also enrolled.

Arthur had to pay $250.00 representing the full cost for *a one-student* enrolment but for any additional students {like me} coming from the same household, I only had to pay $190.00. "What a deal", plus a bonus of having a job guaranteed for me at the completion of the course.

Now my being a Diesel mechanic was the furthermost thing from my mind as I wanted to be a "mounted policeman, an RCMP" officer, but at $190.00, this mechanics course was just too good to pass up.

Try and remember that there was no such thing as guidance councillors back then.

We sort of flew by the seat of our pants when it came to vocational selection. Most times we crashed.

On the plus side, most of the boys from the Branch worked at cars in one way or another and I would probably need some mechanical knowledge if I ever wanted to earn a living and support a family.

It was an excellent course; CVT kept their commitment by correcting our completed lessons and mailed back *the marks* of our success with the following lessons. CVT never failed to provide the new lessons on time. I am confident that had I {and my brother} completed the course, that CVT would have honoured their contract in finding us employment.

Alas, it was not to be.

If my memory is correct, Arthur completed over thirty {of the approximately fifty-lesson course} I completed only thirteen.

It turned out that I could never be an RCMP officer, as *back then* you had to be at least five foot nine inches tall physically to be considered enrolment worthy, and no matter how much I stretched myself I couldn't get beyond five foot seven and *one half* inches.

It just goes to show how much *an inch or two* of body height was worth back then.

Some years later while employed as a car salesman at a local GM dealership {Hebb Motors Ltd} the owner W P Logan enrolled me in a truck specification course. Those thirteen lessons that I had *under my belt,* acquired from the previous CVT course, helped me pass the latter course with flying colours.

Arthur is also a runner, a determined one. He ran *to and from* church many Sundays, a distance of about two miles one-way. But it's not the distance that Arthur ran that is significant it's the way he ran. He ran barefoot.

He did something few North Americans would ever attempt, that was accepting a challenge {from me} to run "barefoot" from his home in Branch LaHave to the Bridgewater Exhibition grounds in Bridgewater, a distance of about seven miles.

He was scheduled to do his run on what turned out to be the hottest day of the summer.

His idea was to raise some *seed money and* to increase local *awareness* to filling *the need* of installing a roof over a*n outdoor* show area at the local exhibition grounds.

His effort {and hope} was to initiate community fund raising that would ultimately provide he much needed shield over *the pulling ring area*, keeping both sun *and rain* off the attending patrons.

I tried to talk him out of this *crazy* venture but his resolve was *to do what he said he would do.* As I said earlier, he was determined.

Both he *and his feet* survived the hard gravel, the hot asphalt, the suns searing heat *that* day and he completed it, in "record" time, as no one else has tried anything *close to it* since.

As I write about his efforts, some fifteen years later, the outside *show arena* is still without a roof.

Marguerite and Marjorie The girls, in the Young family.

Back during the early days of my life, it seemed to me that girls were not considered important in the educational scheme of things It was less than essential that girls receive an *advanced* or *formal* education, *other than that* being taught in the local yellow, or red, one-room schoolhouses *that were by now iconic* in every rural community.

"Grade school was good enough for the mothers and grandmothers of the past" They, the girls, could learn all the *important stuff they needed* to know, from their mothers, and in turn, continue to pass their knowledge on to *their* girl children, thus providing *all their basic educational needs,* beyond that of *their knowing* the basic, *three R's.*

The girls *could learn everything else they needed to know*, mostly about household and culinary skills, from their mothers, as other, *more important* skills, *were not taught* in school. *Those skills* were; how to find a good man, and being knowledgeable in providing a *safe and nurturing home environment* for *their* future husbands and children. Those, and other personal skills, were, the responsibility of the mothers to instil in their daughters

After all, *it was the responsibility of the boys*, later to become men, to learn, and earn enough money to provide for the family. It was *a tradition that seemed to work well* for our forefathers and mothers. In short it was an established fact that girls needed less academic skill*s and more "family" skills,* so why not continue with a *proven* tradition.

Marguerite was the first girl to be born into the Kingdom of boys.

She never had it easy, being the first girl-child born into a male dominated family. She was treated much like us boys. When manual chores needed to be done, Marguerite was considered as part of the male workforce.

Marguerite was strong and healthy and was expected *to do her share* of carrying wood and pulling weeds from the garden. She also participated in doing many of the other chores; most were labour intensive and most were outdoors.

If I were Marguerite I would have hoped *and prayed to God* to be taken away {as soon as possible} from this slave like environment that was known as the family farm.

And that's what she did.

Marguerite married young {as was expected of her} to a good husband, Gerald. They have three children and several grandchildren.

Marguerite merits *my greatest respect* for working *so hard* at home breaking away from the traditional farmer wife syndrome and for the many duties and responsibilities she has accepted since then. Marguerite and her husband took on an awesome responsibility in recent years, when they agreed to offer their home as a refuge for our uncle Donald and his wife Maud, when it was vital that *they* find a secure and nurturing home environment in their senior days. It was a commitment and responsibility that is not easily managed or can it be lightly discharged.

Donald *passed away* at ninety plus years but Maud is still going strong at ninety six and should easily reach *the goal* of centenarian, much to the credit of my sister Marguerite.

Marguerite is an honest sincere, caring, sharing, never complaining mother, grandmother, faithful and loving wife.

Perhaps her home training was superior, after all, to that taught in the schools.

Marjorie, the last and therefore the youngest of us five children, came to share our lives later than most.

She thinks *she wasn't planned* {"like the first four were?"}

Marjorie was the only sibling who was born late enough to attend the newly built New Germany Rural High School for a *prolonged* period of time. She ultimately graduated from there. Brother Rex had attended NGRHS for less than three months.

Like Marguerite before her, she also had to live with the boys and experience *daily* seeing the boys "being treated like royalty" But Marjorie was smart enough to know that she had to break free of the *old, stay at home* traditions, of only learning *the home skills* of sewing and cooking, of finding a man and marrying young.

Just how smart was Marjorie? Smart enough to land a good paying government job, including health benefits, short hours, close to home, early retirement with a big pension.

Only kidding Marjorie, but in all honesty, we are all just a little jealous of your retiring so young.

What counts is that we all still love you - a lot

Marjorie is an accomplished photographer. She along with her husband Gerald have taken many *unusual* photos, several that have been purchased by *business* interests, to be reprinted and sold commercially as marketable prints.

Unidentified Flying Object

"Space may produce new worlds" John Milton 1608-1674

If there are any extraterrestrial advocates out there who are craving for another hair raising spine tingling *true* tale about spaceships and body transference, you will love these next two stories.

Marjorie kindly consented to allow me to include both of her {only once in a lifetime} events, for you the readers of this book. In relation to the objectives of "YOU should have been with me when I was alone" the reality of her experiences and eventual consequences, are, compared to mine, eerily the same.

The following are excerpts from letters I have requested and received from my sister Marjorie with verbal permission to use them for reprinting in this book. The letters confirm, in her words, two extraordinary experiences that she has had.

A – UFO, as seen by Marjory {Young} Zwicker dated April 4th 1985 {the Thursday before Good Friday}

It was a very foggy, misty evening.

My husband Gerald had taken his truck to go bowling and after bowling, I took our car and met him at our friend's house {Marie Sarty and Dolly Wambolt} in the town of Bridgewater to play Canasta.

Gerald drove home ahead of me.

Enroute home, even though it was only a short distance of a few miles, the fog lifted and the sky became clear.

As I proceeded up the highway through Wileville {the community just before Auburndale} a bright moving light caught my eye, {looking out my right window.}

I thought it was perhaps a low flying airplane.

I slowed down to get a better look, and I could see *whatever* it was, it was moving very fast and it was not one light, but three - then four lights.

I accelerated my car very fast and drove into my brother-in-law and sister's driveway. {Gerry and Marguerite Cross}- rushing to the door and frantically ringing the door bell, because I wanted them to witness *whatever this was* that I was privileged to see.

Before my brother in law could get to the door, this huge spaceship came directly over their house.

It actually slowed down when directly over the house; *I believe that it did see me.*

It was cone shaped, the surface looked like stainless steel {very shiny} with three brilliant, absolutely dazzling large white lights on the bottom and there were three brackets which came out on each side.

There was also a light on the top of the craft.

There was no noise whatsoever to this craft, just a *swish* in the wind.

If this object would have landed on my brother in law's house it would have flattened it as the circumference of the ship was good the size of their bungalow.

The UFO then speeded up, it was at a height that it could just clear the tree tops and with *amazing speed* flew into the night in the direction of Mahone Bay, N.S. {Mahone Bay is located about eight miles to the East of Auburndale}

My husband, thinking that I had run off the road, came looking for me and found me in my sister's yard.

Needless to say I sat up most of the night looking out of our windows to see if it would return and I could get a picture of it.

I might add that all my life, whenever out at night, I was always looking up at the sky, hoping and praying to see a UFO.

I still keep looking, but have not seen another one.

It certainly was an *"encounter"* I shall never forget.

"YOU, should have been with Marjorie", CWY

The second extraordinary experience that my sister Marjory lived to tell about is "in a way" even more amazing then her encounter with the UFO.

I will entitle it; Body Transference

Marjory's *first marriage* was to a man *who may have become possessed* by a demon or demons. Prior to his metamorphosis, he, *for many years,* was a loved and respected member of the Young family.

Whatever *claimed and changed* his *good* personality, replacing it with an *unpleasant one,* may have been initiated from the stress of his work as a Provincial Fisheries Officer; but more likely, the change was *probably* caused by his personal use or misuse, of illegal {non prescribed} drugs.

He was "a manic depressive" *as acknowledged by his Doctor* and some years later, after numerous highs and lows and many horrors in between, he took his own life, *in a very violent manner*. Marjorie is considered to be *very lucky or blessed* to have survived this *too long* and *increasingly negative*, noxious union.

I repeat for you in her words my sister Marjory's *amazing* story.

Transference

By Marjory Young {Joudrey at the time}

I cannot recall the exact date that this took place, but it happened during the years when I was still married to my first husband.

He had me trapped in the bathroom {the door was closed}.

He had both my arms pinned behind my back with his one hand and with the other hand he proceeded to choke me with the handle of a tooth brush, "he pushed it down my throat"

"He was talking in a different language".

I remember gagging *and I silently said in my mind*: "GOD HELP ME"

The next thing I knew I was standing out in the hallway of our home. The door to the bathroom was still closed and I could hear him saying; *"Where* did she go?"

*I was then given the physical st*rength to flee our home.

How I passed through a closed door I have no idea, but I know GOD knows and I thank Him for saving my life.

You may not believe her; *as no one else other than her husband* was in the house.

"**You** should have been with her, when she was alone" CWY.

Grandfather

"I am fortunate indeed, I knew my grandparents and my grandchildren know me" CWY

My Grandfather, Elvin Harris Young was the King of the mountain. {Young's hill was one of the highest in the county} He was a proud and handsome man, had excellent stature, owned a *commanding* voice, walked with long meaningful strides, had an easy *healthy* laugh and maintained a perceptive mind and memory until the day he died at the age of ninety-four.

He had what is now commonly known as *charisma*. That same charisma led him to be involved in a few uncharacteristically *Young type* activities, but men and women, having the same desires back then as they do now, sometimes stray, looking to greener pastures for a new or different entertainment.

I was married and a father myself before a friend related to me the whole truth about Papa's extra curriculum experiences.

Dad and mom {and Grammy} knew about his escapades but no one else ever told us kids; *it was none of our business* anyways.

What's that they say about ignorance being bliss?

Papa was always an *old man* to me as he was over sixty years old when I was born.

I now can more easily relate myself to papa's age and thinking *back then*, as I can now at age seventy, compare my thinking and my 2009 lifestyle to the how's and whys of his day, while being old, and having seven grandchildren and several great grandchildren of my own.

I guess my grandchildren too will *only remember me* as *always* being old.

Some things never change much; do they?

Another old saying; *the more things change the more they stay the same*, confirms this.

But I don't feel *that old* and I don't look that old {my opinion only} but then again, neither did papa.

In truth, the generations come and go, as they should *and must*.

Elvin could, by hand, mow an acre or two of grain *or meadow hay* like a well-oiled machine, only stopping briefly to drink some water or sharpen his scythe.

He could also handle {*train*} an unbroken horse in the shortest time and drink more rum "straight from the bottle, with no mixer" than most men.

There was *an unwritten law of the land back then* that every man had better be honest and trustworthy in all his dealings with others, as there wasn't any time or money to solve disagreements through the courts. And so both my dad's family *and my mom's family* had little time or respect for liars and thieves.

To give one example of how severe local justice could be back then, a relative of my mothers, a young man by the name of Cyril Rhodenizer {Mom's mother was also a Rhodenizer} was charged with stealing a chicken. Now I do not know much about why he and the two other fellows stole the chicken, but I do remember the family telling us about papa sitting on the jury that convicted him; giving him a *severe* jail sentence.

There were few punches pulled when it came to lying or stealing, particularly amongst family members.

You had better be honest and tell the truth *and be quick about it.*

Papa always seemed to have *some* money and was among the first few people to own an automobile, this from an area encompassing several other small rural communities, some having two cars and other villages having no cars. Pretty elite company, wouldn't you say?

The first car I can remember him owning was a 1931 black Chevrolet four-door sedan. "That was some car" I was born in 1936 so it had to be purchased {as a used car} sometime after that date. I can remember that it served the family well for many years.

The next car on the hill was a 1941 Ford.

I can remember the Ford being used for peddling {selling} young pigs. We travelled as far away as the next county, a distance of over forty miles from home. There wasn't a lot of room inside it, once you loaded in two adults, a couple of kids, and a litter of four-week old pigs; but it sure made for an interesting trip.

The car broke an axel while dad was driving up through *the Branch* one day, with the whole family in it. The left rear wheel and axel came *out* of the rear *housing* and the left rear side of the car fell down, hitting the road surface.

I can recall a man by the name of Earlen Crouse holding up the side of the car to keep the gas from running out of the damaged tank. Gas was selling for about thirty cents an Imperial gallon, so saving every drop was important, and besides the cost, there weren't any gas stations around for several miles.

It was not the environment that Earlen was concerned with when he held the car up to keep the gas from leaking out; it was the cost {a full day's pay was around one dollar} along with the scarcity of gas, as gas stations were few and far between

Gas still sold for less then forty cents per Imperial gallon up until around 1953 or 54.

Our next car was a grey coloured 1948 Plymouth *sloped back* sedan. It was big and quiet and you never felt a bump in it; that car also lasted several years.

Papa's last car was a 1957 Chevrolet Impala V8 automatic sedan that he purchased around 1960. I sold papa this car as I was working as a salesman for Hebb Motors Ltd. at the time.

I think he just wanted to patronize me, and to give me some commission money, as I was married then and had a family of my own to support.

It was a beautiful turquoise colour with lots of chrome on it; it was *by far* the smartest looking car around.

We never thought *back then* that the 1957 Chevy would become the *iconic* car of the age.

General Motors was *flying high* at that time and GM was producing over 60% of all vehicles sold in North America. No one knew, not even the principals at GM that this was near the peak years of their popularity as an automobile manufacturer, and that *they* {GM} would begin a slow slide towards oblivion.

It was no accident that a new kid on the block, a car company called Toyota *has recently* bested General Motors in producing and selling *the most cars* worldwide.

The first Toyota car showed up locally in the early 1960's. It was a black four-door beauty, well built, well appointed, and it did not rust out like most of our North American built cars were doing.

The local GM dealers all laughed at the upstart import; look who's laughing now.

Post note

"Change is the only thing that stays the same" certainly is true in the automotive world.

After writing the last paragraph, several months ago, about the near demise of GM a taxpayer funded bailout has since pumped new life into that once mighty but troubled company. GM has since replaced many of its large gas-guzzlers with improved fuel-efficient downsized cars, while continuing to improve quality. On the other hand, the Toyota Corporation has been a victim of its own success, having production outpace their vigilance for quality, consequently, having to recall millions of their vehicles for alterations, all because of their overlooking a simple but important content; that customer safety must always come before volume and profit. {End of note}

Pop also had a few "*unrehearsed*" *incidents* himself.

Once, I saw him go cart wheeling off the top of a full load of hay, when the horse that was pulling the rubber-tired wagon made an unexpected and sudden lurch ahead. I can still see him go flying "head over heels" through the air and then hitting the soft sod below, a bit annoyed but with only his pride damaged.

His second tumble "that I know of" came in later life when his eyesight was *not as good as was his physical ability* to move, sometimes too fast. He failed to see *an open trap door* to a basement in a home where he was visiting.

They are called trap doors for a very good reason, as they are located in the floor.

Many older farmhouses had, and still have, trap doors.

Papa went tumbling down, this time, and legs first, into the cellar below, for a drop of six or more feet. He got bruised and skinned up pretty badly from that encounter, but again he survived with only his pride damaged, as no bones were broken.

Perhaps Papa's happenings or mishaps were a precursor to what would eventually become a litany of "major" miracles, *in several survival incidents* for his grandson.

Prove me wrong?

Grandmother

"Grandmothers should be called Greatmothers" CWY

Grandmother Elva Mae was the one that seemed to hug and love me *the most,* she hugged *all of us children* often and she seemed so soft and cuddly. Grammy said many times that she would rather die than to have anything bad happen to anyone of us children; and I believed her.

She did the knitting of all our woollen winter socks and mittens, she also spent several hours every school day evening, rehearsing {hearing} mine, as well as my brothers and sisters *next day's* lessons.

One memorable *learning lesson session rehearsal* was the times she spent teaching Rex how to read. His assignment was a *continuing* story about a boy named Jimmy Dale and his dog-named King. It seems that Jimmy Dale's dog King would search to find objects {as dogs are supposed to do} by sniffing them out. King would go sniff sniff sniff and Rex was supposed to repeat Grammy by saying sniff sniff sniff. But Rex, having a bit of a problem in pronouncing *sniff*, would repeat instead, saying "niff niff niff" instead of sniff. The evening repetitions became hilariously funny, something our mother and the rest of us kids have never forgotten.

We still say niff niff niff when we are around Rex.

When the men were working *away*, Grammy Elva was responsible for seeing that the barn work was done. She always counted on the boys to help her.

The men {dad and papa} stayed away for most of the winter, usually working with the Mersey Paper Co {now Abitibi-Bowater} in another County for a period of up to three months.

Grammy was the world's worst "or best" *worrywart*. She worried about everything; from us kids getting hurt or sick to our going *too near* the mill-dam and drowning, or fears of the house *or barn* being hit by a lightning bolt during the few thunderstorms we had yearly.

Grammy would worry so hard that she sometimes got sick and "threw up".

Perhaps that is why I never worry. Grammy did all that worrying and nothing ever happened.

Perhaps I mistook what she was *really* worrying about.

Grammy was also the one in the family that disciplined us most often. She even threatened us with "that if we weren't good children and behave as children should behave, that either God or the devil would surely get us".

I thought for many years that God wasn't much better than the devil, as both of them sounded like *pretty bad* guys and that both wanted to get me.

Today, *I know differently, I know the devil lost out* on getting me.

My wife doesn't share my confidence.

Our grandmother also spouted political logic {wisdom} that stuck with me over the many years.

She had a *negative passion* for most leaders, especially the ones from Quebec.

Every Federal government {in her mind} bowed to their whims and wishes and was always doling out additional money to them. "They would take it all and still not be satisfied" I can remember her saying.

When it came to the issues about the Arabs and Muslim countries she also reminded the family *and anyone else that might be listening,* that "they will never stop fighting with each other *over there*" "because it says in the Bible that there will always be wars and rumours of war, and *it will be that way* forever".

She never could understand what they were always fighting about.

History sure has confirmed her slant on things, hasn't it?

Perhaps it was my grandmother that inspired me to try a few {failed} attempts at politics.

All five children loved both of our grandparents dearly; we saw few of their faults and none of their problems, *as any faults* were well concealed from us kids.

I still think of Grammy a lot.

Grammy was the first on the hill to die and leave the family.

Even today {at the age of seventy-three} when I think of her, I never feel quite alone.

A shocking experience for me was the time I was making what turned out to be my last visit to the hospital to visit Grammy. She was confined to a bed in the old Dawson Memorial hospital in Bridgewater.

I parked my car and went jogging up the wide, white, wooden steps to the hospital and continued to walk briskly down *the only aisle* towards her room, happy and light hearted as any young person might be under the circumstances.

I intended to visit with Grammy; *if only for a brief moment*. Instead, I found her dead; and worse, if anything could be worse, she was completely wrapped up from the top of her head to the tips of her toes, in white linen.

When I was a little boy Grammy seemed to be such a big and strong woman, one moment filled with energy and ambition, the next quiet and loving. Now *in death*, bound tightly *like a mummy*, she appeared so small.

Why had no one stopped me and told me of her passing on my way up and into her room? Perhaps I moved too fast for anyone to stop me. I was ill prepared for that experience.

As no one else in the family knew that she had died, I phoned them to break the news. I was hurt, I was mad, I was sorry: *I still am*.

No one was with Grammy when she died. No one should die alone.

No more hugs and kisses. It still hurts.

Dad

Dad was a small man in physical stature but he sure had a big heart, one that kept him doing "big man's" work, at home on the farm or in the lumbering woods, for close to seventy years.

He along with a partner, spent several months of the year cutting, *delimbing* and sometime yarding the logs out. {*"Yarding them,"* meant hauling the fallen trees out of the woods} The act of felling the gigantic hemlock trees, and then sawing them up in *yard-able* lengths using only an axe and a hand pulled Swede or crosscut saw to do the job, was daunting, especially for a small man like dad, in the heat of the summer.

I can only recall one *relatively* serious accident that dad had while working away in the woods and that was the time he came home from the Mersey woods with his face all bloodied up. He had cut off a spring pole, a small tree that was bent over and was being held fast by another object. When he cut the small tree off, it sprang up fast and forceful and hit him under his nose with an upward trajectory.

It was a severe blow but dad shrugged it off and was soon back doing what he had to do, cutting hemlock, earning a living, supporting his family.

Most responsible husbands and fathers of that period had little leisure time to spend with their families, because of *never ending farm related responsibilities,* and when they did find time, it meant working away from the farm at whatever job was available, at whatever compensation it paid, all *in order to provide* some money for *store bought* necessities not provided from farm produced products.

The memorable fun times were when he and I, Rex and Arthur, would go trout fishing down below the old milldam. We all had our poles and lines with hooks attached. Dad baited our hooks with rain-worms and then placed us up, standing us far enough apart from each other so that if a fish did bite at one of our hooks, that in our excitement to pull the fish out of the water we didn't snap our line out too fast and hit *one or the other* in the face, or worse yet to be hit in the eye by a wayward hook.

I have fished quite a bit since then and can confirm that old habits die-hard. I still retain the habit of *jerking my line* out of the water as soon as I feel a fish bite.

We usually went home proud, carrying with us a seven or eight inch trout or two.

Another exciting time around the farm was when it was announced that we were going to be having homemade ice cream.

Having homemade ice cream meant that it had to be wintertime and the way dad made it, there also had to be a snow bank around.

At our home, we never had one of those new fangled hand powered crank operated ice-cream freezers, although, I believe that they *were around* and available at the time *"at a price"* from the town's hardware stores.

What dad used instead, was an eight-quart metal pail.

The ingredients of cream, sugar and flavouring, usually vanilla, because the Young's had no coffee available, as we did not drink coffee, were mixed together by stirring all the ingredients together inside the pail. Then the *covered* pail would be placed into a hole in a snow bank and dad would begin moving the pail back and forth until the cream was set up, and eventually frozen into ice cream.

It seemed to take forever. It probably seemed even longer for dad, who was creating all the gyrations {the back and forth motions in the snow} to eventually freeze the cream.

With the invention of electrical operated freezers, we, the ice cream eaters of today, can never come close to appreciating how much effort it took to make it the *original-old fashioned* way.

Dad *worked hard* up until a few years before he died, he was a man of honesty and of excellent character, he had a powerful faith and unwavering belief in God, a man with *uncommon* common sense; a man that any child would be proud to called "father".

He knew when his time and usefulness on earth was complete; he was willing and ready to move on..........but Dad, we still miss you".

Dad bought a white gold wedding band for mom when they were *getting* married.

She lost the ring in the snow while crossing the wooden pole bridge that spanned the local brook down below the shingle mill. The ring slipped, unnoticed, off her finger when she stopped to remove her gloves to *adjust* the clothing on one of us kids, while crossing over the bridge and brook on our way to church.

She never expected to see the ring again, when, several years later it was returned to her under the most unbelievable set of circumstances.

Brother Rex started to write a song about the missing ring, He got bogged down and ask me for some assistance, and between the two of us, here is what was composed *and sang* to the family several times while dad was still with us.

Mom's Golden Wedding Band

My mother wore a wedding band, quite simple by design
It became a symbol; the whole world to remind
Of love my father gave her when they exchanged their vows.
But now the ring was missing, she knew not where or how.

A gypsy fortune-teller who was grey and old
Said worry not dear lady, you will find the ring of gold.
My mother failed to understand the story she foretold
Long afterwards remembered the mill and bridge of poles.

Mom stopped upon the bridge one day to fix the children's clothes
The ring slipped off her finger and fell into the snow
Then came the gentle rains of spring to melt the winter cold
The ring fell through a crevice towards the stream below.

A shaving from a shingle like a mighty saving arm
Firmly held the ring secure, safe from natures harm
Young lovers strolling over the stream, first thinking it was sand
To see it shine and then to find, mom's golden wedding band

Two winters long had passed beyond, when first the story heard
Someone was known a ring to find; they knew no other word
Dad's heartbeat fast, his mind was sure; he knew that it must be
The ring they found so long ago fulfilled the prophecy.

Sixty five years have come and gone, ten thousand memories
Five kids and more are here to share this anniversary
The symbol of their love once lost, again upon her hand
Lives on forever from that day in one gold wedding band

For love to have a reason, God surely plays a part
Through all the many seasons to hold two sharing hearts
The circle still unbroken, not ours to understand
Love's universal symbol; mom's golden wedding band

This song, written by Rex and me, was given to mom and dad in a glass-covered frame on December 5th 1999. Although there is no-one living in the old house at this time, the song along with hundreds of family pictures and other family keepsakes, still adorn every available space on the walls of the living room.

Mom

We children were always and still remain mom's pride and joy.

Mom was always dedicated in making sure the children were kept physically clean and always had clean clothes to wear. I can very clearly remember her saying to me and to my brothers and sisters {every-time} before leaving the house "make sure you wash *behind your ears* and make sure that you have clean under pants on, what if you should happen to get into an accident?"

Mom was our greatest source of family strength and dependability by always *being there* whenever we came home. She was totally dedicated to the well being of us children.

How else could she have lived in one house with five kids, another woman {our grandmother} two men, several cats and a dog?

Mom's time was taken up by either baking large loaves of white bread, patching torn or worn clothes, scrubbing the children's necks to make sure they were clean, or else she was washing our dirty clothes. This was a *none-stop* job with no pay other than the personal satisfaction she got from *just doing it* for us kids.

We bought baking flour by the one hundred pound bag, either Robin Hood or Five Roses, and mom must have had strong arms and hands, as I can still remember her mixing, rolling, kneading, and then pounding the readied flour dough into what turned out to be, at least six to eight large loaves of great textured and tasting bread from each and every batch.

The bread didn't last long as it always turned out excellent and if any of us could sneak a slice or two of it when it was fresh, and hot, right out of the oven, then to coat it *thick* with homemade butter or jam, made it even better, *if that was possible.*

Patching the holes in our shirts, pants and jackets was one big job. Our old worn out pants and shirts were always saved, and the best pieces were then used to patch the rips and tears of the ones that we were currently wearing. Mom was an excellent "patcher" matching up the torn garment with a *like piece* of material so as to make the finished product look *original* and *acceptable* to her or anyone else that might see it.

Back then women took a lot of pride in their patching ability.

For many years mom washed everything, every sock, shirt, towel, pants and bedding by hand, using only a scrubbing board to remove the dirt. To get the excess water out, she used a hand-operated wringer to squeeze out the soiled water before hanging the wet clothes out on the wash-line, which was located outside, near the back of the house. The wind would do the rest.

It was not until years later that the family was able to afford a gas powered washing machine. It was purchased from Fred Rhodenizer's Electrical Store in Bridgewater.

It was paid for "on time" by dad, with Fred co-signing a contract with him at the Canadian Imperial Bank of Commerce on King Street.

Fred also made a verbal contract with dad that if we were ever to have electricity "put in" at Young's hill, that he would exchange the gas operated engine from the original washer with a new electrical motor.

It was several years after the original washing machine sale when the power finally came to Young's hill. Fred kept his promise.

It was one great day when that gas engine was finally converted to electricity as the power poles and lines found their way in the one-half mile distance from the main trunk line up and connected to the Young's home.

Now we too could have many of the new fangled utilities that our friends had, like brighter lights, an electric radio and mom could now have an electric *steam* iron.

Getting back to the gas washing machine, I remember the exhaust hose from the washer being extended up and out through the kitchen window and the *foot type push pedal* {like that of a motorcycle} was necessary in order to start the engine It had to be pushed down hard and fast by using the power of only one leg. It was relatively easy for a man to start but difficult for a woman.

Most times it started easily but there were times when it took several or more pushes to get it started.

It certainly was a happy day for mom when she finally got rid of that smelly {dangerous} and difficult to start gas powered washer.

Mom still hasn't parted with her old wringer type washer, it can still be found sitting out in the porch of the {now vacant} house.

There was one period of time that mom did not get off the hill {except to go to church} *for over a year.*

Mom wasn't quite as naive as she put on, when she sometimes insisted that the United States really wasn't telling the truth when they said they put a man on the moon back in the early 1960's

The country still had lots of sceptics about *whether the Earth was round or flat,* as it looked flat, so far as anyone could see. Remember this was in the mid to late 1940's.

TV and space travel were not the daily conversation items.

Mom was a very resourceful woman, one who saved everything from wastewater, plastic and paper bags, cards, papers, all sorts of bottles and containers and just about everything else that she came in contact with.

She also had a great perception of *things and events*, and she could read people's actions like a book; she still can.

The one and only time I can remember of seeing mom cry was the time she had an enormous abscess develop in the roof of her mouth. What caused it I do not know?

It grew larger and more painful as time went by. There seemed to be little or no interest, or money in taking her to the doctor to have it removed.

As a child I can only remember her pain and suffering and how glad we all were when she finally got to go to the doctor to have it *lanced.*

Mom remained a dedicated mother and faithful wife, a joy-filled person to all who knew her.

She always had a smile and a memorable laugh, one that made everyone around her feel happy.

Children, especially boys, judge their mothers {and grandmothers} more rigidly than they do their fathers {as fathers were not always around the house and homestead} so mothers were the *natural* teachers and administrators of ethics and discipline.

Most boys do not appreciate social training, direction, or discipline, and boys resent it *even more* when their mothers insist that they must watch their posture, wash behind their ears, clean their teeth and always, always, wear clean underwear.

The last of the hated disciplines was, never to make an ugly face while having your picture taken, and lastly, make sure you *behaved properly* when company arrived.

"It sure was tough being a boy"

A late but hopefully not too late "thank you mom" for even at your ninety plus years you still defend and watch over us kids. You made and moulded us to be good citizens; you still give us reason to be proud of the Young name.

Living with your parents and /or in-law in one house seemed to be the order of the day back then, and we, like most families, lived with mom and dad together with his parents, *our grandparents,* making a total of nine. Families living together under one roof was convenient, foremost, it provided a ready made home, plus it provided additional manpower to help work the family farms, knowing full well that in some future day you too would marry and raise a family of your own and keep this sensible tradition.

For the most part things went smoothly. There was always enough work to go around. It was only when papa Elvin had too much *free* week-end time and went away, I never knew where, and then returned home hours later, a little, or a lot, drunk, only then did things become heated and somewhat unhinged.

I recall one *hairy* incident when papa came into the house inebriated and Grammy confronted him verbally and physically. Grammy was strong and Papa not wanting to be too physical, ended up having his backside pushed out through and breaking the glass in the kitchen window. Dad and others soon got involved in the melee.

I was sixteen years old at the time and having some boxing ability stepped between the combatants {papa and dad} and ordered them to stop such foolishness. At the time, I had no idea other than the fact that papa was drunk, what acerbated or who instigated the conflict.

Grandfather was quick to tell me *"you will never be worth the sweat on my b--- 's"*

I had never heard that phase before but I instantly knew that he did not respect *my interference,* or me.

I have never forgotten those reproving words coming from my much loved and *previously* respected Papa.

I can only accept them as words spoken by a man too drunk to argue logically, for to believe otherwise, that he would think, that I, his grandson, was *that worthless,* was more then I was ready to forget.

It was a brief but hard learned lesson in human *mis*behaviour; I would like to put it behind me, but I cannot.

Dad met and married mom when she was very young and *very beautiful* "the most beautiful girl I had ever seen" he repeated many times, when telling us about seeing mom for the first time It was probably at a church function in Midvale Branch, her home village and a neighbouring community.

Dad maintained that "beautiful" opinion of mom until the day he died at the age of 94

If I were asked to make one statement of dad's life and worth to our family and the world, it would have to go something like this.

As stated previously, dad was a small man physically, but he was a giant in honesty and integrity, a God fearing, Christ loving Christian, a man with impeccable work ethics, one holding to *absolute marital fidelity*, a person of solid reasoning, unparalleled in having and using common sense in all dealings.

I hope that I can live my life mirroring that of both my mom and my dads. Lives of honesty and integrity in every area of work and dealings with others, so that when my time comes to leave this earthly place, my children would have need of finding similar words when speaking of me.

"What a legacy that would be".

Life is upside down—sometimes.

When you are young, married, have children of your own, in need of a home, a car, food, insurance, clothing, medical coverage, etc. and no matter how hard you work or how much you scrimp, you never seem to have quite enough money to go around.

Contrast that to when you get old. Your family has grown up and moved away, your spouse is gone, you have little need for any extras, your health has failed, you have lost your desires to travel or to see the *wider* world and your most ambitious project is going out for groceries or to visit your doctor.

Isn't it true that now when you have need of only the barest necessities to support *your present* life-style, you now have more income *and surplus wealth* than you need, or know where to spend it.

That is the way life seems to evolve, both for our family and for many of my friend's families as well.

This holds true, especially for my mom, who is now home alone on Young's hill. The old house that once was filled with the sounds of voices and laughter, the hustle and bustle of five kids coming and going in and out, is now sadly quiet except for the movements of her dog or the occasional ring of the telephone and every so often an old friend or family member who decide to pay her a visit.

It's apparent that dogs are not only man's best friend but also a best friend for mothers as well.

Mom has the bare minimum in radio and television services and she still watches TV using nothing but rabbit ears. Her TV only *brings in* two channels.

She reads everything written in the local and provincial papers, with very little *getting by* her keen mind and eyes. But mom's health is failing, she doesn't hear so well and she doesn't like wearing a hearing aid. She leaves the security of the house sparingly except when she goes to the village church or to visit with her doctor in Bridgewater.

She uses a walker to assist her in moving around, both inside and outside the house.

She takes her multiplicity of medicines and goes to bed early and alone.

It has to be torturously lonely but mom is one that never complains, as she doesn't want to leave the hill.

Mom probably has a thousand stories to tell about being alone.

Postscript

Since the writing of this book began several months ago, mom has now decided *"on her own"* that she would be better off living at another location. Young's hill, as much as she loved it, is remote from the larger community, and with her health failing at an accelerating rate; she needed constant {around the clock} monitoring and *she* knew it. This came as a revelation to most of us, as I had said only recently, {and most agreed} that mom would *never move away* from the hill.

In retrospect, I feel that mom *thought* that she was beginning to put too much burden on the children {mostly Arthur and the girls} who were using a lot of *their family's time* in looking after her needs, needs which could be alleviated if she were to move to a {seniors} home, where others {not being family members} would take care of those needs, thus releasing the family from having to be concerned for her well-being.

I may be wrong in my assessment of the reason why she *so suddenly* decided to leave, but mother, wanting to stay independent to the end, made a decision, her decision, and no one was about to try and change her mind.

{End of postscript}

Last Post – script

Today, Friday April second {Good Friday} in the year 2010, at twelve minutes past eight in the evening, Mom passed away.

After an attempt at a life prolonging surgery, Mom succumbed to a litany of complications with pneumonia being the final phase. All five children and four spouses were at or near her bedside most of the day. She was alert and of sound mind to the end.

It marks the end of a remarkable life and era. Mom had told us before entering the hospital that she would not survive; again she was right.

I am writing this Last Post, script, late at night, {3AM AST} as too many Mom memories kept me from sleeping.

I know that Mom has joined her favourite Saints in Glory and will await the coming of we whom she left behind. We, your sons and daughter, who remain to carry the torch of life, thank God, for blessing our lives by giving you to us, as a mother, a mentor and a friend, for almost ninety two years.

I personally will hold many regrets of things I should have or should not have not done; the last being, that I did not complete this book in time for your perusal and enjoyment.

It would have been great to hear your laughter, *just one more* time. "Goodbye Mom".

To confirm the fact of my earlier statement, *about needs and surplus*, two years ago mom handed out envelopes to all five children, *each containing* four thousand five hundred dollars.

We, *her* children did not want to accept it, but she insisted *that it was dad's wish* that *she do it* after *he was gone* and that she was only doing what *he wanted* her to do.

She could have kept this *vast sum* of dollars. I for one never knew it existed and never expected any money, but in truth *if she had not given it to her children*, what would mom have spent it on? Herself? Not likely.

Perhaps it may have been better if the money had been used when she and dad were younger and in better health, but that's not the way life works, is it? So that is the reason why I said earlier "sometimes life seems upside down" This act of generosity may have been a prime example.

When you are young and need money you never seem to have quite enough to go around and when you finally live long enough {if you are fortunate or lucky} to have accumulated *some measure* of wealth, you have now *passed* the time and reasons to need or have a use for it.

That thought aside, many parents scrimp and save for a great part of their lives, just to leave a monetary legacy for their children. They sacrifice many of life's comforts and *all* luxury to provide a better life for those that come behind. That too may have been the motivating factor in the decision to fill those five envelopes with money.

Whatever the reason *or reasons* mom, dad? Thanks.

Not having much money back in those early days never seemed to be much of a problem to us children, but in retrospect, it had to be an enormous burden for the parents of many families to bear.

No wonder a great cheer rose up from all across Canada when the Federal Government brought in the Family Allowance, a stipend of up to seven dollars a month, to be paid to the parents for every child in the country.

I know it was a great day for our mom and dad and for us their children.

Mom spent every penny of the money she received from the family allowance services in purchasing school supplies and clothing for us children. Talk about a legacy; that's an example of what a legacy should be; honesty, diligence, love, appreciation and sharing.

I recall stories of dad, telling us of the times that he worked a 9 or 10 hour day for $1.00 {that's one dollar- about ten cents per hour} His father {our grandfather} Elvin worked for even less.

Mom told me recently that dad once brought home eighty dollars for a full winter's {three month's} work.

Fred Penny, an insurance agent from Bridgewater, made a call to our home around about 1947 and sold dad a one thousand dollar

"Twenty Pay Life" insurance policy that would pay dad back one thousand dollars when he reached the age of sixty five. A "twenty pay life" is a policy that "for a *minimum* premium" insures the life of the applicant {dad} for one thousand dollars, should he die *at any time*, no matter how long he lived.

If the policyholder lived, the policy payments *ceased after the 20 years* and with *accrued interest* over the remaining years, or until dad became sixty-five, the policy would then pay out the full sum of one thousand dollars.

I can remember dad telling mom "now we will be okay when I reach the age of sixty five, we will have enough money to see us out".

It was serious business back then, kind of funny now.

The strange thing is, we children never thought of ourselves as being poor as we went to school and mingled with children of families who had even less than we had. We never judged others that had less; children just did not see poverty as an issue back then. *Perhaps our parents knew*, but we kids thought *that* was *the way* it was supposed to be.

Only when we became older did we realize just how good we as a family had it. We always had lots of food to eat; we had clean and warm clothes to wear {always some Sunday best clothes} and a loving supporting family. Some of our friends were not so well blest.

We never had a mealtime without a meal, but a dollar had to be stretched a long way back then.

I recall Papa coming home from Doyle Meisner's community store one evening and relating *this statement* to the members of *our* family. "Would you believe what Freddy Veinot told us tonight "why he said that *they* {meaning Fred his wife Etta and their only child Pauline} cannot live on a dollar a day any more, can you imagine that?" and Grammy agreed that the Veinot's were spending far more than was necessary.

Sundays

"Remember, what the Sabbath taught, *every* day" CWY.

On Sunday the family did little in the way of manual work. It was time to be in Sunday school at 10 am and for Church service that started at 11 am.

All dressed up in our Sunday best we usually walked the one and one-half miles through the woods and *up* the main road to the *modest sized,* white, {*with a high steeple},* community church.

St James Lutheran was located a fair distance away from the larger community of homes and farms that comprised the village of Branch LaHave.

I was never given a better reason for the church being built in such a remote location, away from the main community, other than the fact that the cemetery is located immediately adjacent to the church and that the cemetery property was given *free* to the community by a Mr Paul Veinot. Perhaps he also donated the land that the church was built upon.

On second thought, chances are good that *nobody* in the community wanted to live close to a cemetery.

Ringing the church bell

It was Fred Veinot's {unpaid} responsibility for many years to ring the church bell, not only on Sunday mornings to remind the community residents to come to church but for other occasions as well.

The bell was also used to announce any deaths in the community.

The church bell served as the community clarion, as one pull of the heavy rope that led up from the church entry to the bell tower represented one ring of the huge brass bell. This heralded the news to all within hearing distance, that someone from the Branch had died and the number of years that the person had lived.

I can still recall hearing the bell being "tolled" and of our family listening intently *and counting the number of "gongs"* to establish which person from the community had died.

I guess that is where the term "for whom the bell tolls" came from

Vacation Church School

Church and Sunday school was a major ingredient in and during my youth years. Every Sunday morning Mom would make sure that we kids were all dress up in our Sunday best, including bow ties and hats on the boys and bonnets on the girls.

We had lessons to do, the same as in regular school, and always a nickel or a dime for collection. We usually walked the one-mile plus each way and never seemed to think about the distance or it taking too much time to come and go. We accepted what we considered *the norm.*

During the summers of my youth, for two weeks of the summer, St Paul's was active with vacation Bible School, when as many as 20 children from the Branch, plus a few from another community {Wentzel's Lake} would gather daily for a few hours during the mornings to learn more about God and Christ.

For several years the Missouri Synod of the Lutheran Church in the United States would send up two or three teenage youths {missionaries} to lead us. They usually came from the states of Iowa or Nebraska.

The visiting youth were always *billeted* {the term was *stayed* back then} at Fred and Etta Veinottes as Etta was always the leader of every youth movement in the Branch, including our 4-H club

Etta was a 4-H leader before 4-H leaders were deemed necessary. She was a youth leader before anyone even considered that youth needed leaders. Her home, her yard and the ball field {which was located in back of the barn} were welcome beacons to every boy or girl from the Branch who wished to visit.

Her mentorship and leadership efforts did not all fall on fallow soil. Thank you Etta, you were like a *second mother* to most of us. You left us long before you should have.

1950 – 1955 "Those were the best of days" we were young, carefree, and filled with high hopes. We never wanted them to end.

When *my* generation of peers refers to "*the good old days*" it included activities like vacation church school or 4-H activity and the thousands of other fun filled moments, all garnered from either group singing, playing board-games, playing softball or skating on the ice that covered the old mill dam in winter. The dam, which was located only a few hundred yards in back of the Veinot home was the catalyst for those *priceless memory moments* that many of us shared together, all under the love and guidance of Etta Veinot.
"*Thank you* Etta".

Pie Sales

At least once a summer the community had a fund raising event called a pie sale.

It, like most everything else that happened in the Branch, was held at the home of Fred and Etta Veinot's.

It was a time when all the girls in the community would bake a cake or a pie, and the boys from the Branch would bid to see who would pay the most to win the prize. Now the prize wasn't so much the cake or pie, but what went with it. The successful bidder would get to sit down and eat the cake or pie with the girl who baked it.

Talk about incentive.

I have been told that the competition was so fierce at times, that a pie or cake would be bid as high as twenty dollars. Can you imagine how much money that would be in today's dollar?

Every once in a while a girl would deny making the sweet tasting pastry, if the successful bidder was someone she didn't prefer to dine with. All in all there was only the occasional scuffle and the money was well received and was saved up to go towards building a hall for similar future community events.

I have a notion, that a pie sale, using the same incentive and format, would be a worthwhile fund raising event even today.

Halloween

Both adults as well as children looked with anticipation as Halloween approached, some for playing tricks on others, while others, wondered what hell-ry would take place in the community by some over enthused Halloweener or *Bellsnickle,* as anyone wearing a mask and visiting others on Halloween was known to be out Bellsnickleing.

Most pranks were harmless, like knocking on a door and then running away, or dislodging an outhouse from its foundation or moving a wagon or other farm equipment to a site other than where it was placed by the farmer the night before. A more serious prank might include upsetting the outhouse or hauling the wagon a goodly distance from where it was found, causing the resident some measure of aggravation or constipation.

One serious but laughable prank took place in a neighbouring community.

A certain farmer had an ox wagon loaded with a substantial amount of lumber sitting in his yard. Only hours before he had delivered it there after picking it up at the local sawmill with his team of oxen. He was planning to remove it from the wagon and stack it for drying, the following morning.

A good plan, but not, for the eve of Halloween.

It seems that once the farmer and his wife had settled down for a good night's sleep, several ambitious Halloweeners went to work.

Under the cover of darkness they first pulled the wagon closer to the barn. Then they removed the lumber and disassembled the large and lumber laden ox wagon.

Then, using country hardened muscles and a long strong rope, several of them up on the roof of the barn, and several down below, did the aforethought unthinkable.

They reassembled the wagon on the barn roof, by straddling the wagon over the peak of the roof for balance. They then replaced every piece of lumber that had previously been on the wagon, in the yard, to its new location, high up on the barn roof, almost exactly as it had been previously, when it had been sitting on the ground.

Can you imagine the gasp of surprise the next morning by the farmer and his wife upon seeing such a spectacle?

I cannot confirm whether this tale is true or not, but knowing the times and the folk of the area, it is quite likely that it did happen. After all, who would have an imagination to make up a tale so colourful and preposterous, so memorable and laughable to all that heard it, all, with the exception of the farmer and his wife?

Christmas Activities

Christmas was different back then. We always had a tinsel trimmed tree with an array or traditional trimmings. The tree, a balsam fir, was always selected and cut by dad, only a few days before Christmas and the tree always came from off our own property. There was no such thing as a sheared or an artificial tree.

Every kid believed in Santa, and to keep that belief alive, every parent would do his or her best to provide that one special request that had been made known to them.

My most memorable gift was a wind up horse pulling a wagon. My grandfather's brother's wife, Alice, gave it to me. It was so beautiful and delicate. I cannot remember breaking it, but someone must have, as it disappeared never to be seen again.

My second best gift was a Buck Roger's Atomic pistol. It had a red Plexiglas window and flashed like fire in the dark when the trigger was pulled.

We kids always had a sock hung, that on Christmas morning had been filled, by Santa, with candy, crayons, a colouring book, and always a large orange. We always received clothes, like shirts, riding breeches, socks and mittens, but we knew those thing didn't come from Santa.

The Branch School always managed to put on a concert around Christmas.

The older kids would do recitations and dress up in costumes and play acting parts that would bring laughter to the jam packed one room school.

At the end of the concert Santa would always show up, and true to his word, he had a gift of a candy-cane and an orange for every kid, good or bad.

No wonder, that to this day, I still believe in Santa Claus, and he hasn't let me down yet.

I discussed the reason for Santa with one of my church pastor's many years ago, as he frowned mightily, on anything that had to do with Santa.

My belief was that many people, including parents, find it difficult to express love to their children or their peers. But they can do so through an intermediary. Santa is that conduit. Even if we cannot tell someone that we love them, we can always show love by giving a gift, and giving Santa the credit. After all, actions do speak louder than words.

I think that God will agree with that statement.

Birthdays

Birthdays were never a big deal around the Young's household, after all there were many of us and everyone had a birthday. It would become meaningless to celebrate too often.

But for us kids, on our special day, there was always an icing covered cake, and it never failed to contain money, or a least one slice of it did. The cake was always carefully pre-cut into equal sized slices, and everyone at the table was sure to have a piece, the kids going first, with the adults holding back, until one of the children was lucky enough to get the slice with the loot in it.

The coin was always wrapped in wax paper, usually a dime, as anything larger was difficult to conceal.

Why do we recall such trivial things? Remember what you were told as a child, it's the little things in life that count, even if it amounts to only a dime.

Fighting for Life

At about age fifteen I became interested in boxing. The Branch already had two successful pugilists namely Bob and Lawrence Grace. Both were "stars" in the community, the town of Bridgewater, the County, and *rising stars* in the Province.

Bob went on to become a serious contender for the Canadian lightweight title.

In my first summer job {during our school vacation time} I had the good fortune of working alongside Bob at Russell Sawler's White Rose Service Station in Bridgewater.

He encouraged me to try the "sweet science" and for the next several years I got caught up in the fervour and the excitement of the sport. To me, the greatest motivator of all was to be in top physical condition and to win every bout, as not being in top condition meant that you might take a physical beating plus the embarrassment that went along with losing.

I had a strong body, conditioned from running, bicycling and doing farm related work. To build more strength and stamina our manager Frank Manthorne encouraged Bob and me to go into the woods {his woodlot} and cut logs and firewood.

It was hot and it was back breaking work, but I had a goal. I wanted to box, I needed to get better, I wanted to win, and if winning meant improving skills building up muscles, improving wind and stamina by working hard at cutting Frank's logs and firewood, along with running long treks uphill and down, all bundled up in a sweat suit, I would do it.

I trained diligently to improve my boxing skills, which ultimately led to 15 bouts spread over several years.

I sparred with Bob and *other hopefuls* and practiced diligently daily, always remaining dedicated to the Marquis of Queensbury rule; of *"being* able *to protect myself at all times,* and to *never foul* an opponent intentionally"

My "fighting" career ended with a record of 12 wins and 3 losses.

I always regretted *two* of those losses.

In my first loss I received a cut above the left eye from a head butt in a bout I was winning. The cut from the butt bled profusely and the bout was stopped at the end of the third round. Under today's rules I would have been declared the winner.

The second "regrettable" loss came in Nova Scotia's "fight town" Sydney, Cape Breton This loss was my most difficult to accept.

I had never fought three-minute rounds as an amateur and I entered the ring that night *not being told* that this bout was scheduled for four *3-minute* rounds.

Everyone hates to lose but when you lose and the playing field is level you have no one to blame but yourself. In this bout that was not the case.

I did great for the first round and a half, hitting {sticking with a left jab} and moving well, avoiding being hit and wondering just how long *I could keep up this pace.*

I could duck and I could weave *side to side* with the best, and I had a strong stiff left jab with a great right hand cross. I used all my skills and strength to take advantage of a bad situation that evening; at least I was winning the first round of the bout.

I cannot remember the other guy, *Bobo Bonaparte,* hitting me *even once* during the first round and a half.

But Bobo was a big guy. My opponents always seemed to be bigger then me and after the first round and a half, I was suddenly dead tired and Bobo was just coming on. As hard as I pounded and punished him for the first half of the fight, *he* pounded and punished me *twice as hard* for the next round and a half.

He knocked me down *to a sitting position, which means I* only had one knee *touching* the canvas. Bobo knocked me down three times by hitting me with a heavy right hand *right smack on my heart.* Something like this had never happened to me before. As I felt no pain of being hit, my head remained clear, so I bounced back up on my feet after each knockdown and continued fighting.

As the third round *dragged on* I decided that if Bobo didn't *knock me out* it wasn't from his lack of trying, so in order to survive the round I waited until he was starting to swing his powerful right hand usually at my head, and then I would deliver a straight jab to his jaw for all I was worth.

I hit him hard every time, but Bobo was relentless; I know that my jabbing manoeuvre saved me from being knocked out *and from an even worse* beating. I believe that he was going to kill me by beating me with his powerful punches or else I would die from a heart attack trying to defend myself. I must have been in excellent physical condition that night or *one of the two* scenarios would have been a certainty.

At the end of three rounds I was finished, *still on my feet* but dead tired-*totally fatigued.* I lost that bout by not being able to "come out" for the forth and final round.

I was barely able to talk, or walk to the dressing room. There was certainly *no fight* left in me.

I wanted to lie down. I wanted to sleep; I didn't even care if I died as I was completely depleted of energy. "Leave me alone and let me go to sleep," I pleaded, to my handlers Tremaine Fraser and Frank Manthorne. But they insisted on keeping me awake and prevented me from going to sleep. I found out later *that they thought* I might have died in my sleep from the beating, had they let me drift off and fall asleep.

In summary, I remained bitter for a long time afterwards all because of the way I lost that fights. My anger was directed primarily towards my corner persons for their not knowing that I was fighting four *three minute rounds,* instead of four *two minute* rounds, when I entered that ring, not *even as the bell rang* to start the bout.

Had I known that I had to fight three-minute rounds I would have paced myself better. I still may not have won but I would have applied a *different* strategy *to* allow me to have competed for the *scheduled length* of the bout.

I competed and completed nine minutes of a fight that I thought was only supposed to have lasted eight minutes. Wouldn't you be upset?

Even after the beating I took that evening, I was still in better shape then most of my friends who had accompanied me to Sydney, Cape Breton that day.

I was one of two drivers {we had two cars} that remained *in good enough physical condition* to make the return trip back to Bridgewater, a distance of about two hundred and fifty miles.

I arrived back at my place of employment, Hebb Motors Chevrolet Ltd, around noon of the next day and immediately went back to work. I had two black eyes and my upper lip was busted up and stuck out almost as far as my nose.

Don't talk to me about the Marquis of Queensbury rules, the love of the sport, conditioning, superior skill and killer instinct, I had them all and it didn't do me any good that ill-fated night in Sydney Cape Breton.

Bobo almost killed me that night.

The third fight I lost, I was knocked out cold, and I cannot remember where it happened or who did it. In my opinion, this was the only fight that I *justly* lost.

During those several years of actively pursuing the sport of boxing I had *two main events* and won most of my matches *against odds* that I would or could win. There were some very tough guys and some very worthy opponents on the local fight scene back then. I was fortunate to have escaped that *rough and tough sport* with minimal damage.

I loved the competition of the sport and never disliked an opponent, *win or lose.* It may sound strange but if I could, I would do it all over again.

I have never been considered "punchy" so I guess that means *I must be crazy.*

4 H Years
Character building times and events.

The 4H Pledge
I pledge my Head to clearer thinking
My Heart to greater loyalty
My Hands to larger service, and
My Health to better living, for
My Club, Community and Country

My youth years were also my years in 4 H
The Branch had an active Garden Club of which Mrs Fred {Etta Veinot} was our 4 H Club leader.

My highlight experience as a member of 4-H came to pass when Bill Grace and I were selected to represent the Province of Nova Scotia at the National 4-H Convention competitions in Toronto.

Billy was always my best friend during "growing up" and going to school years.

He was bigger, taller, stronger, better looking, and smarter, he could box {fight} effectively, and he even ran faster than I could.

He also got into more street fights {outside the ring} then *any other* of my friends.

As he did not live on a farm he had no garden *to speak of,* so, because of no fault of his own, he had very little knowledge of gardening. But Billy *caught on* fast, and as *co-members* of 4-H *we combined for a winning entry* at the local and then won again at the county level. We then entered and won the Provincial gardening category competition.

Surprise! Surprise! Through a series of tests and elimination events held throughout Nova Scotia, Billy and I had won the right *to represent our Province* at the National finals to be held later on in November in Ontario, Canada

Now being selected as Provincial representatives posed a bit of a problem, as all Provincial representatives of 4H attending the Royal Winter Fair in Toronto had to comply with a strict dress code.

We along with every other representing member from across Canada were told that we had to wear white shirts, ties and grey flannel pants, along with blue blazers. The girls had to wear blue pleated skirts with matching blue blazers.

Neither Billy nor I owned grey flannel pants or blue blazers, nor could we afford them. We both were okay in the white shirt and tie requirements.

After hearing about *our plight*, the Lunenburg County Federation of Agriculture came to our rescue; but *their rescue* came with one stipulation. They *{the Federation}* *would provide funding* for our clothing needs, but, upon returning home from Ontario, we, Billy and I, had to appear before the Federation members, and tell them all about our 4-H experience.

The Federation met in a large wooden building on Pleasant Street in Bridgewater. It also served as the County Court house, a building that *neither of us had ever been in before*, but this was no time to worry about repayment. We needed those blue blazers and grey flannels and we needed them now.

The pants and blazers were supplied by Rofhies Men's Wear, a store located on King Street Bridgewater. {The same store, carrying the same name, still exists on the same corner of King Street some fifty-seven years later}

We were never told how much our pants and blazers cost the Federation, but we sure were appreciative of their generous gesture.

The trip meant going from Halifax by train to Toronto, where accommodations were made for our stay at the Royal York Hotel, Canada's premier hotel From there we would travel to other venues and cities, attend the Royal Winter Fair, touch the waters *that rush past and over* Niagara Falls and visit the Parliament buildings in Ottawa.

Another {*less famous*} place on the agenda was a visit to the Grey Steel Mill Co in Hamilton Ontario, where I, for the first time in my life, saw dozens of women working under the most severe conditions that one could imagine. In this *immense factory* there was *molten hot iron and smoke* everywhere.

If you can imagine what hell is like; now you're getting close.

In one section of this mill *women* were wheeling around heavy containers of burning metal while in another section they were handling heavy steel girders {just like men} all this while working under terrible conditions.

The incredible heat emitting from the giant blast furnaces was bad enough *but equally bad* was the lack of visual ability caused by the smoke and dust arising during the production of the steel.

Some things one never forgets. Most vividly etched on my memory were the difficult work and the awful working conditions experienced by those women.

"Man oh man, was it hot in that factory! I was more than happy to get out".

Those women *were big* and *strong* they had to be. You should have seen their muscles! I sure wouldn't want to tangle with any of those gals in the ring.

But best of all, was *first seeing and then touching*, the waters of Niagara Falls.

I had seen pictures and read about it, but there is no substitute for being there and seeing *the real thing*.

I met my twin on this trip. It happened while I was sitting and chatting with other 4-H ers in one of the many large ballrooms that dot the Convention Centre area of the Royal York.

He was a young man, *having my exact age and identical birth date;* {September 25th 1936} He was from somewhere out west {Alberta or Manitoba}

What a shame that neither he nor I *followed up* on this unique experience.

Speaking of unique experiences, while visiting the Hotel Chateau Laurier located in Ottawa, Billy and I decided that we would do some hotel *exploring*.

No one has ever heard this story before as both of us were a bit hesitant about telling *too many people* about it, but Billy and I ended up sitting outside, *on the roof,* of the Chateau Laurier.

No one stopped us {we never saw one security personnel} to ask us questions, on why we were wandering around from floor to floor of the hotel, so we just kept going higher and higher up inside the Hotel, until we found *this hatch* that appeared to lead out onto the roof. *It did.*

We could hardly believe our good fortune. Slowly and carefully we slipped up past the now open hatch and carefully *crawled out* on to the metal covered roof. We spent the next several minutes just sitting there, looking out over the sights and lights of the city below and around us, before returning later to join the other less adventurous 4Hers.

How times have changed when it comes to security *or lack of it*.

It's a good thing that Billy and I weren't terrorists; at least not of the destructive type.

Billy had several girlfriend *experiences* on the ten-day trip. I had only one.

I became infatuated with a girl from Prince Edward Island. I never even touch her, not even for a kiss, and I cannot remember her name for certain; I think it was June.

I ate my first meal of mutton, at least I intended to. It turned out to be my first and last as I had never eaten mutton before and I have not eaten mutton since, not in my whole entire life.

The "none meal" happened while I like the rest of the 4Hers travelling from the East was attempting to have dinner in the train's dining car at the very beginning of the trip.

The incident came about while travelling on the CNR passenger train running out of Halifax, going non-stop to Toronto. The meals on the trip were all *free* and I never had eaten a "free" government paid for meal before.

It should have been the best meal on the train, {or so I thought} as it was the most expensive of all the meal items listed on the menu; at least that is what this down home country boy *contemplated.*

The staff in the dining car *must have had* other ideas and consorted against me, {let's fix that little *whippersnapper*} for ordering *the most expensive dinner* listed on the menu.

They *probably* figured that I was *"an extravagant free loader",* a burden to the tax system, of which they were a part. In truth, they were right.

What they presented before me on my plate for dinner was a plate piled high *with blubber,* nothing but fat. I never did find any mutton meat to eat.

The dining car staff had fixed me good. From then on I ordered nothing but sandwiches, cheap but edible.

From that *none* meal on, I was probably the least expensive kid to feed on the whole trip, and as I said before, I have never eaten mutton since.

When we returned to Bridgewater it soon came time *to pay up* for those blue blazers and grey flannel pants. Remember, those that the Federation had generously provided for us, for our trip?

The day quickly arrived for us to make our presentation to the Federation members *"in that big old courthouse"* and guess what? Billy backed out.

I know I was just as nervous or terrified as Billy, but someone had to do it, to repay our debt, and do it, I did. I kept *our* commitment and *we both* got to keep our clothes.

Perhaps it's the unexpected events in life like this one that has made me less dependent on others and more dependent on myself. Over the years when things needed to be done, many times I found myself doing them alone.

'Thanks a lot Billy, but, you still owe me one'.

Palm Beach; Pulpwood and Pigs

My mother was an avid collector of country songs. Country songs, was about all anyone knew or sang around the Branch back in the forties and fifties and she collected hundreds of them. They were included in a section of a monthly farm magazine; I believe it was called the "Free Press".

She cut them out with scissors and then carefully pasted them into *a lined* scribbler.

Mom, Dad and Grammy were all good singers and Mom's *song scribbler* came in handy lots of times.

I listened to the radio to learn most songs. I liked those sung by Hank Snow and Wilf Carter as both Hank and Wilf were once residents of the local area. They left the area to become international celebrities. Both were successful and became famous, their records are found in the Country Music Hall of Fame in Nashville, Tennessee

It was their singing that became the motivating force for me to *want* and *need* a guitar.

I searched through the Eaton's and Simpson's catalogues countless times to find the smartest looking, most affordable and best-equipped guitar.

I settled on a Palm Beach. I liked the name and the price seemed right.

It came with everything, a carrying case with a steel bar for playing Hawaiian style music, an instruction book and even an extra set of strings. Extra strings were very important in those *beginner* days, the total cost was $13.95, a princely sum in those days, and I had little money - only a dream.

So, how was I to obtain my Palm Beach?

Being only thirteen years old and not having more than fifty cents at the most to my name, I needed a plan.

It's good to have an older brother – with money.

Arthur always seemed to have money, even when he was young. My parents and grandparents said, Arthur saves *his* money, why can't you?

My only reply was that I never had any to save.

Now Arthur, being no pushover, wasn't about to give me $13.95 for something that held no interest for him, but Arthur was a budding businessman. He told me that he would give me the money if I would cut a cord and a half of pulpwood that he could then sell to Dalton Mailman {a local buyer of logs and pulp} for more money than the $13.95 We never knew much about the word *profit but Arthur knew it was necessary* if he was to lend me money. *He needed* to make a profit - nothing wrong with that, and I wasn't the best risk in the world.

Fair enough, as we were brought up to believe that if you wanted something badly enough you should be prepared to work for and earn the money to pay for it, which I was *now committed* to do.

The big hitch in the verbal contract was, the pulpwood that I was about to cut, had to be hauled out from the woods area from whence it was cut, to a spot located between two apple trees located at the upper end of our orchard, a place where Dalton's pulpwood truck could drive to and be loaded without problems.

If I wanted my Palm Beach I had to not only cut enough wood to pay for it, but I must agree to deliver it to where Arthur wanted it delivered.

I agreed.

But, still another problem. Brother Arthur was the only one who was big and strong enough to yoke *and handle* the steers {young oxen} that were needed to pull the spruce and fir pieces of pulp from the forest where I cut it, to the *specified* orchard location.

I wanted that guitar so badly that I not only cut the spruce and fir trees down with a small hand saw, I cut them up in four foot length pieces and then using a leather belt, I hauled those four foot pieces of wood, by hand, up through the rough terrain of the pasture and neatly piled the pieces between the two trees in the orchard that we earlier agreed to in our brotherly contract.

How long it took for me to cut and haul that wood up and out of the pasture I am not sure. I bet Arthur and my family know. It was not easy for me, but I knew then as I now know, nothing *worthwhile* in life is ever easy; nor should it be.

Doing what I did back then was to me not work, but a mission of accomplishing something worthwhile, making it become a reality, of gradually reaching my goal *against odds* that *I could or would* ever finish the job.

I still feel pride in that one simple act of accomplishing something meaningful, by working alone, *without help*, to earn the money to pay for my $13.95 Palm Beach guitar.

The Palm Beach was now mine and mine alone. Wow, what a good feeling!

Learning to play my Palm Beach took longer than I thought. It was almost as difficult as earning the money to buy it.

I had to first learn how to *tune* it and then learn to pick and play something on it, by using the included handy instruction book.

I was determined to learn how to play the Spanish version and I eventually learned and earned {suffered} every blister {several times over} before even the simplest cord was mastered.

I made so many awful sounds during those first weeks that the family banned me from practicing on it in or near the house, and *suggested* that I ply my trade out in the pig barn.

Now that isn't quite as bad as it sounds as the pig barn was a new section that had just recently been added to the existing barn, and for me and my Palm Beach, it was the best place to be.

Sitting there above the pigs, amongst the feedstuffs of pumpkins and hay I practiced and practiced {through blisters and all} until finally the day came when I could play something.

The first song I played and sang was a song called Jimmy Brown; it came from out of mom's scribbler and was one of her favourites.

I still remember most of the lyrics.

Like many other amateur musicians in this world I now play mostly for the love of playing my guitar and singing to myself.

Leo Conrad, the only other boy on Young's hill {other than our family} lived just down the hill from our home. Leo was a bit older and had amazing story telling talents that made the hundreds of walks *too and from* school seem more like adventures. With his verbal talents and vivid imagination he seemed destined to be a great orator.

He and I made two 45 rpm records with me playing my Palm Beach. The recordings had to be made at the local radio station CKBW, under the direction of one of their technicians, in Bridgewater, and cost the princely sum of $12.00 each.

"Life is Like a Mountain Railway" was the title of the first record we made. It sounded great *to our families and us.* We never did made more then one copy. I wonder if that copy still exists.

Later on Leo moved out to western Canada where he got married, had a family and became an Anglican minister. His destiny had finally been realized.

Over the years I have owned several other guitars in both six and twelve string versions. I have written several songs, some that I have sung in public. Some were pretty good. I have included several in this book. Sing them if you like them to whatever tunes that suit you.

Unknown to me, my mother had kept my $13.95 Palm Beach for me over the many years since I had left home. It was stored in the attic of the old farmhouse and the heat from the kitchen chimney, which extended up through the attic, caused the top to dry out and crack. I sold it for $75.00 at an auction several years ago.

It was worth a fortune in memories to me.

"The buyer of that old warped Palm Beach guitar can never appreciate its real value".

Saturday nights

Saturday was the red-letter day of the week back then.

That was the day the men {dad and papa} came home from the woods. But more importantly to my brothers and me, it was the day that we {the boys at least} got to go to town on the back of Calvin Snyder's converted log truck.

For 25 cents Calvin could carry up to thirty or more residents, gathered up along the way, from the several communities leading from his home in Upper Branch on route to Bridgewater. He would leave his home around six PM and return us back home again around midnight.

But just going to town didn't hold much allure if you couldn't afford to go to a movie {25 cents}, at the old Capitol Theatre, or buy a hot dog {10 cents} from Mrs Simmons hot dog stand on King Street, or to buy a comic book or two, at 10 cents each, making a grand total of 75 cents.

So how did a kid get the princely sum of 75 cents a week back then?

In my case I was given the opportunity to earn it from the adult members of the family.

I did this by doing my regular chores of *getting in the stove*-wood and the drinking water, plus *behaving* myself.

Those actions might account for twenty-five cents, still far short of that which I needed.

To earn the extra money I had to wax the kitchen and dining room floors.

I know now that the family *invented the need* for *excessive* wax jobs just to give me the opportunity to earn the extra money I needed to go to town. The wax was so thick on that old kitchen floor covering, that you could have scraped it off with a knife. I am sure it could have gone for a year without needing wax, but I gladly waxed it every week.

I could *get by* with a minimum of 65 cents per week, and some weeks when I earned up to 95 cents I could afford an extra comic book or two and a box of caps for my cap gun.

I cannot remember ever having more than ninety-five cents.

Comic books were popular. I liked the Two Gun Kid, Superman, Batman and Robin, Captain Marvel, and The Lone Ranger.

I had dozens maybe hundreds of comic books, had I saved them all, they would be worth a small fortune today.

Confusion, in choosing: a vocation

Like most country boys my talents were few but I had *more than my share* of great ambitions.

I was a pretty good singer and a fairly good guitar player so I thought about being another Hank Snow or Wilf Carter and hitting it big in Nashville.

I loved boxing and I was better equipped at that time both in body and talent than anything else. It would have been simple for me to continue in this rough and tough sport, but the money wasn't *good* and my parents and friends said it was *too hard on the eyes*, so I abandoned those ambitions.

Becoming an auto mechanic seemed the top choice for a vocation as many of my friends and I like most boys, did acquire *some* general knowledge *of the workings* of gasoline engines. In a pinch I could always find employment in *that* field.

My grandmother was adamant that I would become a minister. I never was quite sure of why she thought that way. Perhaps she saw something in me that I failed to grasp back then.

Why should I not *become* an RCMP officer? It sounded great and everyone in my peer group {especially the girls} admired their red and black uniforms. But I had to turn that dream down when I found out that I wasn't quite tall enough back then, or that I ever would be.

Becoming an airline pilot seemed exciting and meaningful, but even back then I figured it was unattainable for me, so I quickly diminished those thoughts.

Farming was never a serious consideration, as I knew first hand the long hours, the hard work, *the low, to no*, pay etc *as the rewards* for farming.

Woods work was another vocation that didn't appeal to me. Wonder why?

Sales seemed the only vocation that I was really suited for and one that would give me and my future family a decent *living wage* and I did have lots of experience, *garnered and honed* from a kid, on up.

Drunk, on my first real man's job

I turned sixteen on September 25th 1952. It was now time for me to go to work.

I had worked at a few *paying* jobs during the summer school vacation periods like picking strawberries for Caroll and / or Lee Wentzell at 4-cents a box, plus pumping gas and other service related work at the White Rose Service station in Bridgewater. Later on, as *I grew older and up in size* I was able to help the older men paint the large iron bridge that spanned the LaHave River at Wentzells Lake, about three miles from home.

We started working at eight AM when the mist was rising off the river. The mist made it uncomfortably cold in the early mornings. Then as we worked on through the day the hot sun would come, bearing down on us with no shade until quitting time, which came at four thirty. We only stopped work for one half hour at noon for our lunch break. No one slacked working for even a minute as every man was expected to complete his *allotted portion* of the work. An inspector {sometimes dad} hovered over us like a fly.

Sitting or standing on a narrow plank suspended only by ropes, hovering out over the 120 ft. wide and swift flowing river and not being able to swim was daunting at best, but having to leave the plank at times in order to crawl higher up into the bridge's iron framework in order to reach every crevice on that 20 ft high bridge was quite fearful.

Dad and I and brother Arthur along with six to eight other men could scrape and pound the old paint off and repaint a bridge that size in about five or six weeks.

You first had to pick off *every particle* of the original black paint using a small hand-held pick and a large flat file, sharpened at one end. Once the iron was scraped bare, you then painted over the scraped area, first with a bright orange rust proof paint, then once the orange paint had dried thoroughly, another coat of heavy oil based black paint was applied *over* the orange undercoat.

If you missed any spots with the black paint, the orange undercoat would show up like a brick outhouse in the fog.

I believe that the government of the day invented those bridge painting jobs just to keep the local natives quiet, allowing them {the workers} to feel useful, by having them earn their keep, instead of having money dolled out to them in the form of welfare. Whatever the case, it worked.

My first "*real man's* job" came *after Christmas* in 1954.

At the age of sixteen years and three months, I, like every other able bodied *man* from the country was expected to leave the comforts and security of home and family and go into the lumbering woods and mill camps of the province to harvest the abundant supply of wood products that was needed in the construction of almost *every building in the province* and in the *creation of wealth* for everyone involved

The pay was five dollars a day plus meals. When you worked you got paid, if it stormed or you were sick you didn't get paid. The workday spanned the hours from daylight to near dark.

You only stopped working for as long as it took you to eat a hand delivered lunch, usually twenty minutes before returning to work.

On days when it snowed *too much* or the wind blew *too hard,* some loggers for safety reasons stayed in the camp; Arthur and I and dad did not. Sunday was our only day off.

On the journey down to the woods to the sawmill and woodlot operation, which was located in Leicester, Cumberland County {about 160 road miles from home} I got sick. Dad decided to stop by the home of one of our relatives who lived in the village of Shubenacadie.

When they asked dad, "What are you going to do about Caroll's {that's me} sickness"? Dad told them he planned on stopping in the town of Truro to pick up a bottle of Brandy *for me*, which he did.

The trip from Truro to the woods camp took another hour or more by car and every so often dad would open the flask of Brandy and give me a drink.

I had never tasted Brandy before, but *this stuff* tasted good. I was soon looking forward *to the drinks* and anticipated getting better but by the time we bedded down for the night I was still quite sick.

One of the men in the camp also asked dad what he was doing *to fix me up* so that I would be able to go to work in the morning. He again said that he was *giving me Brandy* and with that he proceeded to pour me another drink.

"Why don't you pour him a *real man's* drink?" one of the men spoke up. {I believe it was Floyd Lowe} and with that encouragement, dad continued to pour me an even larger portion of Brandy.

I swear to God that I can still hear that Brandy flow, as it gurgled out of the glass flask into a large metal mug, and when he handed it to me, I drank it down without stopping and then I *flopped* backwards into the comfort of my bunk, with grave doubts of what the next morning held for me.

You must remember that *I was not a drinker* of alcohol, at that time, and had never been drunk before.

The last thing I remember was using my fingers, twisting at the ends of the hundreds of *bent over* nails that protruded through the camp walls. The nails were used for keeping the black tar paper fastened down securely to the outside of the camp walls. There was no insulation in any of the woods camps to keep out the cold. A wood burning fire drum took care of the heating.

For some *drunken* reason I was trying my best *to straighten out those nails* with my bare fingers. Then I passed out.

Sometime later I awoke *abruptly* into what was *by now* a totally black cabin; I knew that *something* was wrong. I was sick and I needed to throw up, and fast.

To *do that*, without making a mess on the floor of the camp, I needed to first find the camp's door. Almost all woods camps only had one door. Thank God my bunk was located closest to the door, as I had no sooner fumbled for the latch, found it and quickly opened it, when I threw up. Whatever I had in me to throw up, was thrown up, mostly Brandy.

Morning came and I was a zombie. I cannot remember eating any breakfast only doing what I was told.

I was already dressed as I had not removed my clothes from the day before and I soon found myself following behind my brother and dad and a woods boss, a Mr Creelman, back along a snow covered woods road, with only a smidgen of daylight silhouetting the tall trees and the three men walking ahead of me.

I tried my best to keep up.

I remember thinking, My God! Caroll, what have you gotten yourself into.

Needless to say I survived the three *long* months of work without taking a break. At the end of the first six weeks all but a few of the men including my dad and Arthur, left camp and went home for a few days, as the Company allowed *a brief break* at the end of the first six weeks of employment.

I thought that if I went home I might not come back- ever, and so I stayed behind alone in the woods camp putting in time by washing up some of my dirty clothes and handkerchiefs, and doing some patching to my boots, rubber boots, that, by the time we left for home had accumulated almost thirty patches on them. It probably was a record number of patches.

I had a head cold for most of the winter and my weight went from a soft 160 lbs. down to a muscled up 141 lbs.

If ever I turned into a man it was that winter.

I cut my big toe on my right foot with my axe. It was on a cold snowy morning and the woods boss picked me up and delivered me to a clinic out in the town of Amherst. There I was to have it examined and stitched up. Sitting there that cold winter's morning in the clinic's *waiting* room I must have looked like someone that had just stepped out of a Dickens's tale, all dressed up in my rough looking woods clothes and wearing my pair of *multiple patched* boots.

I was the only male amongst several *well-dressed* ladies that came into the clinic that morning. I felt more *out of place* sitting there, waiting for the doctor to arrive than I had ever felt in my life.

When the Doctor *finally* arrived at the clinic, he poked his head out from around the corner into the waiting room and asked, "Who will be the first person that I attend to this morning"? One lady, looking at the doctor first and then at me, quickly said, "You had best take that young man first".

I was never so relieved.

I respect my elders and all those of every past generation for their unquestioning dedication to working under such conditions; but, I would never want any of my children *or their children's children* to do what *our ancestors did* in order to earn a living:

And I *only did i*t for one winter.

The girl next door

There were only a few girls in my age group "to pick from" living in the Branch. I never *loved* more than one. Her name was Pauline

Veinot. We *first kiss*ed at about age sixteen. Wow! You can never forget your first kiss, nor should you.

I didn't know there was such a thing as *puppy love* and had it all figured out that this was going to be the *one and only* girl for me. This had to be "the real thing". It turned out that other boys from the Branch and elsewhere had the same ideas as I had about Pauline.

I was hurt, I was jealous.

I got over it, *somehow,* but it wasn't easy.

Aurora-borealis

Much has been reported in science magazines about the aurora borealis, you know, that band of lights that flash across the northern sky on cold winter nights.

On many a night I not only saw those lights but in spite of what the experts say, I *heard* them.

I would stand and wait quietly at night, on the snow covered fields of Young's hill, watching and listening for those lights to appear, with their "swishing" sounds as they passed overhead.

Scientists say that the lights are created by the reflective rays of the sun bouncing off the ice packs in the Artic Circle.

They should have used their ears as well as their eyes, when they were exploring this wonder of wonders. They too may have heard *what I heard "when I was alone"* on those cold and *frosty* winter nights.

Then again perhaps those men of science never found a place as quiet or as peaceful and as totally silent as those nights on Young's hill.

You should have been with me...........

People and events that have impacted my life

The dropping of the first and then the second atomic bombs by the USA on Hiroshima and Nagasaki, two cities in Japan
Sputnik

Astronauts from the USA, first setting foot on the moon and then being able to returned home again.

U S President John F. Kennedy's assassination.

Robert Kennedy's assassination.

Martin Luther King Jr. assassination

Roger Bannister breaking the four-minute mile *human* time barrier.

9/11

California earthquake.

Worldwide disasters caused by flood, famine, drought and tropical storms.

The flooding and aftermath of the city of New Orleans

My accidents {incidents}

Famous People I have met

Mohammad Ali - World heavyweight boxing champion

Jimmy Ellis - World-class boxer.

Gordon Howe. -. Mr hockey

Tensing of the Mount Everest expedition

Pierre Trudeau – Prime minister of Canada

Events and locations that I have been privileged to visit.

1967 World Expo {world fair} in Montreal

1984 World exhibition {world fair} in Vancouver BC

The 1952 Royal Winter Fair in Toronto

Niagara Falls

The1988 Calgary Stampede

Port a Rico

Haiti

Hawaiian Islands 1960

The Mediterranean Islands

Mexico and Haiti

Most Canadian Provinces and US States
The Strip at Vegas
The Grand Canyon
The Rocky Mountains
Disney World

Prologue on Incidents

The following pages contain *my narrative* of the "near death" experiences that I have had over a span of several years.

Many of *my close calls* took place during the years that I spent traversing the continent's highways, *picking up* recreational vehicles from RV manufacturing plants located both in Canada and the United States and returning them to Bridgewater, Nova Scotia.

The greatest proportion of my incidents occurred on the highways of Ontario, New Brunswick and Quebec in Canada.

When travelling the highways of Eastern Canada and the northern US routes of Maine and Michigan during the wintertime, *you can expect* to run into *an assortment* of dangerous driving situations. A *certain* amount of undesirable highway conditions are a constant expectation when driving as many *and sometimes more* than one thousand miles in a day.

While wildlife, humans, traffic congestion, detours, drunk drivers, speeders, slowpokes, and inattentive drivers are *a constant*, the most dangerous highway conditions originate from changing weather patterns that produce anything from heavy rains, wind, downed trees, icy road surfaces, to total white outs from blowing snow.

It's the *unexpected* that can cause the most violent and life ending accidents.

Black ice is one of the unexpected; it scares the daylights out of me. It appears suddenly on the road surface in front of you, testing both your driving skills and courage to the limits.

Or, when *wind blown* snow causes momentary "white outs" you can do little except hold your breath and maintain a steady hand on your steering wheel; keeping your vehicle moving ahead, firm and straight, until the blindness subsides, while praying that there are no other vehicles stopped or going *too slowly* in the roadway *in front of you*.

There are times when you must slow your car or light truck down to a crawl until the tempest blows over.

It's the *big rig* truckers that cause the most discomfort to us *mere mortal drivers* as they pass us by, *in bad and sometimes* God awful, driving conditions. In their haste to make *on time deliveries* they need to cover sufficient miles during allotted and limited driving hours. Both miles driven and hours of driving must be filed in a logbook, confirming that their daily driving hours comply with the government's mandate. To exceed mandated driving hours carried a heavy penalty.

The National Departments of Transportation have not taken into consideration the hazards *that they have created on the highway* by placing truckers into none compromising positions.

The big rig drivers *might choose caution over expediency by reducing speed when experiencing hazardous weather* and *road conditions* if they had a choice

The DOT has inadvertently added to an even greater possibility for highways accidents.

There is not one long haul trucker in this land that has not driven past smaller and lighter vehicles *under unsavoury driving conditions* that would take offence at the previous statement.

My Incidents

I will now relate to you *"from a vivid* memory" *one of the several* incidents that came *very* close to ending my life, with *the potential* for ending the lives of others.

You will find most of my tales very difficult to believe and for that, I cannot blame you for doubting, as I too can only wonder why so many of these *almost unbelievable* "incidents" happened to me and how and why I survived.

"You should have been with me--- when I was alone"

The first incident I will tell you about *did not happen* on some cold and lonely *weather affected,* stretch of highway, *but in my own backyard; the place* of business that I owned and operated, on a bright and sunny autumn afternoon.

For identification purpose I will rate my incidents in order of level of risk
There are a total of eleven {11} incidents.

The # 1 incident is rated being the least life threatening while the # 11 incident {the last} I consider to be downright scary. You can decide for yourself.

Incident # 1

Out of Control

It is difficult to find words to explain the horror of "life out of control".

This is one of those "life and death moments" that should never have happened and mathematically can never happen to any one person more than once. And, as in most of *my incidents* there was no one around to bear witness.

This "incident" happened when I was attempting to start and move a 40ft Intruder Diesel *pusher* motor home from one location to another on our recreational vehicle sales lot.

A simple task under normal circumstances.

A pusher is a motorhome where the engine is located at the rear section of the chassis or frame and "pushes the vehicle forward" instead of pulling it from a frontal location.

It is constructed that way because the diesel engine weighs thousands of pounds more than a gasoline powered engine and needs the carrying strength of a heavier rear frame assembly with extra large tires to support it, as well as contributing less weight up front to assist steering and handling. The weight of a large "up front" diesel would create a major steering problem because of the extra pounds and cumbersome assembly needed to allow for safe manoeuvring especially when Motor homes are sitting still or moving very slowly. .

The *Intruder* had been parked and had not been started for a week *or more,* sitting in between a row of other "none motorized" RV's at the rear of our sales lot.

On both sides of the MH {motor home} we had parked other *non-motorized* RV units. The two RV's sitting parallel along *both sides* of the Intruder were parked at a distance of approximately three feet *or less* from the unit I was about to remove.

Immediately in front was our metal fabricated office and service building.

Another row of RV's was parked along the side of this structure, facing the Intruder at an angle. The distance from the front of the motor home that I was about to remove and the row of RV's parked alongside this building was about 60 feet, sufficient space to manoeuvre if you are moving at a low speed.

To complicate the removal of this motorized home even more, was the fact that the front section of the RV parked on my drivers side, left side, was sitting angled slightly ahead and *in front of* the MH that I was about to remove.

The RV unit parked on my right side was also parked near the front of the 40-foot MH, as it was a much shorter unit than the Intruder. This was to create an eye *appealing straight line of RV's* for the customers to view.

Had everything gone according to plan, I would have started the Intruder and moved it slowly forward, with a slight turn to the right, then proceed *straight forward* for approximately 30 feet before turning a bit further right and then proceeding straight for several more feet before making a hard left turn towards the front area of the sales lot, where I had intended to re-park it.

I was alone on the lot at the time. It was approximately 4:00 pm

I put the keys in the ignition, which was located on the steering column slightly below and to the right side of the steering wheel.

With the ignition on, I waited for the glow plug to alert me to the fact that the diesel fuel was warm enough to ignite. I then twisted the key to the right.

The MH started almost immediately. I then put the MH into drive position and proceeded to push my right foot down on the accelerator pedal to move the MH slowly forward.

The accelerator did not move.

Without thinking I pressed down harder and again *not thinking of the circumstance* that I was unwittingly creating, I then pushed down even harder, all the while the large Diesel engine was running and the MH was now in a forward drive gear position.

What I recall next will stick with me as long as I have a memory.

I remember hearing an enormous roar as the Diesel sprang to life with the acceleration much the same as that of a jet plane, as the powerful engine had been suddenly injected with a *maximum* amount of fuel.

I was sucked back into the driver's seat and was about to be taken on one of the shortest but most traumatic rides of my life.

The Intruder bus, with the automatic transmission engaged in a forward drive position, suddenly sprang forward, giving *a shocked* me no time whatever to change the gear lever position into neutral or turn off the ignition as both of my hands were planted firmly on the steering wheel as I had to use them to try and control this, now, out of control, monster.

Because of the sudden acceleration the front end of the Intruder nearly lifted clear of the gravel-based lot and I knew right away that this was going to be *big* trouble.

My first response was to push down hard on the brake pedal but I found out immediately that the brakes were no match for the torque of this 275 hp Cummins Diesel running at full throttle. I could only steer this "thing" and I had to do it fast.

With less than the blink of an eye, steer, think, steer, think, steer, survival at all cost.

Amazing things happen when your senses take over and your mind goes on automatic pilot initiating an action directing your conscious and subconscious to work as one. You do not realize it in that moment of crises how the mind and the body are interconnected and co-ordinated.

My mind's survival mechanism was suddenly and without warning on full alert, my hands were automatically turning the steering wheel, first to the right as there was no time or opportunity whatever to seize the transmission lever and move it into neutral and certainly not that extra second of time that it would take to reach down by my right knee and find the key to the ignition in order to shut down this run-a-way *juggernaut* that was about to do me and my business in.

With hands spinning one way and then the other, hand over hand in rapid motion I was aware that by steering too far to the right I would hit the front of the RV parked to my right and rake the side off of this very expensive *customer owned,* Intruder Motor-home.

Going forward was not an option, as it would cause me to collide with the front of the RV parked to my left side exasperating a now uncontrollable situation into total disaster.

Faced with no time to turn right as planned and then take another slow right, I had to invent a survival route and do it fast because at this increased speed any prolonged action would have meant hitting several RV's before ploughing into the sales and service building and at the speed and torque "this baby" was now generating, everything, even total disaster, would have taken less than 3 or 4 seconds.

As the MH jettisoned forward, my eyes and mind took full control, steer right! as that appeared to be the *one and only way* out of my predicament.

By turning right I would at least avoid hitting the RVs parked in front of the office and service building leaving only one medium sized RV left to tangle with.

"I just might make it out of this mess alive".

First right, then left and now right! There was no possible way that I could miss hitting some RVs, so I chose to hit the one parked at the rear of the building and even though this was not such a great idea, it was the best of all the scenarios that might have been.

Did I mention to tell you that this MH was placed in my care on my sales lot to resell, by a personal friend and valued customer?

With a scrunch I heard and felt the left side of the motor home swipe against the rear section of the travel trailer.

"God, I almost made it," but somehow I still felt *satisfied.*

Now finally I had nothing but wide-open space ahead of me for the next 100 feet. It could have been worse, much worse. I was still travelling quite fast but now I had time to react.

I quickly reached down and turned off the ignition. After what I had just experienced, to say the sound of silence is golden, was an under statement.

As bad as this incident was there was not even the slightest consideration in my mind that I could have done any better. My heart was still pumping like crazy and felt like it was going to burst with elation at what my body and mind had just accomplished.

"What just happened back there"? was my first thought? Next thought; "How in heaven's name did I survive this nightmare, suffering only minimal damage?"

I remember being very much relieved after the visual damage assessment, mostly superficial, to both the travel trailer and the MH.

I immediately phoned the local detachment of the RCMP. {Royal Canadian Mounted Police} After relating my experience, they told me that they would investigate.

I then called the Mallard Manufacturing Company, the company that produced the Motor home. They told me that they did not build the Diesel engines but only installed them onto their chassis.
The Diesel equipped chassis is delivered to them, the MH manufacturer, who proceeds to construct the home onto the chassis.
After a brief conversation with a Mallard Company spokesman I was assured that they would take care of the costs *of all damages.*

Next I contacted the *local* diesel service experts, who after hearing my story warned me not to try and restart the diesel engine. A mechanic told me to wait until they assessed the diesel engine to see what went wrong.

To make a longer story short the mechanic pointed out to me that the malfunction was caused by an engineering fault. He found that the linkage to the accelerator was jammed against other operational linkage at a point where it was connected to the engine and the accelerator could not return to an idle position without a mechanical altering change.

Because of my having pushed the accelerator pedal down, diesel fuel was being forced into the cylinders *at full throttle* because the foot controlled fuel pedal was now in a max position, and could not return to its normal position because of the jammed linkage.

The mechanic told me that I was really one lucky fellow as he had heard *of much worse endings* to similar incidents.

I later had several conversations with the DOT {Department of Transportation} in both Canada and the USA.

Both authoritative bodies confirmed that this or similar problems were on record, that several accidents with diesel powered vehicles had occurred before, apparently because of the *same or similar* circumstances.

In conversation with several additional *diesel informed* persons, they too confirmed that Diesels can do mean things when the engines are running out of control. They also told me *that I was very lucky.*

They told me that normally a diesel generates *so great a torque* when this type of malfunction happens that the vehicle *usually* breaks a rear axel rendering the unit immobile This did not happen in *my incident* as the rear wheels were located on gravel which provided enough traction for a quick lift-off, but the gravel base, not being as solid as concrete or asphalt did not supply friction sufficient to create adequate traction *to snap* an axel.

I did not feel it immediately, in the moments of my terror, but shortly after the incident my mind and body began to be traumatized by what had just happened, as neither my mind nor body would function singularly or cohesively; this weird feeling lasted for several hours after the incident.

If there was any good thing to have come out of this, it was the fact that *I was fortunate* to be alone at the time, for if there had been anyone standing in front of this "juggernaut" when it took off, they would have most likely been run over, and had anyone been in the way of the route which I was taking during those several runaway seconds, they too would have been in grave danger.

I was incensed; *I could have been a killer* at no fault of my own making
Time has not soon diminished my inner anger.

Later that same evening when my wife and I attended a dance class that we were enrolled in, my feet would not obey my mind's command and in spite of how long and hard I concentrated, I just could not make my legs move to my mind's direction. It was a weird feeling; one that I never had before or since.

The total cost of repairs to the travel trailer and motor home was in the $20,000 range. The manufacturers never contributed a dime to the repairs.
The Mallard Coach Company is no longer in business.

The Department of Transportation in both Canada and the U.S. may have provided letters of awareness to those responsible for the existing problem of this Diesel engine and the chassis Manufacturers.
I do not know, but I hope they did.

In summary, neither I nor anyone else was physically hurt and both my Company and I survived the ordeal, all to the wonderful apparatus that comprises the human brain and body working together, *as they are designed to do* when danger overtakes us.

Was something or someone guiding my mind and *human* physical movements that day, who's to say for sure?

Just maybe, someone or some power was there, with me and within me, guiding my hands, my eyes, *my mind,*

"When, I thought I was alone" CWY

Chapter Three

Incident Section

Incidents

The original intention for writing about *my* **incidents** was to comprise a record in print for personal and family use of the many *near* fatalities that I have had in my life.

As stated elsewhere in this book, tens of thousands and perhaps *even tens of millions* of individuals worldwide have had similar singular *incidents* during *their* lifetime but there is where the similarity ends. What differs is this.
I have exceeded the national *average number* of survival incidents by a country mile.

Most *incidents* happened **when I was alone,** without any witnesses.
I can only swear to a higher power that what I am about to write and you are about to read, that "I am telling the truth, the whole truth, and nothing but the truth".

I have chosen eleven {11} incidents to tell you about. The level of personal risk escalates, as the numbers grow higher. Number one {1} incident was related earlier in this book and was *sort of a preview* to the remainder. I think that you will be mesmerized by several of the ensuing ten {10} incidents, how they unfolded and finally the *profound* question, to you and to **YOU- God,** why am I still around to tell others about them?

It is far better to have been born lucky, than rich. Word's repeated to me, many times, by my grandmother Elva.

Incident # 2

As a child of twelve years old I had the usual amount of *close calls*, one of note being a *near* drowning incident at a summer fun spot located about a mile below the town of Bridgewater at a place, now a public park, known as Horse Shoe Point, where, but for a few spindly reeds extending themselves out from the side of the riverbank, I would have been washed out to sea.

After making the easy jump *downward* from the mainland to the small Island we soon decided to leave the Island. Getting off the Island wasn't as easy as getting on, as the mainland was situated slightly above the landmass of the Island. In returning to the mainland my one and only jump attempt was not quite long enough to breach the distance to the opposite bank of the stream. In desperation I reached out and grabbed hold of the only thing that was there to get a hold of, the reeds. With my right arm and hand fully extended I clung on to them for dear life.

Had I missed clutching those sparse and fragile lifelines in my *one and only* attempt, and had they not been strong enough to hold my floating body weight, I would have been swept out into the larger stream by the current and then downward towards the picturesque but deadly LaHave river and then onward and out into the Atlantic Ocean several miles down river and no one may have even noticed that I was missing, as I was the last one in a group of ten or more kids that made this sojourn on that sunny Sunday afternoon, first jumping over the stream onto the Island and then back again to the mainland. Being a swimmer may have helped but I was no swimmer, then or now.

I never told my family about it.

I almost didn't make it.

YOU should have been there with me.

Incident # 3

I had another close call when walking over an ice-covered lake when the spring ice was starting to break up.

I believe the lake was called Fitch Lake and I was taking a short cut across a portion of the lake to save time instead of doing the safer but slower and longer walk around the snow-covered land that surrounded the lake.

Once out on the lake I realized that I was in trouble as my body weight started to break through the top layer of ice downward to another layer of older ice about a foot below the more recently frozen top ice.

Going forward towards the nearest shore was the only sensible option available to me, but had it not been for a long *needled* branch from a pine tree that miraculously appeared near me on the ice I would have had a difficult time of making shore. By using the branch to spread my body weight out over a larger portion of the rotting ice I was able to make shore. And there were no witnesses.

YOU should have been there………...

Incident # 4

This was the time that I was walking alongside a school friend {Harold Conrad} through the woods that was not a part of the school property but was nearby and adjacent to our old yellow schoolhouse, which Harold and I attended. We were walking along side-by-side talking quietly on the lookout for squirrels or crows to shoot at, as we had done on several previous occasions. All of a sudden the gun that my friend was carrying accidentally discharged and the bullet went directly across and in front of me. It may not have been fatal as it was only a 22calibre rifle, but if it had hit a vital part of my body it was certainly close enough to me to have enough power to kill or maim.

I thought it worthy of *incident # 4*.

Incident # 5

Driving through New Brunswick on our way to Hensall Ontario to pick up an RV, recreational vehicle, almost became the day of demise for me and for one of my company's youngest employees.

My young employee {name withheld} had never been to the Province of Ontario before, so I invited him to go along on the trip with me as it would give him an opportunity to see the landscape and scenery beyond our home Province of Nova Scotia and to enable him to tell his friends that he had seen both the larger cities of Montreal and Toronto.

The pre-trip plan was for him to assist me in the driving, as it was a long and tiring trip up to the General Coach RV factory which was located approximately a one hour drive northwest of Toronto in a small town called Hensall; a distance of about twelve hundred miles from home.

A short time before we left to go on this trip my young employee became attached to his first serious girlfriend. Along the way we had conversed mostly about his infatuation for his new friend and finally I got bored with the conversation and *crawled* back over the front seat of the Oldsmobile station wagon to the rear section that had been converted into a sleeping area with blankets and a pillow.

I had driven for several hours and it came time for my young employee to take his first turn at driving.

It was in the early afternoon and the road traffic was light, so I thought it was safe for both him and me, if I was to take a *rest* before again taking over the driving.

After a short time in the bed area of the Oldsmobile wagon I found that I could not rest so I again *crawled* out over the front seat and sloughed back in the passenger's seat to relax, if not to sleep.

There was no conversation between him and me, which is not unusual for many male drivers, who would rather drive than talk. But this quiet time was eerily different; my young companion was *too* quiet.

A large maroon coloured car, either a Ford or a Chrysler product first came into my view from a good distance away, heading towards us on the two-lane highway. The road was dry and pencil straight as we approached the car.

It was about this time I noticed that my young driver was either in some sort of a trance or had a mind fixation as he had a blank look on his face and our Oldsmobile wagon was gradually trending towards the left and wrong side of the road.

The maroon car was getting closer rapidly and my young driver did not seem aware that our vehicle was gradually heading left across the white centre dividing line.

We were travelling at the standard highway speed of 60 miles per hour and I tend to believe that the approaching car and driver was doing a like speed

What to do? Grab the wheel from him, only to have him yank it away from me by suddenly pulling left and right into the oncoming car, or what else might I do?

I shouted his name, loud and clear!

At once he snapped out of his hypnotic state and with less than the blink of an eye he, seeing the large maroon car, now nearly in front of him, pulled hard right on the steering wheel and away from the big sedan.

Now an Oldsmobile station wagon is not the most agile vehicle at anytime and at sixty miles an hour it would be difficult if not impossible to keep it on the roadway after an unplanned and sudden sideways jerk on the steering wheel.

The heavy wagon responded by lurching hard right as the maroon vehicle whizzed past us, then it swung back again left and then right as my young driver battled to keep the Olds under control and on the highway.

He did magnificently.

I let him drive for another half mile or so and then I asked him to stop and suggested to him that I would drive.

We never discussed that incident afterwards but I know in my heart and mind that *his mind and his body* were back home either sitting in his car or resting on a soft comfortable lounge cuddled up with his new found love, as he was totally *oblivious to everything* except the scene back home.

I was angry.

Had it not been for me getting out of that *makeshift* bed in the back of the Oldsmobile, coming forward and seeing what was about to happen, both of us and whoever was in he other vehicle would have surely died that day.

I had no time to see the number of passengers in the large maroon sedan as it sped by.

I wonder if the other driver also saw what was about to happen and reacted by steering right to avoid us.

After taking over the driving I proceeded to drive to the General Coach factory and back home again *with only one hour rest,* stopping only long enough to pick up the RV, gas and some food.

I remained angry at my young driver *and just as angry at myself* long afterwards for helping create a situation that could have caused the deaths of several people and change the lives of many others.

When I read about *head-on* collisions between two vehicles on straight dry roads, I now understand how they can happen.

YOU should have been with me

Incident # 6

This incident happened in the Canadian Province of Newfoundland on one of my many fishing trips to this wild and rugged Island which is found one half a time zone north of my home Province of Nova Scotia. It was on or about June 24th 1997.

Our pilot, Jean Ploughman, gently landed his Beaver floatplane on the seven-mile long lake known as Lake Jubilee and had taxied up to a half demolished wharf to assist our party of four in the unloading process of our fishing supplies. He wanted to make our *carry* as labour-less as possible.

The wharf had once been a functional structure but only a few months before our arrival the Provincial Department of the Interior {I think that is what it is called} had decreed the dismantling of the wharf in order to discourage *outsiders* from landing on the lake and littering the once pristine surroundings.

A noble thought but the reality of their decree was like just about every other venture that governments manage; it was a mess from start to finish.

The Department's employees used chainsaws to cut through every plank of the wharf through the middle in order to render the wharf useless. That part they did get right.

We did manage to find several post s still standing having enough stability to tie up the Beaver, unload it, and then send it airborne again without any mishaps.

We would worry about reloading the plane when it returned to pick us up six days later.

What the Beaver float plane left behind was four very excited and anxious fishermen and a week's supply of food staples setting on the crippled wharf, waiting to be moved, as soon as we saw that the small floatplane was again airborne, up to the confines of our fishing camp, which was now regulated to being only a canvas tent, erected on a wooden platform. The Department had burned down the sturdy and colourful log cabin, which had been our previous shelter.

The tent was located near the burnt out remains of the cabin, about a few hundred feet up from the lake.

The floatplane was hardly out of sight and we had made a few "carries" from the damaged wharf up to the tent when it happened.

I was carrying an *overload* of fishing gear and was walking *timidly* across what was left of the wharf towards the shore, when I inadvertently stepped on one of the sawed off planks, a short plank that was not nailed down to any supporting beam whatever.

Without warning I went into a free fall as the unsecured plank tipped over and I, and my load, headed downwards towards the water below, or so I thought.

I had no time to control or change what happened next.

Falling down sideways and backwards with an armful of fishing supplies towards an unknown destination was bad enough, but hitting the back of my head on one of the wharf's remaining support timbers of the partially dismantled wharf below was even worse.

My body hit hard enough but had some flexibility; my head had no flex whatever as it hit the wooden beam with a sickening thud that left me feeling a bit dazed and more then a little embarrassed.

I may have never mentioned my fall to anyone had it not been for my good friend, Reid DeLong, who was just returning from the tent to the wharf to get another load of supplies and was watching me as I went flying through the air.

Reid said later that he was amazed to see my acrobatics and more relieved to see that I regained my upright posture so quickly.

Upon getting back on my feet and checking around to see why and what had happened we found a large rusty spike protruding out of the beam only an inch or two from where my head had hit it.

Had my head hit that spike it would have been curtains for me for sure, as that old rusty spike being about four inches long would have easily penetrated my skull from the force of my body falling and my head hitting the beam. Even under more favourable circumstances I would never have made it to a hospital in time as we had no way of contacting our pilot or the plane until it was landed back at its home base in Clarenville, about an hours flying time from Jubilee Lake.

We re-spiked as many of the other loose planks as we could find on what was left of the wharf and from then on we were a bit more cautious where we placed our feet when walking on them.

Since that time we have secured the services of a satellite phone service, "just in case".

They say an inch is as good as a mile, in my case *that spike being an inch away* from my head was as good as it gets.

Incident # 7

After several days of rain, the bridge over the west bank of the LaHave River on the road leading to Branch LaHave was washed out. The demise of the bridge was precipitated by the weight of a large truck crossing over it, and because of the fast moving water, erosion to the bridge supports was fast and furious. The bridge gave way and both truck and driver were swept down into the swollen river, along with the bridge.

The driver escaped but the truck did not.

The washout happened after dark as I can still remember seeing the truck's headlights shining brightly for several days after the accident. It must have had a fully charged battery to last that long.

The truck had come to rest several hundred feet down river from where it and the bridge had fallen into the swollen stream.

After that, any access to the Branch, and home, from the town of Bridgewater, meant travelling a different and longer route. It also meant crossing over a much longer bridge traversing the main artery of the LaHave. It also meant using a road that contained a *much* longer bridge and a much longer and steeper hill leading up and away from the bridge, than the one previously used.

Both the bridge and hill were named after the Wentzell's, as several families by the name of Wentzell lived in the area, and they owned the land and a lumber sawmill near the bridge and on the river. The mill was located approximately five hundred feet below the bridge and immediately in front of and at the base of a high dam that was constructed over the river to supply waterpower for the mill and also for control of the waters of a lake, also named Wentzell, which was located a thousand feet or so above the mill and bridge. The waters behind the dam and under the bridge were deep, dark, with a powerful current.

The hill on Wentzell's road, near and around the bridge, can still be a bit of an adventure, even today, over 50 years later, especially in the winter months when the hill is icy. Vehicles entering the high narrow iron bridge must slow down to a crawl and once across the bridge you are immediately at the base of the hill. The road makes a slight turn to the right as you exit the bridge before graduating up unto a couple of higher plateaus before finally reaching the summit, a distance of approximately one quarter mile.

The turns in the dirt roads at either end of the bridge discourage all motorists to a minimum amount of speed.

When my *incident* took place it was a far different and more difficult road than it is today.

To drive a car up Wentzell's hill when it was covered with ice was almost impossible, unless you had steel chains on your rear driving wheels. Back then there were only rear drive wheels and you had better have a good *run on* as you approached the base of the hill to have any hope of ever reaching the crest, and the best time to try this manoeuvre was in the daytime.

I approached the hill *that night* at a cautious speed and I didn't get more than a hundred feet up when I could go no further, as the rear tires were spinning, and worse yet, I started sliding downwards, back towards the lake, and the high, narrow, iron bridge, awaiting me at its base.

Arriving safely back on the bridge I gave a sigh of relief and decided then and there that I must increase my car's speed to maximum if I was ever going to reach the summit successfully and arrive back home on Young's hill at a respectable hour.

That wasn't about to happen.

I proceeded to reverse my 1954 Studebaker six cylinder automatic back as far as possible, while still having my rear wheels remaining on the bridge. I then started to accelerate forward as fast as possible. Too much speed meant getting into additional trouble upon reaching the far end of the bridge, because of the sharp turn at the base of the hill.

Once I was safely off the bridge I kept accelerating forward in a valiant attempt to successfully make it up and over the last plateau, when low and behold, while my rear driving wheels continued spinning forward, my Studebaker was again starting to slide backwards.

The backwards slide began slowly at first; possibly the sliding might stop.

I didn't want to think about ever sliding all the way to the bottom, with what might await me down there, in the dark and alone.

No such luck.

Faster and faster the ice, which is now polished smoother and even slicker from my spinning tires as I moved forwards and up the hill, is now carrying the Studebaker and me backwards even faster than on my first attempt, and all I can do is sit there and hold tightly on to the steering wheel. All the while, I have the car's brakes jammed hard on, and can only wait and hope for some miracle to save me.

I pray that a similar *incident* never happens to you or anyone else.

I was frozen in position, waiting, holding my breath, needing this nightmare of a ride to end soon, but not really, the end results could never be good.

Did I tell you that directly at the base of the hill and immediately above the large iron bridge that straddles the river, nothing exists to stop an out of control vehicle, nothing but very deep water as there were no guard rails or posts or anything else to prevent me from going off the road and into an icy grave.

Some years before a car carrying three people from one family, drowned in this very same spot.

I never gave it a thought of jumping out of the car, as I should have done. All I did was continue to hold tightly to the steering wheel with both hands while my right foot remained clamped down hard on the brakes.

My carefree night of dating in Bridgewater followed by a routine drive home was about to have a very sorry ending, for both me and my Studebaker.

As the night was moonless and pitch black I was unable to see anything that was happening around me.

What seemed like an eternity was probably less than a minute or two as the car and I continued to slide backwards down the entire length of the hill and then continued backwards even further onto the bridge, without ever slowing down, until all of a sudden the car came to an abrupt stop!

My Studebaker and I were somehow spared an untimely demise, as we were now stopped unhurt and sitting at least two thirds of the distance across that old iron bridge.

My firmly braked and *non-rotating* tires had finally found something beneath them that wasn't slippery.
Elated, would be the best one word explanation of how I felt.

I cannot remember praying at any time but I do remember breathing a long and deep sigh of relief when the car had finally stopped.

But the story doesn't quite end there.

I then proceeded to put steel chains on the rear drive wheels and tires.
Most winter drivers carried chains along *just in case* but before I was able to finish installing them on my car, the battery went dead.

I had left the engine running to keep the battery charged but the headlights must have drawn more current from the battery than the generator was producing.

I can tell you here and now that patience was not one of my virtues that night.

I could not leave a stalled automobile sitting overnight alone and blocking the bridge and roadway, so I had to sit there on the bridge in an increasingly cold car and wait until morning arrived.
Thank God it came early!

At around five o'clock a. m. Mr Roy Joudrey, a man who lived at the upper end of Branch LaHave came upon me on his way to working in Halifax. He gave the battery a boost and I proceeded to back out of his way to let him pass by and then I successfully passed over Wentzell's hill and was home within fifteen minutes.

I have never forgotten a second of that scary experience. What kept my car from sliding out of those icy tracks and prevented me from going off the road and into the lake as had happened the Beeswanger family?

The only sensible answer that I can arrive at is this.
I must have made the correct driving procedures by keeping the brakes of the Studebaker locked on, causing the tires to slide like a sled and by holding the steering wheel straight and firm.
These two simple but vital actions kept the car in a sliding pattern not allowing the front wheels of the car to roll out of those icy ruts and better yet, not allowing the car to go sideways off the road and into the deep water above the bridge.
I even missed hitting the wide steel support beams that anchored the bridge to its cement footing.
Was it plain old good luck or was it Providence?

If you have a better answer I am willing to listen.

I visited the bridge and the hill site a few days prior to this writing and found that several large trees have since grown up in the *danger area* above the bridge. A 200-foot guardrail with sturdy support posts has also since been erected providing a safety barrier along the road next to the lake, thus protecting any unsuspecting driver and vehicle from doing th*e unthinkable.*

In the meantime all I can say is this,
YOU should have been with me that night when I was alone

Incident # 8

It is what did not happen that makes this incident noteworthy.

Driving Eastward from Quebec city towards the New Brunswick border in the winter is no picnic at the best of times but when the fields along side the roads are covered with a fresh dusting of light snow and a wind is blowing off the St Lawrence River it can be an adventure that no one needs.

This was *one of those days*.

As usual I was pulling a large RV and the roads and fields were covered with a dry powdery snow that requires caution but beyond that the roads were drivable as long as you could see them. Anyone that has driven on those roads under such conditions knows what I mean, all is well until an eighteen-wheeler or an even larger truck passes you at over sixty miles per hour. Then driving visibility is God-awful.

I have often wondered how the drivers of those big rigs can see to drive under similar blowing snow conditions but with deadlines to keep they have little alternative then to keep the hammer down and keep moving at posted highway speed limits, come hell or high water.

I believe that sitting high above the roads in those huge truck cabs gives them a vision advantage that smaller lower vehicles do not have.

I trust that they, the semi drivers, must realize what is happening *inside* those smaller vehicles that they pass containing drivers with less "bad road" experience

Many car and light truck drivers are intimidated and therefore more cautious when being passed by those big rigs, which generate enough flying snow to cause several seconds *or more* of sightless driving.

It is a frightful experience.

The first thing I do is slack off of the fuel pedal, keep the steering wheel straight and hold my breath until the tempest blows past.

This was one of those blowing snow days and as I drove further east the wind kept increasing until I was unable to decipher the main road from an exit or entrance road to a small town in Eastern Quebec called Degelis.

Degelis is situated at the eastern end of route 185.nearing the New Brunswick border town of Edmonston I *mistakenly* entered one of the town's entrance roads leading into Degelis.

As soon as I noted the error I stopped and attempted to turn my truck and RV around and again return to the 185 and continue eastward towards home.

I successfully turned the truck and trailer in the blowing snow and was accelerating fast forward towards what I thought was the only road ahead when without warning a car sped past the front of me and my truck, snow flying high and continued on without ever seeing me.

I never saw any stop sign or the road that was passing directly parallel in front of me, nor did I see the car that was on that road while continuing to travel forward in what I thought was my right of way.

Not only was the snow blowing but the sides of the roadways had high snow banks obscuring visibility.

To repeat how bad the driving conditions were that day; I was in the wrong and didn't know it, as I had no sight of that cross road or the car that almost hit me.

If I had been *one second* further ahead that car and driver who was definitely in the right and doing nothing wrong would have driven squarely into the driver's side of my truck.

My God! I thought as I jammed hard down on my brake pedal slowing my truck and trailer somewhat, I could have been killed and probably killed others but for one second, or less, I would have been directly in the path of the other vehicle.

A "close call" could not cover describing this one; this was *really* close, the closest I have ever come to ending my life and no one was around. Not even the driver of the other car that I had narrowly missed colliding with was aware that he/or she came so close to disaster. And I would have been solely responsibility.

I have told few friends {and none of the family} about this one and the few that I did tell didn't seem all that impressed.
YOU should have been with me when I was alone.

Incident # 9

I had a dream.
No I am not Martin Luther King Jr. but I did have a dream.
I had a reoccurring dream that perplexed me immensely over several years.
The scene was always the same, a big highway with lots of trucks, big trucks.
What was it about? It never ended, only suspended until it returned.
Was someone sending me a message and if so, how do I prepare?
Was I about to have an accident on a busy highway; a highway where a great number of big trucks travelled?
What was the dream about, what was the final message to be?
Did I survive or not?
Always questions but never answers.

This dream or vision was not on my mind that September 12th morning in 1986.

I'll let you mull over the next statement as you continue reading.

This *incident*, that almost killed me, ended up saving my life.

On September 11th 1986 I and another employee {Barry Myra} left Bridgewater Nova Scotia with plans of picking up two new travel trailers from a Canadian Recreational Vehicle manufacturing plant owned by the General Coach Corporation.

General Coach was located in Hensall a small town west of the city of Toronto.

To travel together in one vehicle {to save time and fuel} we hooked the two tow vehicles together one behind the other. The one being towed was a 1975 Oldsmobile Vista Cruiser station wagon. The towing vehicle was a 1980 Chevy ¾ ton truck with a 427 cubic inch engine. Both vehicles were in excellent condition having excellent tires and large gas engines.

The trip was over two thousand four hundred miles return. The Olds wagon was converted into a sleeping unit by lowering the rear seats and installing a foam mattress, pillows and blankets. It also contained extra gas, tools and a change of clothing for both drivers.

Picking up RVs from distant locations meant trips that were non-stop except for food, fuel and toilet services. We had made similar excursions before without problems.

I had driven several hours during the previous night and when morning came we found ourselves on highway 401 in Ontario, one of the safest highways in Canada.

At 6AM we stopped for breakfast. The roadside Plazas in Ontario allow for a quick food and fuel stop and back on the 401 with a minimum loss of driving time.

I had pancakes and sausages that morning of September 12; As soon as we gassed up we hit the road again.

The time had arrived for Barry to take the driving wheel for the next several hours.

"Do you want to lie down on the bed in the station wagon?" Barry asked. "No", I answered, "This is bad enough", I said with a laugh, I then took two pillows that were in the Oldsmobile wagon and proceeded to make myself comfortable by *stretching back* in the truck's cab. I then pushed my seat back as far as it would go and, placing the pillows underneath my head and closing my eyes, I quickly dozed off.

But I do not sleep well in a moving vehicle.

I tried my best to get some rest in this upright position but, needing to find a more comfortable resting place, I managed to find enough space on the seat in the cab between the driver {Barry} and the passenger's door. Using one pillow under my head, the other pillow on top of my head and by covering my left ear to drown out any road noises, I finally dozed off.

The pillows may have saved my life.

Before dozing off I had previously removed both my seat and shoulder belt to find the most comfortable lying down position.

That action could have also helped save me.

To set the scene, it was now about 6 AM, the skies were overcast, the roads were wet {not raining} and the ditches along HWY 401 were filled with water. We were told later that it had rained steadily for almost a full week prior to our visit.

As I said earlier, I am not one for sleeping in a moving vehicle but everything seemed safe and secure and I was tired and if ever I fell asleep quickly this was the one time.

In what seemed like only a few minutes but was more like an hour I was suddenly awakened by the voice of Barry saying, "Oh my God! Oh no!"

I immediately raised my head and asked at the same time and motion "Why, is something wrong?"

It took me almost four months before I remembered that brief conversation with Barry, Barry says he has no recollection of saying anything to me.

As my head rose up from the truck seat with my eyes wide open, I remember a surreal sight.

The metallic brown Oldsmobile wagon that was originally being towed by our red Chevrolet truck was now almost adjacent and alongside the red Chevrolet tow truck, only it was going backwards, the rear of the Olds was almost parallel with the cab of our towing truck.

What I will write about next are words and thoughts that were hidden for several months somewhere deep in my mind.

The inside cab of the truck impacted the top of my head and hit directly on the memory area of my brain. It tore away a large portion of my scalp from the skull that took several hours and hundreds of stitches to replace.

Neither the Doctors nor I knew at this time about the more serious injury of my having a vertebrae in my neck broken. This was discovered several weeks later.

I am a living witness that your subconscious mind will never allow your conscious mind to tell a lie. I will explain.

What I remember first was the bright lights and *semi loud* whistles.

My eyes failed to comprehend anything other than basic bells and whistle sounds.

My only recollection of feelings is that I had no pain, only that my back seemed to be propped up against something firm and I had a muted sense of hearing a distant jumble and jingle and mingle of musical notes.

If this was dying it was not all that bad.

"Did you have your seatbelt on?" a firm voice asked. It came from someone sightless to me.

It was probably an Ontario Provincial Police officer who was on the scene asking me that question but I never confirmed it. It may have been a fireman or a paramedic.

Looking back today at what must have been a horrific accident scene, it seems strange to me that there was more interest in my wearing or not wearing a seatbelt than there was for my physical condition; strange indeed.

I had to be a mess; unless skulls don't bleed. But the question was continually repeated...

The accident scene made the nightly TV news and a large picture complete with a write-up made the local newspaper {I was given a copy of the picture and story line and I may still have it somewhere}

The Oldsmobile had broken loose from the truck's tow bar and ended up down off the highway some distance from the truck. The truck had impacted cab first into a solid rock wall that ran parallel to the highway. After hitting the wall of rock it then overturned and ended up in water filled ditch along side the 401.

The newspaper headline read - Tire Blows but Seatbelt Saves. It was a crock from the beginning as neither statement was true, as no truck tires blew out and no seatbelt saved.

Since then I haven't put a lot of stock in accurate journalism.

I am now and have always been an advocate for wearing safety belts but on that day in that particular accident I am sure that I would have been crushed down and killed instantly had I had my seatbelt on as that portion of the truck's cab where I had been sitting was smashed inwards towards the passenger's seat.

So what saved me from the initial impact?

Having no seat belts to hold me in place and in my seat under the crushed cab, I ended up being thrown over and across to the driver's side of the cab where I was knocked unconscious from my head hitting the top of the cab above the steering wheel.

The two pillows also cushioned me from full impact as I remembered much later of rolling over and over but there was always something soft {my two pillows} cushioned me.

By my being jettisoned over and in front of the driver, Barry received only a minor scratch on his forehead as his body was thrown against me and my body then cushioning him from hitting the steering wheel and the front of the inside of the truck's cab.

The cause of the accident was never determined other than the newspaper headline.

I have my own theory, which I will not discuss here, but the 401 near Brockville where the accident occurred had a slight incline, poor banking and a curve in it. The truck travelling at highway speed of 110 kilometres per hour and pulling a heavy vehicle behind did nothing to alleviate the situation.

By the truck leaving the highway and slamming into the nearest rock wall the Oldsmobile wagon broke free from the tow-bar and continued on past the impact scene.

Upon impact and first crushing the passenger's side of the cab, the truck then rolled over and ended up in one of the water filled ditches along side the highway, up side down.

The Oldsmobile wagon ended up battered and bruised beyond repair further down the 401.

The company that towed both our red Chevy truck and Olds station wagon away from the highway accident scene to a storage depot near the 401 settled up with me several months later by keeping the two damaged vehicles and paying me one hundred and fifty dollars to settle the costs of the towing bill.

There were several hundreds of dollars worth of tools and other equipment in the back of the Olds station wagon when it was towed away to be stored in the towing company's compound but I was in no position to argue.

I also carried only PL & PD insurance {public liability and property damage} but no collision insurance on either vehicle as I had always said, "If we ever have an accident it will not be because it is our fault," so sure was I of the safety of our vehicles and the competency of our drivers.
So much for saving money, by not buying collision insurance.
The loss was almost more than my fledgling company could bear.

Authorities who first arrived at the scene were confused about what really happened as they found two smashed vehicles but one vehicle didn't appear to have a driver.
It probably did not take them long to put the accident picture together and come to a conclusion of why there was only one driver.

What I relate to you now took several months of mental rehabilitation before my mind awakened to these facts.
The memory portion of my brain was damaged far greater than first thought as it took almost two years before my memory returned to "before the accident" normal.

On initial impact with the rock formation my body flew across the interior of the truck from right to left ending up still inside the truck but lying on the roof of the now upside down cab. My face was in the water that was now filling the overturned top section of the cab.

Barry {the driver} remained fully conscious and aware of my predicament. Luckily for me, he came through the crash with only a scratch on his forehead.

He asked me "Are you hurt?" My answer was, "I cannot move," and my head then fell face forward, unconscious, into the water.

Had Barry been seriously hurt, I would not have survived, as my nose and mouth were now submerged in several inches of water.

According to Barry he struggled {he is only a small man,} to lift my *dead weight* body and bones, up and out through a door window of the cab of the truck.

In simple terms Barry saved my life.

I kidded him many times afterwards that he almost killed me so that he could save me.

I remembered nothing more until I heard a voice asking me if I had my seat belt on.

What a strange question under the circumstances. There must have been a better question like "how are you or are you hurt etc" but no "did you have your seatbelt on" instead.

No I did not have my seat belt on, I remember responding. And again in response to the same question "No I did not have my seat belt on"

If I had been answering using my conscious mind I would probably have said "No", or "I don't know," knowing that the rules are severe in Ontario as well as other Provinces of Canada and states of the U.S.A. should you be stopped by the police while not wearing your seat and shoulder belts.

But being guilty of any crime was of little concern to me at that moment.

Someone spoke up and said, "Yes; yes he did have his seat belt on". It was Barry.

"No I did not," I disagreed with Barry to the point of arguing with my only *one line* verbal reply. The debate raged on between "my subconscious," the OPP {Ontario Provincial Police} and Barry until I must have passed out as I no longer remember this *insane* conversation.

The first inkling that I was involved in an accident was when I came to my senses lying in the back of an ambulance. I can recall some sort of crazy thought like "I must be having a bad dream" because I *reasoned* that as long as I did not wake up, I did not have to deal with what seemed to me to be a very bad experience.

But restrain as much as I could, my mind continued to clear enough to allow me to open my eyes. Sensing that I must have been in an accident I must deal with it; as I was strapped to a backboard and riding in the victim's section of a speeding ambulance.

A young man with Asian characteristics was with me in the ambulance and seeing my eyes open, asked me how I felt.
"What happened?" was my first question.
You had an accident and you were hurt *bad*. "Bad" I thought, why would he say *bad*?

My second question was, "How is the other fellow?" as I knew that there was someone else travelling with me but I could not think of his name. "He's okay," the young man answered, but I mistrusted his answer, for had he said the other person was dead I would not have had an extra heartbeat; such was my condition.

My third and final question, "Was there anyone else involved?" "No", he answered, not as far as he knew, but that the two smashed vehicles added to the confusion of the rescuers involved.

I then closed my eyes not knowing if I had arms or legs or if I was about to die but with sense enough to know that there was nothing I could do to change the present situation.
I was strangely *content* that if my life was to end here and now *I would be okay.*

I still think about that moment when I was confronted with accepting death over life and the contentment of that decision. I surrendered all.

The first ambulance stop was only for a brief period at the Brockville city hospital {the nearest hospital to the accident} where the Doctors assessed my condition as more serious than they wished to deal with and sent me away to the Kingston General, a larger hospital which was better equipped to handle cerebral or head injuries.

By the time the ambulance arrived in Kingston I was fully awake and aware of my circumstances, but try as I might I could not remember my name or where I came from and I still could not remember the name of my employee and passenger, Barry. I kept referring to him as "the other fellow".

"I know I am from a long ways away," is the best answer I could come up with for several hours but before noon the hospital had identified who I was and where I was from.

I was asked if I wanted them to contact my wife and family back home in Bridgewater Nova Scotia.

I told them to wait until they had me stabilized, when they knew that I would be okay before making the phone call. I did not know until later that the hospital called back home as soon as they spoke with me.

I had no plans other than spending some time in the hospital {how much time I did not know} and I had no idea that my wife Dolly and son Darren {who worked for Bluenose RV} would book passage by plane and arrive at the Kingston General at 10 o-clock pm that night.

They arrived at my bedside only moments before a Doctor had finished putting the final stitches in my scalp to reattach it to my head. It was a slow and exacting job and nearing the end of the ordeal I asked those that were doing the stitching to try it without deadening the tissue as it did not seem to hurt much and by not having to deaden my flesh helped speed up the stitching process.

They {the hospital staff} had worked on me from around noon until after 10PM

If I live to be a thousand I will never be able to repay them or the dozens of other medical "angels" associated with the Canadian Medical Association for their sincere concern for my well being.

I will detail more on the *medical miracle* of this accident later.

My neck, shoulder and upper arm area was swollen so much that an accurate X-ray could not be taken.

It would be a few weeks later back home in Bridgewater, during a routine X-ray of my upper body confirmed that I had a fracture of the seventh vertebrae and surgery was immediately needed or I may end up paralysed.

In medical terms I was a walking time bomb.

A short time after entering the Kingston General someone from the police department confirmed that seven hundred and forty dollars had been picked up at the scene of the accident and they were returning it to me.

The cash had been lying loose in an open cubicle in the dash of our truck and upon impact and roll over many of the twenty-dollar bills were scattered around the accident site area.

I had seven hundred and sixty dollars in total lying in a cubicle in the dash of the truck.

All but twenty dollars was returned to me. I never expected to see much if any of the cash returned. My faith in humanity and honesty was again confirmed.

Within a day or so my son Darren continued on to Hensall and picked up a motorized home at General Coach, had a rear hitch and ball installed and hooked a travel trailer behind it and made his way back to Kingston.

He had never driven a Motor-Home with a trailer attached before but was determined not to be deterred by my accident when it came to delivering new RV products to our sales lot. He was planning to drive these two units back to Bridgewater.

I was determined that he must not attempt this perilous journey on his own as he also might have an accident because of his inexperience and the unfamiliar highways.

If anything more should happen, both the family and the company would be in jeopardy; even destroyed.

The city of Montreal, Quebec is a beautiful and friendly city to visit but for a stranger the maze of roadways can be confusing especially if encountered during daytime traffic. Montreal is located smack in the middle of Canada's main highway heading East towards home.

To have Darren travel that route alone while driving a motor home with a large travel trailer in tow was a foreboding thought.

That thought combined with my own personal experience of having travelled that route, I was fully aware of Montreal's congested confusing traffic routes, quick blind curves and difficult to read signage. It was bad enough for drivers with experience and intimidating for those who only make the journey occasionally.

When towing RV's I usually schedule my driving through Montreal either for late at night or on weekends.

That thought was initiative enough for me to find a way to avert Darren from making this trip alone.

Back at the Kingston General I was roomed with three younger men all suffering from a similar fate as all three had been in motorcycle accidents. All three accidents happened from different causes but all ended with the same results, broken limbs and missing skin.

I only drove on a motorcycle once and after seeing the multiple injuries of my three roommates it was probably for the best.

After a few days in the hospital I was feeling pretty healthy and I decided to go home. I had held my son Darren up as long as possible as he wanted to get home and back to work.

I knew I could not drive but I could navigate, especially through Montreal.

So away we went with me sitting on my knees on the floor in the centre of the motor home watching for whenever there was a decision to be made on which road to take for the shortest and safest route home.

We drove through Montreal without a hitch.

I was at home for approximately ten days when I received a phone call from the local hospital in Bridgewater. I was to go in to have an X-ray taken of my injured neck; of which I complied.

I had to walk to the hospital and back home again as it was not yet considered safe for me to drive a car.

I had very little sense of speed and had little perception of distance. When crossing a street I had to wait until any oncoming vehicles were almost out of sight before attempting to walk across.

I had also lost my memory for many commonly used words and had *forgotten* the names of many of my friends.

I broke out in a cold sweat when answering the telephone, caused by the mental effort of straining to concentrate to finding the proper words needed to carry on an *understandable* conversation.

I made a written list of all my friend names and as time passed I was able to reacquaint my mind and memory with their faces.

I walked around at home and I traveled as a passenger in cars not knowing that I had a serious break in my neck.

If I had slipped and fallen or been involved in even the slightest accident I could have ended up paralysed.

The X-ray showed that I had broken vertebrae and that I needed to be in Halifax to be examined and interviewed by a noted *spinal surgeon* in a day or two.

I went to see a Dr. Holness on a Thursday morning and when he showed up {he was late getting into his office and I was anxious to leave} he wanted to put me into the Victoria General for immediate surgery. I refused to go.

As this was near the end of the workweek I had several necessary things that needed *tidying up* before I could go to the hospital and no one else but I could do them. I told the Doctor that I would return on Monday, which I did.

I took a scolding from the doctor and a verbal bashing from my wife for my stupidity. She {Dolly} was afraid to drive home with me as a passenger in the car.

When I arrived at the VG on Monday morning, members of the staff immediately took me downstairs where several persons went about installing one of those halo devices around my neck and head. I had not expected it.

Do you have false teeth someone asked me, "No" was my answer.

Do you have any contact lenses was the next question. Again "no" was my answer.

At my final *no* answer they took a good-sized mallet {either wood or composite} and started driving some nails or studs into both sides of my skull.

I soon found out why they asked me those earlier questions as both my eyeballs and my teeth rattled at every impact of the hammers blows.

"I may forgive you but I will never forget what you are doing to me," I remember saying to a couple of the female hammerers and true to my promise I have long ago forgiven them {but not forgotten them} for what they did that day.

Back upstairs in a hospital bed I found out what those halos are used for as I was soon attached to a harness that was then attached to a pulley that was again attached to a weight that was intended to produce sufficient tension to pull my fractured neck back to it original form. The operation would take place later.

As I am about five foot seven and one half inches tall at the best of times, my wife wanted them to stretch me out to be taller; about five foot ten would have made her happy.

"How long can you go without using the bathroom?" a nurse asked me.

"How long do I need to have *this thing* on before you take it off?" I asked her.

"About three day," she answered.

About three days meant to me that it might be off in less than three days.

"I can stand three days of anything," I answered her.

I resolved then and there that I was not going to use one of those bedpans for three days for anything other than to urinate.

For the next few days everything went according to plan. I was tied to the bed and I did not need to go to the toilet.

Strange things happen in a hospital but how those *dinner attendants* thought I was going to reach any of the food they delivered to my room, I never did figure out because when they delivered my meals, they usually set the food tray on a chair that I could not reach or worse yet they placed it as far away as setting it on the window sill. If it hadn't been for other patients in the room or a family member showing up around mealtime I would have had little to eat.

Three days passed and I asked when I was going to be released. "Not just yet": was the answer.

In the meantime I had used the bedpan only for urinating and at least once I upset it causing a need for a change of bedding. I was embarrassed...

The forth day came and went and still no release and remember I still had not gone to the toilet.

On the morning of the fifth day they released me but low and behold I still had no need of the toilet.

This mind control stuff really works I thought.

The most unfathomable and momentous thing that ever happened in my life was about to start unfolding.

While I was lying on my back tied to the weights above and behind my head and bed and unable to lie down in any position except on my back, a nurse who was bathing me said to me; "My you have such interesting moles on you, do you mind if I have a doctor take a look at them?" As this was only my second day of being confined to the hospital bed I was in no condition or position to go anywhere else for a while and I really didn't care who looked at my torso so I said to her, "Sure that's okay by me".

Soon after that conversation a doctor came and took a look at the moles on my chest and belly and left the room. Before long there were several additional doctors or interns surrounding my bed conversing excitedly about my moles. You would have thought they struck gold.

"Do you mind if we take a sample core of some of your moles?" one of the doctors asked.

"No problem" I said, not knowing at the time that taking samples of moles can be plenty painful as no deadening is used when extracting mole samples.

It was explained to me by one of the doctors that the Victoria General Hospital was presently doing research on the potential deadly but hopefully pre cancerous melanoma variety of body moles and my moles had all the characteristics of what they were looking for.

The mole samples were to be sent to a research laboratory somewhere in the United States where there would be a biopsy to determine whether or not they were of the melanoma pre cancerous variety.

It's a move that probably saved my life.

Ironic isn't it that after I survived a near fatal accident over one thousand miles away from here, to end up on another hospital bed tied to a halo tree with my chest area exposed and then to have a nurse notice the unusual shape and colour of my moles.

This happened all because the VGH was one of a few hospitals in Canada that had been selected and funded to carry on research on melanoma; it was "mind-boggling" to say the least.

Melanoma moles can develop into the cancerous variety quickly when a body is exposed to too much sunrays, something that was a natural for both adults and children of my era.

We kids removed our shirts as soon as the sun was warm enough in the spring to feel good and provide us with a *nice healthy tan.*

It was the hot days of July and August probably tipped the scales from sunshine to sunburn which laid the seeds for these potential killer melanoma moles to grow and I like everyone else in the family had experienced my share of bad sunburns, the ones that blister your skin like boiling water and a few days later you peel off the dead outer skin. Every boy in the land did it. It was a ritual of summer to see who could get the best tan or the worst sunburn. We knew that one complimented the other; you had to have the pain of blistering sunburns to have the gain of a good healthy looking tan.

Not too bright either, was it?

When the tests came back I was notified that the biopsy confirmed my moles to be the pre cancerous type and that I would need to have them removed.

My brothers and sisters were also required to have body examinations to see if they also were subject to having melanoma moles.

A scary situation arose some years later when my older brother Arthur was found to have a melanoma mole on his nose that went untreated and had progressed to a fourth stage of melanoma evolution.

There are no higher danger stages in melanoma than four and it was a tense period that he and the family went through until the cancerous portion was removed with a face altering operation at the VGH. Arthur is monitored yearly for any reoccurrences and is considered by the medical authorities as a cancer survivor. He now wears a wide brimmed hat when out in the sun.

As for me, I had approximately seventeen moles removed from my chest and back area over a period of several years. The VGH has since ceased its research programme and even though the public is better informed on the dangers of sunburns, skin cancer still remains one of the most common and dangerous forms of cancer, with an alarming and increasing death rate.

I once met a stranger in the dressing room area of the VGH with his shirt removed and seeing a long line of scars on his back appearing to look something like a railroad track I asked him if he had been in a chain saw accident. "No," he told me, the scars were the results of operations to retrieve all the tentacles that belonged to just one cancerous melanoma mole.

Melanoma moles are a sleeping killer that we can carry unknowingly with us. They are your most innocent appearing moles but if not discovered and removed in the early stages they can suddenly run out of control as the roots of the melanomas go searching for a blood supply and creep deeper and deeper into the blood providing portions of your body and become ever more difficult and sometimes impossible to remove successfully.

One other short story to add to my melanoma melodrama was one that also happened in the waiting room of the VGH.

While I was visiting the hospital for one of my scheduled routine removal operations I saw and spoke to old friend Harry Mosher who resided near my hometown. He laughed as he usually did with me about local events and about our similar situation of both having melanoma moles.

It was the last time I spoke with Harry as the melanoma took his life shortly after.

The lesson you can learn from reading this is; melanoma is dangerous, if you have any moles on your body that look different from your normal moles or if you have a mole that suddenly changes its shape {the outlying contours} I urge you to visit your doctor as soon as possible.

What I have gleaned personally from this whole process starting with my spectacular accident in Ontario only to find out weeks later back in Bridgewater Nova Scotia that I was walking around with a broken neck and finally in the process of being "repaired" and convalescing in the confines of the Victoria General Hospital in Halifax Nova Scotia where a "routine" visit by a nurse at my bedside would in turn alert the doctors at the VGH who would then proceed to confirm {by sending my mole tissue samples to the USA for biopsy} that "yes" I was carrying a deadly skin cancer and a potential killer around with me is mind boggling to the point of being unbelievable, perhaps all the way to calling this life saving event *a miracle*.

The simple reality is this, had I not had the accident and the following incredible chain of events that followed, my cancerous moles would have gone unnoticed and unattended.

The vertebrae operation was successful. I had a choice of clamps or fusion.

I now carry two clamps {much like the clamps that hold your sink in place} in the upper section of my vertebrae tying the sixth and the seventh vertebrae together. I have lost one seventh of my neck's turning mobility but it is something that I gladly live with.

The accident occurred on September 12th and I returned to work in early December of the same year vowing never to lose an hour's work because of my injury.

"So far- so good".

Remember the reoccurring dream, or vision, I spoke of at the beginning of incident # 9?

After the accident on Ontario's HWY 401, one of the busiest and most heavily used truck routes in Canada, I have never had that dream again.

Listen and believe me *because it is true*.

YOU should have been with me

Prelude to Incidents # 10 and 11

I have chosen to list my ***incidents*** not in chronological order but by the order of significance to my living or dying.

As you follow the incidents you must by now be starting to doubt. Could all these near death experiences really have happened to one person? If that is your opinion I do not blame you but should you wish to continue reading, the next two incidents are going to stretch your unbelievable quotient even more, perhaps to the limit.

I have watched America's deadliest police video chases with their many unscripted car pursuits and spectacular endings along with dozens of other high speed racing events that were professionally recorded for National and International TV audiences

I have tuned in to witness the car and canyon stunt jumps performed by the likes of Evel Knievil {and others} and truly believe that what happened to me in the following two incidents will equal and perhaps surpass any one of those highly publicized TV promotions.

For sheer drama, skill, courage or luck, for moments that will hold you in your seat of suspense until the end, you are invited to read on and then you can be the judge.

Incident # 10

This ***incident*** happened on February 12ᵗʰ 2004 on the Trans Canada Highway approximately twenty miles northwest of Fredericton, New Brunswick, Canada on one of the coldest days {if not the coldest} of the year.

I had left Lindsay Ontario the day before under harsh winter road conditions towing a forty foot long SUT {sports utility trailer} behind a 2002 Dodge ½ ton truck with a Cummins Diesel engine.

The trip was uneventful except for the usual snowy and sometimes icy sections of the highways.

Approximately seventy-five miles east of Edmonston, New Brunswick, and the northern most towns on the TCH, the road conditions improved considerably from those of Northern NB and eastern Quebec, and I breathed a sigh of relief that my worst driving conditions were behind me.

The day started bright and cold as I rolled down the newly twinned TCH {Trans Canada Highway} in a light-hearted mood. If everything went according to plan I should be at home in Bridgewater by the middle or late afternoon.

I had not used the cassette player in the truck at all during this trip and remembering that a friend had given me a cassette tape of songs by a folk singer from the neighbouring Province of Newfoundland, I decided to give it a listen.

I opened the glove compartment and searched a moment before finding the cassette.

To do this, I had to glance away from the road for a few seconds while I located the tape and placed it into the cassette player that was located in the face of the truck radio.

I should have paid better attention to the driving conditions.

I missed seeing what was the beginning of a long stretch of ice on the TCH highway. It was black ice.

Black ice is a thin layer of water frozen over black asphalt that camouflages the ice.

I have always feared encountering ice while driving, more so when towing an RV.

The first inkling of ice was the movement of the back section of the truck as it made a slight slide to the left. I sensed it immediately.

I wasn't overly concerned, as I had always managed to compensate and control my towing vehicles when encountering slippery spots on the road surface. I had managed it successfully numerous times before.

But what I had entered upon this time was not just a short patch of black ice as I found out later. It had completely covered a section of highway one half mile in length, running from one side of the wide staked highway to the other.

The highway base was constructed by building the roadbed up by filling in the original terrain. Highways are designed this way to take away grade allowing for level driving conditions. Don't get me wrong, there was nothing wrong with the construction of the roadway; it was just good engineering.

The culprit that allowed the ice to build up for such an extended distance was the snow that was lying along both sides of the highway. It had been ploughed back and to the sides of the road far enough for safety and plenty of space to allow for the two lanes of traffic to function as it is supposed to do.

Because of the elevation of the roadway, safety posts had been installed on both sides of the highway. This was to protect vehicles from leaving the highway and cascading off and down several hundred feet to the valley below.

But the installation of the safety posts did not allow the snowplough driver the convenience of pushing the snow completely off the highway; only back as far as the safety post, and thus any melting snow water was trapped between the two snow dams that had been created on both sides.

The afternoon prior to my arrival at this stretch in the TCH the sun had melted some of this snow that had been recently ploughed back. The melting snow water could not run-off the road surface because of the *dammed up* sides of the road.

When the melted water had no place to run off to, it accumulated in a long thin puddle of water that froze during the night when the temperature dropped, creating a one half mile long skating rink.

It was almost an entrapment situation but had I been watching 100% of the time and had I not taken my eyes of the road for those few seconds while installing my cassette tape I might have seen the ice that had accumulated on the road before me - ice that was now under the wheels of my vehicles.

As truck and trailer twitched I responded in kind and thought that my corrective manoeuvre would be successful.

I was wrong.

The next movement I sensed was that of the 40 foot SUT as its back end slid towards my left {the driver's side} and again I responded instinctively by turning the truck's steering wheel left to compensate.

I was travelling at a minimum of sixty miles {100 km.} per hour, which is considered a safe driving speed for *good* road conditions.

Thank God I did not have my towing truck operating under cruise control for if I had I would have no doubt immediately touched the brake to disengage the control and as any truck driver will tell you, under icy road conditions that move is strictly a "no no" as the trailer in tow would initiate what is known as a jack knife as the rear end of the towing unit would be pushed sideways by the trailer and start a chain reaction.

When the back end of a trailer slides sideways towards the towing unit it creates an accident scene that looks like that formed by the closing of a pocket {a *jack*} knife.

A truck {or any vehicle} heading *sideways* left on any two lane highway allows a very short distance to travel before you must compensate by turning your front wheels towards the road ahead, so that is what I did next, but the trailer was picking up speed in its sliding motion and when it slid too far to the right {the passenger's side} I again responded by turning right.

The rear wheels of the trailer continued to slide back again to the left, something like the wagging of a dogs tail, only this time the swing carried the rear end of the trailer far enough left to hit the protecting posts on the left side of the *wide* highway.

I did not hear the impact of the trailer hitting the posts but I felt it, as I now had to turn my steering wheel left to hopefully stop this now out of control sliding situation.

I knew things were getting serious when the trailer hit the far post but I still had to try and make the correct steering moves and hoped the momentum of the trailer and truck would subside without applying the truck's brakes.

Needless to tell you that nothing worked as the trailer gave another slide to the right and then back left for a final time, this time far left and tight enough that it cleared the complete width of the TCH and the SUT was now going down the road backwards and ahead of my truck.

What a helpless feeling. The trailer is now the lead vehicle. My truck is now pushing *or being towed* by the trailer to end up stopped somewhere God only knows.

When was this nightmare ride going to stop and how was it all going to work out?

Imagine this if you can. I now have the brakes of the truck and trailer on to the max and both vehicles are continuing to slide backwards without diminishing speed or any control whatever

I had plenty of time to think about things as the two uncontrolled vehicles slid backward down the TCH, only now I am travelling along on *what was* the left side of the highway gradually moving towards the posts on what was earlier the right hand side of the road.

This situation is as surreal as anything can get; and I am in it.

I can remember seeing the snow piled high along the posts that bordered the TCH as the truck is now starting to be pulled by the trailer sideways and backward towards them, to an unknown fate awaiting me on the other side.

Both vehicles slammed into the snow covered posts bounding up and over them in an almost soft rolling motion, almost as if they never existed at all as both vehicles disappeared from view from any drivers and passengers that may have been following in the East bound lane of the TCH that cold February morning.

As the truck continued to roll over and over I wondered where the SUT could be, was it still attached to my truck and if so what would be the outcome if the two landed at the same time in the same location. I felt sure that if it was still attached to the truck that it had a good chance of ending up on top of my truck and me.
A sobering thought but a realistic one under the conditions.

Unless you have had a similar experience {and I hope you haven't} you will find it hard to believe that when you experience *uncontrollable* incidents such as this one, there comes a time of peace. It happens when you finally come to the realization that you must finally give in and give up control of your life and the situation at hand.

Some people say "time seems to stand still" and I guess that is about as near as I can say what happened to me.

I thought about my life, that I had lived longer than many of my friends that I always treated others honestly and fairly and there was little doubt that my family would manage without me.

I had so many close calls before; I just didn't deserve another chance. Besides that, the law of averages was strongly against me and I am a firm believer in the law of averages.

During my *thinking time* everything around me turned from daylight to dark, I wasn't sure why but later the reason became quite apparent. It was the deep snow that was being tossed around and over the vehicles as they spun and cascaded down and over the side of the highways long embankment.

The tossing and turning and blackness finally stopped.

I was *pleasingly shocked* to realize that I was still alive and that there was light again.

The truck had broken free from the heavy ball mount on the trailer hitch that towed the SUV, but the safety chains held firm.

The large trailer was still attached, lying on its side behind the truck.

The deep snow that covered the sides of the hill saved me.

When the darkness turned back to light again and the wild billows of snow subsided, everything was quiet and still.

"I am alive," I thought joyfully.

I found myself sitting in my truck parked upright on all four wheels still with my seat belt firmly in place and again I thought, "How in God's name did I survive this one?"

I noticed the passenger side window and the large rear window of the truck were missing.

My coat, other clothes and traveling supplies that *earlier* lay beside me on the seat of the cab of the truck were missing and that a good portion of my head and body was soaked in diesel fuel.

"Strange," I thought as I removed my seatbelt, "not even a scratch; how can anyone be that lucky?"

I quickly removed my seatbelt and removed myself from the truck.

Once outside I was surprised to hear a voice shouting down at me from up on the highway. "Are you okay?" "Yes" I yelled back. "Is there anyone else with you?" "No", I returned.

With that brief conversation I returned to my truck to see if there were any papers or personal items that I should take with me before moving on. Only then did I notice that the truck's Cummins diesel engine was still running.

Because of the snow covering the cab the sound of the Diesel was barely audible. I turned the key to the off position and slowly walked away.

I paused to look back several times at the truck, at the trailer now lying motionless on its side at the scene, at *something* that only several minutes before appeared to be the instruments of my death.

Somehow that *old snow covered, beat up Dodge* truck *had a different look about it* - one of friendliness and strength. It certainly protected me in my time of need.

I felt truly sorry for what I had done to it.

As I struggled upwards through the deep snow towards those voices on that cold winter morning, I realized that the deep snow is what saved me from contact with the rough and rocky terrain underneath it and the 40 foot RV that was now lying on its side in almost perfect alignment behind my truck.

It had acted as a parachute saving both me and the truck.

The soft deep snow produced enough friction against the flat side of the SUT as it slid down the incline to slow the momentum of both truck and trailer and stopped us even more gently than had I been out on a highway on bare asphalt and applying brakes in a stopping procedure.

It was the trailer sliding on its side that kept both units from going even further and faster down the steep embankment.

The factory installed safety chains attached to the front hitch of the trailer and hooked on to the trailer hitch of the truck were twisted from the truck turning over and over. Had the chains not held firm, my little old white Dodge would have had clear sailing all the way to the bottom of that long incline; it would have bounced around just like a tin can, and with me inside it.

Have you ever held a kitten in your arms and dropped it upside down to the floor? Cats always land on their feet. After being tossed over those guard post and rails of the TCH so many meters above where I ended up, landing so gently and unharmed, you never need to talk to me about having nine lives.

Someone with a cell phone on the highway above must have called the RCMP [Royal Canadian Mounted Police}

After arriving at the scene, noting the slippery conditions of the highway, speaking to a driver or two who had been following behind me that morning they never did ask me for a statement; not even one word.

I guess it was obvious; I wasn't speeding and once upon the ice I did all that was humanly possible to correct the sliding out of control vehicles.

Both truck and trailer travelled nearly one quarter of a mile before finally leaving the TCH.

I am indeed fortunate to have survived.

Strangers waiting on the highway invited me into their nice warm cars {as I had no coat} even though I smelled strongly of diesel fuel. The diesel fuel that had leaked into the cab from the missing rear truck window and spilled over me came from a five-gallon can that was stored on the back of the Dodge.

The *strangers* then drove me to the Fredericton hospital where I was advised to take a shower as diesel fuel can penetrate your skin. Once they examined me I was released

A friend of the family living in the Fredericton area was called and told of my predicament came to the hospital and drove me to his home.

I found out again that day as I did in incident # 9 that *no one kicked me when I was down and out.* Instead they did everything they could to help me out.

I should know; I've been down more than a few times.

Once back home and still counting my many blessings I mailed off "thank you" cards to several angels who befriended me that cold February morning **when I was alone.**

I called them angels that day; I still do.

YOU should have been with me.

Incident # 11

This is the final *incident* that I have lived through {so far} to tell you about.

Why have I kept # 11 for last?

It has a much shorter storyline than several of the other incidents.

It did not happen out on a high-speed high traffic highway.

It never made the news or newspapers.
No one was hurt-not as much as a scratch.

Over the years, Bluenose RV Centre rented out a few RV's, usually to people who were in need of a temporary shelter or a friend or family member coming home for a visit and having no bedroom space available; or more likely someone who was doing a home renovation.
Such was the driving force behind this *incident.*

My renovation friend lived not more than three miles from our place of business.
As he was not going to be at home the day that the delivery was going to be made he made arrangements with me for the time of delivery and instructions on the location of where I was to park it in his yard.

This rental RV had to be checked out for proper functioning appliances.
All RV's have appliances that operate on propane gas. Are you getting the jest yet of where this story is heading?

The truck to be used in the delivery was connected to the Holiday the day before and was ready to roll the next morning
I left our sales lot at approximately 9:30 am with the 36 ft travel trailer in tow.
The Holiday Hijacker had two 30 lb. propane gas cylinders that had been filled the day prior as well as the appliances had been checked out for proper working order.

I had no idea at the time of getting into the truck and driving off that morning that one of the 30 lb propane tanks had been removed the night before and was used temporarily to check out a propane appliance on another RV before being returned to its original location on the front of the Holiday.

In haste to put the tank back on the Holiday from which it had been *temporarily* removed the evening before, it was not fastened down to the base support on the trailer tongue, as it should have been.

It was late in the evening and after dark when the tank was returned to the front of the Holiday and the serviceman who removed it and then replaced it did not know that the Holiday was going out to a rental customer the following morning.

"Oh what a morning".

Leaving the lot and taking the shortest and quickest way to my friend's home was the logical choice of routes.

It meant going down a short entrance road before hitting the main road and then on towards its final destination.

It was almost my final destination.

After a short time on the access road I heard an unfamiliar sound coming from behind my truck as I hurried along on the downhill section of this road.

I looked into the wide side mirrors of the truck to see what was making such a strange sound. The noise continued but I wasn't really concerned as I could see nothing amiss and so I continued on my merry way.

It was about this time that I met my son in law in his truck who was employed in the propane business and we recognized each other with a hand gesture and we both kept on trucking.

On telling him later about this incident, he told me that when he met me he noticed that one of the propane tanks had fallen off and was being dragged underneath the front hitch of the Holiday trailer.

To this day neither he nor I speak about why no attempt was made to stop or alert me to the problem, for at that short distance into my delivery rectifying it was still manageable.

I still had another one and one half miles to travel to my destination.

About five minutes later I slowed down and turned left off the main road and continued on for another minute before putting my right signal light on and stopping opposite my friend's driveway. I was supposed to back the Holiday up into my friend's front yard and deposit it close to his house.

I stepped out of the truck and was shocked at what I saw.

Billowing up and out over the front of the Holiday was a large plume of vapour, propane gas vapour.

When propane is put into a cylinder it is done in a liquid form. When it is used to provide fuel energy for heating and lighting it is released in the form of vapour by turning a manually operated valve located at the top of the tank.

For strict safety control of propane, all tanks and valves are inspected every time the tanks are refilled and the control valves must be replaced with new ones every ten years.

The propane valve was not my immediate problem.

What I found when peaking through the escaping propane vapour was one of the propane tanks lying under the front hitch of the Holiday. So that's what made that strange sound.

The tank was still attached to the trailer by the rubber hose that carries the propane to the trailer's appliances when the valve on the tank is opened to release the gas from the cylinder.

"Good God," I thought as I stared at the sight of the 30-pound cylinder lying flat under the trailer and the large volume of potentially explosive vapour pouring from it.

The tank had fallen free from its securing bracket and had been dragged along under the trailer from the place I first heard the strange sound {a mile or two away} all the way up to my first and only stop.

When the weight of the full thirty-pound cylinder came in contact with the asphalt-based highway, it created enough friction to wear a hole through the metal wall of the cylinder.

It was this hole through which the highly explosive vapour was pouring.

Why it had not exploded I cannot answer as there had to be sparks created from the chafing friction of tank against asphalt.

I couldn't believe that something like this could ever happen and to tell you the truth I was terrified at what might be the end results of this *developing* incident.

I quickly shut down the gas engine of the truck to prevent any spark from the plugs igniting the vapour.

Now what?

I should alert the EMO {emergency measures organization}

Doing this would take time; time that I did not have.

While the road I was stopped on was not a high traffic zone, it did represent a fair volume of traffic when the local residents were going to and coming from work in town and other areas.

The peak time of being to work had already passed.

But what if someone {anyone} came by, seeing the plume of vapour, they would surely stop and ask if they could help.

A spark from his or her car's ignition would blow everyone within a certain distance to kingdom come.

Someone might even walk by and be smoking a cigarette.

I must get away from the truck and trailer as quickly as possible so as not to be seen standing there and initiate anyone stopping out of curiosity and asking questions.

I decided that the only way of averting a disaster was to remove the tank from the trailer and take it as far off the highway and into the nearby woods as possible and do it as quickly as possible.

I grabbed the largest adjustable wrench I had with me and headed for the tank. I would remove it from the rubber hose that was holding it fast.

I pulled the tank out from under the trailer and had the wrench in position to turn the copper fitting to remove it when I thought, "*what if the wrench slips*" under the pressure of hurriedly removing the hose from the tank and the body of the wrench hits the metal case that protects the valve and causes a spark?

It would be game over if any spark {even the tiniest} causing instant igniting of the propane vapour and there wouldn't be anything left of me and very little left of the vehicles or of the homes situated nearby, as the first exploding tank would also cause the second full tank to also explode.

Knowing the explosive nature of propane and the dangers from the slightest spark igniting the vapour that was billowing up and around me I just could not bring myself to put pressure on the wrench that was now placed on the brass nut of the hose connection.

It wasn't worth the risk. Was there another way aside from calling EMO?

The EMO would have taken ten minutes to get to the scene, another ten minutes to close the highways and a large bridge nearby that crosses the LaHave River in Cookville, plus evacuate several businesses and homes in the immediate danger area.

That would take too long.

They say that one's mind works brilliantly when confronted with life and death situation.
I had an idea.

Desperate times call for desperate measures but my idea wasn't complicated at all, in fact it was quite simple.

I found myself running up to the front of the home where I was to make my delivery and rushing into the kitchen through the unlocked door. The wife of my friend was there and wondering what was going on.
Quickly explaining what was happening I ask her for a pail of water in the same breath.

I soon found myself back at the scene of the vapour plume rushing from the leaking propane tank.

This has to work I thought as I placed the tank between my knees and squeezed my legs tightly together to hold it from turning. I then placed the wrench on the brass nut of the connecting hose and began to tighten the jaws of the wrench.

I could barely see what I was doing through the billows of cold vapour wafting up and around me.

Only this time as I put pressure on the wrench I used my left arm and hand to pour a steady stream of cold water down and over the tank and wrench slowly and gently applying pressure, turning the nut and releasing the tank from the hose.

All propane nuts are manufactured with a reverse thread and have reverse threaded fittings so as not to make a mistake in installing and removing the hoses. The valves are made of brass so as not to induce sparks. I am glad I had a bit of knowledge of what I was attempting to do, knowing that any mistake would cost me my life.

Worse than dying was the thought that if ever there were a spark while I was enveloped in propane vapour, the explosion would have blown me to smithereens with nothing but some bones and teeth to be found or gathered up afterwards.

A grizzled description of what might happen but an accurate one.

Needless to say that my plan worked as I hurriedly moved the now free and leaking tank into the trees and bushes away from the highway.

I had just dodged a major sized bullet. The whole ordeal from first assessing the situation to the removal and dispersing of the tank took less than five minutes, five minutes in which not one other person came along to induce a catastrophe.

Again in looking back I ask myself why the tank had not exploded while I was driving along the highway to my destination. The friction from road and tank had been sufficient to burn a sizable hole in the tank and yet no spark from the friction caused the tank to explode.

Perhaps the wind pressure against the leaking cylinder created by the vehicle's forward motion prevented sparks and ignition by forcing the gas vapour away from the perforation created by the friction of asphalt and steel.

Highly unlikely, but there had to be some simple reason that there was no explosion, as anything complicated just doesn't fit.

What began with one small and seemingly simple error, fostered by another more apparent error, in my ignoring those *unusual sounds* while driving, together, could have ended in tragedy.

A disaster of momentous proportions was averted only by a handful of desperate thrown together common sense measures, and reciprocal actions, ultimately bringing a successful conclusion to a story that never even made the news, but one that might easily have qualified for inclusion in Ripley's Believe it or Not.

YOU should have been with me, when I was alone.

Chapter Four

Home life activities

Sleigh Coasting
Bob sleighs "or sleds" were built to seat *two or more* people, one sitting behind the other, for downhill coasting *in* winter. For those who do not know what *bob sleighs* are, they consist of two small sleights connected together by a long board *on top* that served for seating up to four persons. The sled are then controlled by the front passenger, the driver, who is seated behind the steering wheel, which is attached to a post connected to the bunk of the front sled. This allowed for steering and control. There were no brakes on our sled.

Once you neared your down hill destination, you either came to a gradual stop, *or* if a corner was too sharp to get around, or the hill was too steep to slow the sleigh down, everyone had to roll off the sled, together, usually upsetting *and stopping* the sleigh.

It's a wonder someone wasn't killed over the years, as we used this type of sled to coast down hills using trails and tracks coated with ice, generating lightning fast speeds, where only the most coordinated {not the bravest} person was designated as driver.

I always felt safer with Arthur up front and steering, with me *sitting in back as one of the passengers.* He may have upset us *every time* but I still trusted his ability over mine, as not one of us ever received any serious injuries.

One Person Sleds.

Howard Wentzell, a blacksmith of merit and a neighbour of my mom's family who lived over in the village of Midville Branch, built a large, one person sleigh, and gave it to our family.

It was not only big but it was fast, and unless you were strong enough to guide and stop it, it was very difficult to control when travelling at high speed.

Sister Marguerite was only three or four years old at the time, but somehow she mounted this huge sled and *some-how* managed to get it pointed down hill. When I first saw her she was nearing out of control speed and heading straight for a large pile of rocks that was located at the base of the hill where we did most of our coasting.

The rock pile had grown in size over the years.

Every farm had a rock pile or two, as *they* were necessary to dispose of small, medium and large sized rocks that surfaced when the fields were ploughed or cleared.

At ever increasing speed, she neared the bottom of the *steepest hill* of Young's farm.

That part of the farm hasn't changed much over the generations. It was, and still is, the section located at the rear of the old farmhouse, easily visible to the community some half- mile away, but to the residents *of our house* it was out of sight and for the most part, out of mind. The rocks lay waiting *at the bottom* of this steep incline.

I was at *or near* the bottom of the hill that morning. I had just finished a down hill ride on a smaller and lighter sled and was returning up the hill for another run, when lo and behold, I see Marguerite on this big red sleigh heading straight down the hill towards me. The long wide rock pile lay directly behind me.

She was lying on her belly facing forward, and her head was sticking up like a baby robin does, when it lifts its head as the mother robin approaches the nest carrying a worm in its mouth, to feed it. She looked scared to death. Being only five or six years old she had no control of what was happening or what was about to happen to her. I knew that *unless I did something* Marguerite was a goner. But what could I do?

The sleigh was travelling faster by the second.

I had little time to think and act.

As the sleigh was heading towards and hopefully, *past* me, it would give me *one chance to do something. I would try* to give it a kick with hopes of diverting it off to my left side and away from the rock pile but my timing had to be perfect.

Using my right leg, I kicked out as hard and as fast as I could as the sled whizzed past, and to my surprise I caught that old sleight smack on the very front tip of it's left runner and deflected it *just enough* to have it go careening off the icy track and head towards the snow covered field adjacent to my left and above the rock pile.

Marguerite probably doesn't even remember that day I saved her from grave injuries and maybe saved her life.

Funny isn't it but many times *it's not what happens*, but what *does not* happen that changes our lives.

I know my life and the life of my family would have been changed *had I not been able* to divert the direction of that big old red sled with my sister on it.

I do take a bit of pride for doing what needed to be done at a time when there was nobody else around to do it.

Why was I there at that particular spot on that particular day? Some will say fate; some will call it providence, while others will say it was chance or just plain good luck.

Could there be yet another answer?

You should have been there with me when I was alone..............

Early life remembrances.

How far back can you remember? Well if you are anything like me you can barely remember what happened yesterday but when it comes to remembering what happened nearly a lifetime ago, memories are very clear. I am one of those people.

There are two memorable events that I will tell you about.

How many readers remember the song by Little Jimmy Dickens about his Sleeping at the Foot of the Bed?

I can relate to Little Jimmy's song, as I also had a Jimmy experience.

It was not an uncommon occurrence to sleep at the foot of your parent's bed {with them in it} on cold winter nights *in unheated* farmhouses. I had that experience *more than once*.

It would only happen *on the coldest nights* of the year; when the temperature dropped so low that it was unsafe for a small child to sleep alone, as a child *might kick the covers off* and freeze to death in their sleep.

Our old farmhouse home, like all the others in the community, had no heat source other than that from wood stoves, and when they burned low for the night, the fires were never built up again *to last through the night,* as that was considered too dangerous, and so the old houses were left *in the cold until morning* when the stoves were again stoked and relit.

So to ensure that I didn't succumb during those *especially cold* nights, I was place sideways at the foot of mom and dad's bed. It didn't seem so unusual at the time.

Rex was younger and smaller then I so *he* may have slept *up on top* between mom and dad, and I believe that Arthur, my bigger and older brother, slept upstairs with Papa and Grammy. The girls had not yet made the family scene.

Looking back it seems that *it was the right thing for my parents to do.* They probably had a few uncomfortable nights with me lying there at the foot of the bed but *they slept content* knowing that I would still be alive *and not frozen stiff* when morning arrived.

I have another memory *of something that happened* back *even before* the memory of my sleeping at the foot of the bed.

Believe it or not, I can remember being wrapped up in blankets when I was only a baby.

Blankets or sheets were the way small babies were *wrapped up* back then, *as many still are* today. The one difference being, that, in *that era,* it *seemed* common practice to wrap the baby's arms *tightly against their bodies, making* the blanket act as sort of a straight jacket.

It's not so much the tight blanket that spurns my memory but the way my arms were rendered *motionless.*

As my both arms were held tightly against my sides I was helpless. It prevented me from freeing my hands to shield my eyes when I was taken out of the house during bright sunlit days.

I cannot recall the language used back then but it would have been something like this,

"Just look at how cute he is" or "Isn't he a little darling" as I was being *shown off* by my mother or grandmother to some friend or relative who was visiting- *out in our yard.*

As I can still remember *those times and places so vividly-* the harsh sunlight, *of being bound* both hand and foot, the experience must have been horrifying to me.

The family reminded me *about my early childhood behaviour* as soon as I became old enough to understand it. They claim that *I was not a happy child as a baby* and that I cried all, or most of the time. My mother and grandmother used {or ill used} my first cousin Violet Bolivar whenever she visited our home. The job always fell upon her to rock and console me, to quiet me down.

Vi still reminds me *to this day* of those occasions when she and our old rocking chair combined to "keep me quiet". Little wonder then why Vi remains my favourite girl cousin.

Just maybe the reason I cried was because of my hands and arms being bound tightly created a claustrophobic reaction and I just wanted to get even with someone for doing this awful thing too me. Vi, it wasn't your fault, you were just the fall guy {girl}.

Just thinking about it makes me want to cry.

Spendthrift

I thought money was meant for spending; first you needed to earn it, then to exchange it for things I either wanted or needed.

"Are you afraid that quarter {25 cents} will burn a hole in your pocket"? My grandmother would ask me when I was "chaffing at the bit" to go out and immediately spend it.

On the other hand if Arthur and Rex received any money they would save it.

That is typical of the *money mentality* I carried with me for most of my life.

I never took money seriously. It was neither something I worried about having enough of as it seemed to come to me easily, and if I had *only a little or no money* I never worried about that either, it didn't seem that important to me, I was never going to let money be my master.

There have been *some tough times* in my adult life when I basically and systematically weaned myself away from using money.

I always had faith that money would come to me, if, and, as, I needed it. Call it stupid, call it unintelligent, but I refused to let money, or the lack of it, *control me*. You can call it whatever you want, but I never have, nor will I ever, let money be the yardstick that measures wha*t my life or my human principles* are worth. I would like to think that my unusual trait was and still is confidence.

I have always worked long and hard for every compensation I received, from walking the back roads of *the nearby* communities selling household items as a child or driving the highways of the county *and the world beyond* selling *adults things*. I worked and still do, *for the joy,* of working.

I believed back then as I still do today, that if I worked long and hard enough that repayment will come.

In keeping with a family tradition, I always remained forthright and honest with all my clients *and later* with my employers.

I have learned over the years that to be successful, I must first *be respectful of all* those who would be my customers, customers that I *needed* to purchase my products and services, as well, I must be the first to show trust and respect to my employees, because without both, dedicated employees and committed customers, you cannot have a successful company for longevity.

Mutual respect must be the fulcrum between a Company, its employees and its customers, as respect for all, assures success for all.

"Give them more than they expect" is a philosophy that many companies pursue in providing *their customers* with *quality products* and *service.*

Is it any less important then, for an employee *not to treat his / her employer* with the same respect? In this scenario you the employees are the product, your employer is the customer.

I was employed for five years as a sales and branch manager of a successful company {Centennial Mobile Homes} in the selling and servicing of Mobile and Mini Homes.

The owner at the time was Mr. Stan Haville. Stan came to my office in Bridgewater one day and told me that they {his Company} were planning to give me a raise. Apparently they thought that I deserved one.

"That *is not necessary"* I told him, "I am doing quite well on what you are now paying me and should I need additional income, I will just work harder and sell more mobile homes *and earn more* money".

He must have thought I was addled, as I bet every other one of his other managers were more then anxious to receive an increase in pay.

The promise of the pay increase never excited me as much as the thought that my work was good enough to merit such a high level of commendation.

Several months later when I found the monetary increase in my pay envelope - I accepted it, but I never did ask for the raise.

"The world, and my wife, *would call me* crazy".

Observations

Wall-Street Eggheads

I always thought that Humpty Dumpty was an egg, not, an egghead. I never realized until now, the date today is February 14th. 2009, that, Humpty Dumpty was a Wall Street banker.

Since *his* recent fall from *those lofty peaks* on Wall Street, when I, and thousands of others "were recruited" to put *him* back together again, only then did I realize just who the Humpty Dumpty's, *the eggheads of the world,* really are. "Shame on you, every one of you"

"By not having wealth *you* grow accustomed to living without it".

It's an immense burden just trying to protect what little you do have saved, from the robber barons of Wall Street.

Having *nothing to lose* is a freedom, a freedom you do not appreciate, until you have come to the realization that you are spending far too much of your life's *valuable freedom time, just shielding it* {your wealth} from those that have never learned how to live without it.

"Kind of reminds us of the story about the town mouse and the county mouse, doesn't it"?

Opposites attracts

They must, or how else can you explain these real life situations.

At our home on Young's hill both my grandfather and my dad smoked. Papa smoked a pipe most of the time, but *now and then* he indulged in the odd cigarette. Dad smoked all cigarettes, *the roll your own kind* that could be home rolled, and therefore much cheaper than were the pre-packaged *tailor made* ones.

Smoking took place mostly indoors when the men were resting or sitting around, waiting to have a meal.

This was a generation or more away from the modern day alarm warnings, that tobacco is bad for your health and that smoking it, causes cancer.

Dad *chewed* tobacco. I believe the variety that he chewed was called "Club" and it came in a single stick that was configured to fit comfortably in a man's pants pocket for *on the job* tobacco fixes. A stick of tobacco was called a fig.

Dad would chew tobacco around the house and more then once I saw him remove one of the top covers and spit the residue into the stove.

It seemed to me to be a filthy habit; it still does.

There were five of us kids in total in the household and to my knowledge not one of us ever smoked a cigarette, a pipe, or chewed tobacco.

Contrast that to my dad's sister's family who lived about a half mile away "as the crow flies" within easy visual distance from our house, *out on the main road*.

Both Beulah his sister, and her husband Edgar *never smoked* while raising their nine children and I believe I am correct in saying *that in contrast to their parents*, all nine of their children smoked at one time or another.

While Beulah did take up cigarettes when she became a senior, Edgar never did smoke and I think that several of their siblings, my cousins, have since broken the smoking habit.

I am not implying that smoking or not smoking made us any better or worse as a person, but I am sticking to my original thought that for good or bad, *opposites do attract.*

In the Young household we children saw *what smoking was about* and stayed away from it, while in the Bolivar home the kids never experienced the nasty habit and wanted to try it out for themselves. Go figure?

Similar reversals occurred in other households, including that of my wife's parent's home, where *her dad and mom both smoked* but *five of their six children did not.*

So, do opposites really attract?

I asked this question as a younger person and I am still looking for a better answer today. That answer being *yes*, for while *we as kids saw something we didn't like* and *stayed away* from such experiences, while others who did not experience the same smoking annoyances as we did, felt negatively attracted *to trying it for themselves.*

Does the same *anti attraction* process not take place when selecting a wife?

Are not rough and tough males attracted to soft beautiful females?

Are not "smart" girls or boys attracted to "not so bright" boy or girls?

Are not lazy people *of either gender* attracted to ambitious opposites? And the contrast continues.

What did she see in him, is an old saying?

Or, What those two ever had in common is another familiar saying.

I have always insisted that *boys marry girls a lot like their mothers.* If you want to start a *family war* sometime, try saying that to your wife or girlfriend.

"These *old "die hard" sayings* hold much more truth than many want to admit".

Tithing works

Tithing was something that I was encouraged to do by my parents and the family minister when I got my first steady job at age seventeen. For those who do not know what tithing is, it means putting aside or saving a tenth of whatever you earn for *the works* of the Lord to help others who are less fortunate than yourself?

I was employed at Russell Sawler's White Rose service station in Bridgewater where I received thirteen dollars a week, working five and a half days {10 hours a day} for a weekly total of fifty-four hours.

On *every other Saturday* it meant working the evening shift *of three extra hours.*

We were committed to working through our noon lunch break and only ate *it as a lull in the action might* allow. One employee lost his job by eating his lunch out back of the station, sitting in his car. When the owner of the station, who was *working that day,* became overly busy during *the employees lunch period,* the employee *who did not stop eating his lunch and come forward to assist him,* was fired immediately when he did return.

So it meant non-stop work, *or else*. No unions *to help us* negotiate *for common sense* working conditions.

Every week I would put away my 10% and as time went by *and my pay increased* I was soon saving *over two dollars* a week. I bet the Lord was *happy to see me doing so well* and keeping my Biblical commitment of tithing.

Not being a money saving person previously, I had little or none to save. I was now accumulating *surplus money* at an unbelievable rate. *This tithing thing really works*!

The only thing, I wasn't doing right by the Lord was, I wasn't giving all my *extra money* to the church. I kept putting my one dollar a week in the "collection" plate *as before* and I was saving the rest; *I had good intentions* but that didn't do the works of the Lord much good, did it?

I now know such actions are called hoarding.

They say, the road to hell is paved with good intentions, and when I put that extra tithing money aside, *I wasn't planning on an emergency* arising.

Lo and behold, I was getting married.

By now I had a few hundred dollars saved up in my tithing account, so when it came time for me to purchase *both the engagement and the wedding ring*, where do you think I found the money?

So, one sunny summers day, in the nineteenth year of my life, I and Dolly, my wife to be, along with her best friend Sadie Thompson walked into Leon Neima's Jewellery Store on Barrington Street in Halifax and purchased two rings.

Neima's Jewellery store was advertised both on TV and in our Provincial daily newspaper as the best place to buy wedding rings *in all of Nova Scotia.*

Sending Dolly for a stroll alone along Barrington Street, Sadie and I proceeded to walk into Neima's Jewellery store and, with Sadie trying them on, selected the nicest looking engagement and complimenting wedding band that one hundred and twenty five dollars *cash* could buy.

After over fifty-three years of marriage, I believe that I made the best investment decision *that day* that any good steward of the Lord's treasury could ever have made.

Dolly still wears both rings, although they are worn a bit thin in places

After four children, seven grandchildren and several great grandchildren, "I know the Lord has long since forgiven me for investing *His, treasury,* on those rings".

Climate Change

"Climate change" was neither *a catch phase nor a concern* back in the days of my youth. It was not until about thirty odd years ago, {around 1975} that I and most of my peers first became familiar with the term.

It really never hit home that there was such a problem, and if one did exist, that we as individuals could do little if anything to change it.

Then came my first trip to Newfoundland Canada in 1989.

The excursion plans were to take four of us *fishermen on a three day fishing adventure* to the waters of Lake Jubilee. Add several additional days for traveling *too and from* Newfoundland for a total of *about seven days.*

I was fifty-two years old at the time, but the excitement of the planning, just thinking about it, was worthy of a ten year old.

The excitement never waned for over nineteen years.

Jubilee Lake is located on the Southwest side of Newfoundland, a Canadian Province, *one half a time zone north* and situated north east of Nova Scotia, a few hundred miles *further out* in the Atlantic Ocean. Nova Scotia is included in the Atlantic Time zone.

The geographical location of being only one half of a time zone really makes a major different when viewing the sky at night

On a clear night you feel that you can reach up *and almost touch the stars.*

How beautiful, how awesome, a*re the night sights of the universe* viewed from a dark, silent and remote region of the planet, such as we were.

I and my friend Reid Delong, along with his son Steven and Reid's uncle Garnet Burns were the first foursome to make the trip. Since that initial journey Reid and I along with two other friends {always a foursome} have been making the same journey for nineteen years, our twentieth trip is planned for June 2009. Instead of the original three, *we now spend five full days* on the water.

During those early years we planned our trips for the month of July so that the weather and climate *would accommodate us and not freeze us* to death.

We had previously spoken to friends and outfitters to find out the best time of the summer to go fishing there.

The trip was planned for early July.

A great *description of being cold* is one my friend Reid penned in his poem, On The Shores' of Jubilee. It's about "freezing *to death in July*" but after one frosty July night in 1990 it turned out to be more realistic than *crazy,* even in Canada. It happened on the second year we visited *Jubilee*. *It was cold enough that it snowed* and we did not prepare properly by bringing sufficient warm *winter type* clothing with us. Because of the extreme cold we struggled not only to fish, *but to keep ourselves* from freezing while out on the lake.

I had earlier mentioned to one of our new fishing friends, Barry Naugler that he need not pack any *extra warm* sleeping blankets, and to take along *just seasonable clothing* for fishing attire as the previous year wasn't *that* cold. Did I get fooled! Did Barry get fooled!

It was so cold in fact that *in the mornings* we had to break ice out of the pails that we needed for use in preparing breakfast. Breakfast was usually served around five A.M.

I recall Barry saying, "I have never been so cold in my life".

That was the one and only year that it snowed in July.

The only times that Barry said he was warm, was when Reid and I crawled out of our bunks and threw our heavier sleeping bags on top of him.

Once on the water, getting the boats and our-selves ashore *and then getting a survival* fire started was one difficult task. It took several minutes of brisk body movements just to be able to talk, walk, or stand upright, and once that feat was accomplished we then had to find enough dry ignitable material to keep our fire going.

It was those *not so pleasant experiences* that we would have rather left to the early explorers.

But survive we did and the year after that a strange thing happened.

It started to get warmer.

We first noticed it in 1991 and every *consecutive year* since has become increasingly warmer, so warm in fact that in order to insure that we needed *cooler* weather. From then on, we began scheduling our fishing trip dates earlier *and earlier* each year.

The main reason was not so much for our personal comfort as it was to *accommodate* safe storage for any fish we planned to save and bring home after the trip.

After twenty years and hundreds of fish, we did not lose one trout because of spoiling.

On one occasion while fishing with Garnet Burns, Garnet was getting a dose of this *uncharacteristic* Newfoundland weather.

Now Garnet was a world traveller, of sorts, he was a retired air force man and had spent much of his time while in the service travelling to places that had very warm climates. He knew what hot weather was all about.

"I think *there is something* to this climate change"? Garnet said to me, as the afternoon sun continued to *gnaw down on us* as we trolled along in our 16 ft aluminium boat.

Going faster didn't seem to help.

Garnet was right; the sun was burning *any exposed* skin.

Climate change was happening right before our eyes.

To reinforce seeing *climate change* come upon us so rapidly, here is one phenomenon *we actually witnessed.*

In the early years of visiting and fishing in the area of Jubilee Lake, all the land around our cabin and the lake *was brown and desolate.*

In close proximity to the cabin the terrain *was wind worn with dead and downed trees.*

Everywhere you looked there was nothing but brown stunted spruce *and dead sod that* had never received enough warmth from *old Sol, even in the summer season,* to evolve beyond the dead brown to *a live* green colour.

The sod and forest surrounding the entire lake seemed destined to never enjoy any natural seasonal evolutionary change from winters to spring to summers green *and growth*, as we were accustomed to back home in Nova Scotia.

But *climate change had finally reached Jubilee Lake*, the earth was warming, the greening of Jubilee was happening right before our *witnessing* eyes.

Since then, the land colour and climes around Jubilee Lake have changed dramatically, all in only nineteen years, so much so, that our fishing foursome must now schedule our fishing trips to take place in early June instead of the original dates of early July.

That's over one month earlier than when we first began. Remember the snow and cold of those first few years?

As previously stated, our earlier scheduling was necessitated to provide cool enough temperatures to accommodate both fisherman and fish.

I had an opportunity to chat with a friend and carnival {midway} owner Bill Thomas on one of those warm July afternoon back around 1994. His statement to me was this; "We never thought that *we Newfoundlanders* would ever see warm summers like this".

While all the factors are not yet known, on why global warming is escalating at such an alarming rate, one thing is certain. It is happening and *if there is anything that we are doing personally* that is advancing this disturbing global phenomenon, *we must stop doing it, immediately.* Only by being conscious and acting together globally can we make large enough impact that will eventually reverse this warming trend.

You and I and countless others must stand up and say *enough is enough.*

It is the only way we can insure our children, our grandchildren and future generations *that planet earth will still be around* providing clean water, breathable air, healthy soil, unsurpassed beauty and every other life enhancing resource that we now take for granted.

In summary both my friends and I have seen *"up close and personal"* the impact of global warming Climate warming trends are now reported to be progressing at an accelerating rate, and when Al Gore and his environmentally concerned friends tell us its serious, they need not preach to me or my fishing buddies, *"as we have already seen the truth".*

Glad to be born a boy

"The more things change the more they stay the same" is a statement that was intended for *the never changing sameness of our recent past.* It also rings true when related to the history of our ancient past. It's about people and nations never learning from mistakes, thus being historically doomed to keep repeating those same mistakes over and over again.

In other words, no matter how smart we think we are, even in today's *smart* world, our past actions have doomed us to make the same dumb mistakes over and over again. What does that say for human evolution?

Or so it seems.

"Boy and girls are created equal" may be true. But beyond that, to say boys and girls are equal is far different.

The first statement is one that is used frequently for comfort and convenience *and for the most part* it is only a metaphor, a figure of speech.

My slant is on the fallacy of the statement, that, boys and girls *are equal* and have equal opportunities in life, is simply not true. This opinion has been formed based upon what I have personally seen and experienced in over three score years of living *with and amongst people of all ages* of both sexes.

I wasn't always so tolerant.

Being born into a farm family in Branch La Have Nova Scotia was no different than being born *anywhere else. The vast majority of families from there, and from most countries* of the world, the parents hoped for a boy child to be born.

Times have changed but *some things do stay the same*, most of the advantages still remain tilted towards the male of the species.

Male babies were *deemed to be* necessary; female babies were not.

Male children *were essential* to continue the farming and other labour intensive necessities of the era. This, male dominance tradition, was *precipitated in large by the behaviour of many preceding generations.*

"Don't kill the messenger".

Males were considered superior to females, not only in size and strength but also in reasoning and in upholding a dominant family image.

In some countries *boys were expected to carry on the century old traditions* of keeping and defending kingdoms and sheikdoms. Females were rendered necessary for less important reasons, like *personal* entertainment.

So to be King was to be *the ultimate master,* whether it was on the farm, in the jungle, or anywhere else.

We boys in the Young household accepted our "special designation" as normal.

Such an attitude persisted until I became older; about the time that my testosterone started kicking in. It was then *I began to notice the females* of the species. The girls sure looked a lot more palatable in my eye than did those males, *but that is not the direction I want this observation to head.*

It was quite apparent to me that boys being boys, held a distinct advantage over girls. It never seemed fair to me, even back then, but because of the generational biography it was *the unwritten* law.

Consequently, because of the female servitude attitude of countless families like ours, girls have had to face almost insurmountable odds for generations in *their never-ending struggle to become equal* to man.

Girls knew that being unequal to boys, was not right in the sight of God, nor should it be so in the minds of man; they, so, the girls, just had to change the world.

"Sounds simple enough"

They not only had to struggle against their own families attitude, who wanted nothing to be born but boys, they had to challenge the leaders of the countries and the armies of the world, which were restricted to boys only

They had to sit by, even in Canada, and wait, *to be given,* the right to vote.

Then after receiving *that right*, they now were able to vote in elections, but only for *a choice of one man over another.* It took many additional years before the first female candidate was elected. Meanwhile men upon being elected could continue *the democratic rule* of empowerment over them for the next four years.

It was a "fact of the times" that men only must make governing decisions.

No wonder there is an abundance of women's libbers. Who can blame them?

Where under the sun do men think boys come from in the first place, and who was it that placed that crown exclusive on male heads and made them king?

There's an easy answer, why men, of course.

I have seen a lot of unequal treatment of many girls during my lifetime; I see it continuing to happen all around me, as I grew older and matured.

I have witnessed my own daughter's progression beyond adolescence into their teens and beyond, *as they too competed for equal status* in both social and business environment while having less then a level playing field before them.

I am extremely proud of both of my daughters, Margo and Pam, as are countless other parents of other daughters who have risen *above and beyond the expectations of both their peers and their parents.*

Girls still continue to struggle for equal status today, but thank God the struggle is much less intensive and far more rewarding than it was a generation or two ago.

Today the females of the world work in and succeed at just about every vocation that was once male dominated, including machinery operators, truck driving, police and RCMP officers, excellence in sports, flying planes, racing automobiles, managing large companies, as well as scientists and astronauts.

The last male dominated realm has now been breached as a female has recently earned the right to be a commanding officer of a large naval vessel.

"Girls, the world is now your steppingstone; go for it".

Becoming a member of Junior Chamber International {Jaycees} instilled into me a greater awareness in the logic of fair play and a common social sense, that no matter what colour your skin is, what creed you live by, *no matter how or why or where you were born,* that not only are we equal, but, that any and every one of us *can* change the world.

So that is the central reason why I have taken pen in hand and drafted a new anthem for this country; Canada, one that includes, not just "the boys *that stand on guard*" but one that *includes our "girls" who also stand on guard* and who are now doing what only the boys were once allowed to do, keeping Canada strong and free.

Here are the lyrics; the musical notes are not available but are known in my mind and memory. It sounds wonderful. Perhaps sometime in the not so far future it can be set to notes, than you can enjoy it as much as I do.

Canada my Canada

Canada, my Canada, land of Majesty and Grace.
*True Patriot love, the one command for all thy sons **and daughters**.*
With strong and courageous hearts we stand on guard for thee.

From far and wide your banner held high, in pride and unity.
God keep Canada glorious and free.

Hope never dies with peace the prize, for life with liberty.

I love Canada I stand on guard for thee.
O Canada, I pledge my heart to do my part to stand on guard for thee.
Here is where {for thee" can be inserted and the anthem can end; or it can continue with the following............
For the mountains, plains and valleys, shining lakes and rushing rivers.
For all nature and our people and the way of life we choose.
Yes, I love Canada; I pledge my heart, to do my part, to stand on guard for thee.

Written in 1967 on the eve of Canada's first Centennial
First repeated, with pride, to three *other* fishermen on July 1st 1995 on the shores of Jubilee Lake in Newfoundland Canada just prior to the Quebec referendum of Oct 30th 1995.

Canada - the Monologue

The following is a copy of an original script I had written around the time of the Quebec crises {October 1995}

With a large Canadian flag wrapped tightly around me I delivered this short monologue to a small but passionate gathering of local and like minded Canadians, at St Paul's Evangelical Lutheran Church in Bridgewater, Nova Scotia, while millions more from across four thousand miles of land and water, shared a mutual determination for the retention of Canada as our ancestors had designed it.

Prologue

The following monologue represents three emotions that we Canadians share about Canada.

First – the Pride and confidence of being Canadian, of sharing the joy, the excitement and promise, as Canada celebrates its first Centennial on July 1st 1967.

Second – *To be shaken and awakened to a new reality* as the referendum in Quebec unfolded on October 30th 1995

Thirdly – *Canada - the land* speaks.

Where we live and work each day Indian children used to play.
All across this great vast land where now the mighty cities stand.
Once there were no towns at all, only wigwams and trees so tall.
Then the white man came, to toil, to cut the trees to till the soil
Raised his children built his schools, made his own highways, his hands for his tools.

Fought for and loved the land he made, to make it better for us today.

And the land was called Canada.

Then in 1867 like wise men sent from out of heaven, came the fathers of confederation
To mould this land into one mighty nation.

To this day forward from out of the past, the torch of freedom and progress was passed.

Let's hold it high that it may light the burdened nations to freedoms fight.

To walk and talk and think and do what God and conscience asked us to.

That is our heritage, this is our land, let's keep it free for every man.

Canada.

But now a new and wily foe waits, anxious, angry, at the door Discerning sounds, to some unknown, comes not from out but- inside our home A wolf disguised as peace and wealth, would devour our pride and taint our wealth This would be thief would steal a gem that now is his, also his kin How can we show our brothers, sons, our sisters and daughters?

We need not divide what all have won

To choose not hate or hurt as goal, but will from every heart and soul

The bonds of family, the love of friend must overcome mistrust within

Join hand and heart and mind and soul.

Your Canada is mine-my Canada is yours.

The Trial over Canada

Hark now, *what tremors* do I feel?

A knife; *of voices;* of half-truths, half lies.

No equal justice, no sense of pride, *a sovereign land we want*, you cry.

Blind child, behold your inheritance since the first day that I became your home.

From what I hear and feel, it would seem that many of my children would divide or quarter me with haste, without any consideration of listening to my side of this issue. I ask that you please allow me just a few moments of your valuable time to offer my defence.

My birth certificate states that I was born on July 1st in the year 1867.

That too was the date that both you and I were joined together, not for years, but for life.

But as you *probably* know the original idea of *my being,* was first conceived by your ancestor parents.

Of those that came, first to visit and court me were Norsemen, Asians, Africans, Swedes and Danish as well as you French, English and Indian.

Some thought that *I deserved more than a fleeting glance* and decided to court me seriously.

Let me remind you of my preferred suitors.

Your history books have recorded the names of Henry Hudson, Jacques Cartier, Pierre Radison, Marc LesCabot, Pierre deMonts, John Cabot, Leif Eriksson and Samuel deChamplain.

Now, these were men I tell you, men with ambition, men of valour, and men of vision.

Believe me, I felt very proud to attract men of such courage and noble character.

It was not love at first sight as many would have you believe, but more like a covenant, a union of mutual needs, of challenges and responsibilities, *with a mutual promise* that if we remained true to each other, *that together we could become the greatest union of land and people on earth.*

In a nut shell; I needed ambitious responsible citizens, to live, to plant, nurture and harvest crops, to build homes, farms and factories; to be able to admire and enjoy my lofty mountains, to walk in my many green valleys to explore, develop, and yes earn their daily bread from the bounty of my lakes, rivers, forest and plains.

I welcomed you to partake of my abundant supply of wood, water and mineral resources, my rich soil and clear skies *that seemed to stretch forever.*

I also had a need for those that decided to stay, for I knew that it would take their vision and dedication, their endurance and vigilance and seemingly endless labour to make our union worthwhile and lasting.

Attracted by my great land mass, covered with *virtually unlimited* resources, your past parents resolved then and there that *their strength being complimentary and equal to mine* that *a union of bodies and soul and soil* should *be*. And so it was that we were bonded together by *a signed and sealed document known to all people* at the Charter of Confederation.

It was a commitment not taken lightly by your forefathers *or* me. Oh yes we have had our moments, a few that I am not so proud of, like *the time my French and English children* squabbled *over who should have the authority* over my development. I thought it was foolish at the time and I soon forgot about the matter, and I thought that you had also, for not long afterwards *you joined forces together* to drive away an enemy who was considered *a mutual danger to both of us*.

And so it was, that together, we overcame plagues, pestilence, wars, and would be invaders, using good reasoning that our combined strength and resources for the common good, made better sense than going it alone.

So continue we did, working, playing, enduring, enjoying triumphs, having empathy and the comfort of just being there for each other, when troubles arose, slowly growing stronger, more confident, continuing to offer opportunities *and security for all citizens no matter their colour, language, religion, or place of birth.*

Now keep in mind that *I am still only a youngster on this sphere of maturing countries* but already you have cultured and honed me into one of *the most desired place to live on earth.* Not a bad record at any age and would you believe me if I told you *the best is still to be.*

So please my children, my brothers and sisters, sons and daughters, I ask you to consider seriously upon this charge that many of you have made.

The decision and the ultimate verdict *opposing* me should be rendered *not* in haste, *not* by pretender kings, *not* from personal egos, but only from every fibre of truth that your individual heart and mind and soul can germinate.

This country can be *compared to a beautiful jewel,* millions of years in the creation, formed by extreme heat and great pressure, *almost impossible* to find, but once found, can be cut and designed to perfection only by first making careful study, then, by sure and sensitive motions, by rare and talented craftsmen, once perfected, *if* protected and cared for, *can last forever,* offering *beauty, prosperity, security and pride in return.*

But, in one careless or thoughtless moment by one single act of anger, all can be lost or destroyed and can never again, no matter how much you wish, how sorry you are, or how long and hard you try, it cannot be put back together again.

I close my defence with one final thought for you.

Wonderful and unique situations are born, not out of loud beating of chests or thumping of war drums, *but in quietness, gentleness, patience, mutual empathy, love, positive thoughts and positive actions.* If, after due course, when all thoughts and things are considered, *if your decision should still remain resolute- that I should die?*

*Upon you-*I rest my case.

Signed;   CANADA

Self Hypnosis

Once upon a time for a period of several years I experimented with self-hypnosis *of a sort,* just to survive as a functioning father and bread-earner

It was in the late 1950's early 60's that it occurred.

I was selling new and used cars, mostly used for the first few years, for a local GM dealer and for those first two years I had to struggle mightily to *hold my own* against the status quo made up *of three other experienced and more established salespersons* than myself.

I often had to work unusual hours when they were not around, in order to make my sales.

To succeed, I needed to create a "niche" market, one that appealed to new and younger buyers.

That meant being available *when they were.*

In simple terms I made myself available to my customers *when they needed me* that meant working almost any hour of the day or evening, seven days a week.

This non-stop activity continued for two full years before I finally secured myself as one of the top producers for the dealership. But it came at a cost.

As my volume of sales increased, so did the demands of my time.

Physically I was okay; it was the mental demands that were difficult to manage.

Out of necessity I devised a cerebral process that eased my mental stress, saved me from possible burnout and taught me a lesson I had never learned in school.

The hastening of my attempting *this self-hypnosis thing* was punctuated one evening while visiting my brother Arthur and his good wife Betty.

It was getting late in the evening and Betty, noticing that I *seemed more famished then usual,* said this to me, with a questioning quip. "Caroll, *you seem to be awful hungry tonight,* I guess you did not have any supper? It only took a moment for me to tell her that "no, I told her, I didn't have any supper" and as I continued to think about her question longer, *I could not remember having any dinner that day either* and knowing that I usually *took off for work in the mornings without breakfast,* I soon realized *that I had not eaten at all that day* and the time was now nine o-clock in the evening.

That's thirteen hours without food, okay for a hibernating bear, but not so good for me.

Now you can only run so many marathons and I was running too many.

To take control - I had only *my self as a resource* and *as a solution* base.

That was when I started taking short breathers, as brief as ten minutes and as long as twenty minutes, whenever I found an opportunity; *always* at home, and *as a rule, I did this* immediately after having lunch or supper. "That was *when* I was fortunate enough to get home"

I would sit down in my most comfortable chair, we only had one comfortable, a rocker type, throw my head back, put my feet up on something and then *divest myself of every stressful situation* at hand, *by going on vacation.*

By focused concentration and controlled breathing, I could block out all the problems of my world and enjoy the total stress free relaxation, of warm weather, soft breezes and total silence.

As I write these lines it again draws me back to those times of self induced, peaceful moments. I had actually, successfully trained my mind to fool my body, that, upon completing my brief siesta "I felt like I had just returned from a vacation, renewed and ready to return to work, recharged with mental vim and physical vigour.

If I had only enough time for a ten- minute break I could convince myself that I was returning to work *after* having had several days away. *If the respite was more prolonged,* I could convince myself {fool my mind and consequently, my body} that I had just returned from *a full week or more* of vacationing.

I was then refreshed, recharged, and ready to go back to work.

I know it sounds crazy but *I made the process work for me.* I could return to work after being away for less than an hour, filled with renewed energy. My interest in my work remained exciting, my mind stayed focused and I never again thought about mental or physical burn out.

"When we speak about fooling ourselves, *it really can be done"*

My 30 Day Mental Diet

It's very difficult in today's world to pick up a magazine or turn on a television that doesn't assail us with the virtues of participating in one *diet plan* or another.

Most promos have to do with either losing weight or gaining

muscle and how much better we will *all look* and feel after following and successfully completing their *fail proof* diet plan. According to the ad, it can take *as little as thirty days* or up to several months to complete and to attain your expected results.

My plan is different. You can do what you want, when you want, as much as you want, and keep doing it for as long as you want.

On my diet you can gain and lose, *and do both at the same time.*

On my diet your body does not take in food; you take in thoughts, only positive thoughts as only positive thoughts have any value mentally and consequently physically.

Lose all of your old and present "I cannot do that" mental negatives, and gain a mindset that can accomplish remarkable results. All you need to do is sweep out the negatives and welcome in the positives and anyone can do it.

You can change and *you can change immediately,* just like a chameleon.

Starting tomorrow morning, you will only accept thoughts and suggestion that are positive.

Your brain will no longer be a host to any negative thought.

Your mind and body will not be happy with anything but positive actions.

You will, no longer from this day forward, accept any comments; for example "My it looks like rain today" or, You cannot do that, "you're too old {or too young} to do or think, that way"- "The world is in such a mess, crime is *so* bad that I am afraid to go outside my door" "Everything is bad-nothing is good" etc. etc.

Stop!

Accept no negative statements without *immediately* replying "We certainly need the rain" or "Yes I know its raining *and isn't it a blessing* as there are so many areas in this world that need more rain" or "I can at least try to do it" or "yes I can". "My world is beautiful; let me tell you about something good that's happened to me". "I always walk where it's safe" or "I refuse to give-in to criminal elements" etc.

We can be assailed every moment of the day if we want to be, or if we let it happen.

Those examples are just to give you *the thought process* of where I am coming from and where *we* are going with this *positive* line of thinking.

Another more current *verbal negative* you might be berated with in *today's* economic language might go something like this *"Have you seen* yesterday's stock market *decline, if you have any money you had best hide it under your mattress,* or, *if your holding on to any stocks, now is the time to dump them".*

How about saying something like this in retort, but always with a smile. "My friend, I thank you for the advice, I know that you have only my best interests at heart"

By now you must have the essence of what I am promoting; **accept no negatives** and **do it for thirty days.**

Every day in every way, from sun up to sundown we are berated with hundreds of negatives, coming at us *mostly from our friends* and for the most part coming from friends who having nothing but good intentions at heart.

I first tried this 30-day mental diet over forty years ago and the results were immediate and astounding.

I was selling automobiles at the time and experiencing *the usual number* of monthly successes and failures *generally accepted as average* in a life of competitive selling.

But, *during those thirty days* while holding true to my resolve {my 3o day mental diet} of vowing to myself *that I would not allow even one negative thought* to creep into my psychic, you will find it hard to believe what happened.

For thirty days I never failed in successfully closing every sales opportunity that had come my way.

I sold every costumer I spoke to.

Yes, believe it *if you can*, every single person I spoke to in relation to purchasing a car or truck, purchased one from me. My total number of sales was *over forty for the month.*

I myself found it difficult to believe as nothing like this had ever happened to me before. What had I opened up, what amazing secret had I discovered? Can this be what success is all about? *Is this* what all the unsuccessful people of the world are missing out on?

Can success be that simple and easy, and if so, if it is, then why is a positive mental diet *not* on somebody's *must do* list, to be taught in every school, to be shouted from the tops of buildings, to *say it-do it- tell it,* to anyone and everyone willing to listen.

But success sometimes comes at a cost. To remain socially acceptable in today's society we are expected to apply some give and take, to tolerate others as we wish them to tolerate us.

My close friends thought that I was disagreeable, augmentative, a never wanting to lose *type* guy, and that is true. *I vowed to get my positive attitude right ov*er fifty years ago, and even today I struggle every day to retain my positive behaviour, but it's difficult in a negative thinking-speaking-acting, world.

It is still a vital part of me; one that I consciously and subconsciously refuse to let go of.

Staying one hundred percent positive is great when you are in your "work a day" harness where every thought and action can reflect on you or your employers success or *failure*, but there comes a time when you must throw off that *positive* harness and join the other stallions or fillies for the retirement pasture of relaxation and leisure.

For me, that time has arrived.

But, "I can never completely let go or forget what Norman Vincent Peale called the amazing power of positive thinking, I tried it, and it really does work".

Time

It's all we *really* have.

When *we have no more time left,* nothing else matters.

Not our health, certainly not our wealth, not our friends, not of how smart or dumb we are, not the exotic places we have travelled too, or what amazing and wonderful things we have seen, or, what famous persons we have met, be they great, or not so great, or can we boast of the many things we have accomplished.

Time has run out.

Then, it's only our families that matter and *if we haven't prepared for ourselves and them* for a sudden exit from their lives, then that doesn't matter either, as it is now too late to do anything about it, and they, your family, *or someone else,* will eventually pick up and dispose of what remains of you, or me.

So *time, right now time,* is the only thing that matters.

Our time truly does mean everything and we should never waste a single minute of it.

Over the past thirty years of my life I resolved never to waste a single moment of that precious element called *time. Time* is not considered a tangible thing, but nothing, *and I do mean nothing,* ever happens, without the consummation of *time.*

Over the course of those thirty years of being self employed in the vocation of selling and servicing mobile homes and RV's *I cannot recall wasting even a minute* of my time. It probably happened but I cannot recall it happening. I do not consider eating or sleeping or having good conversation and interaction *as a waste of time* as all three are essential to good health and life itself.

I was usually in my office or doing some physical work at 8 AM, no later than 9 AM

When 3 PM in the afternoon arrived I considered my day only *half over,* as I generally worked through to 9 PM.

I worked six days and five nights a week, only taking Saturday nights and Sunday's off.

I believed that my presence was essential to my company's survival.

Some call that behaviour as "workaholic" I never viewed it as such.

In retrospect *I must have been the world's worst salesman and manager,* as few people except my father-in-law, who worked seventy two hours every week for his employer, a man who thought that the company he worked for *would surely fail if he was not there every moment* doing his seventy two hour a week job. The worst part of his job was the pay; he received pay for only forty-eight hours. The Provincial labour laws did little {actually nothing} to protect hourly workers back then, and my father in law never ever complained, he was only happy to have his job.

I worked for myself; so, I have no one to blame but myself

I guess we, my father in law and I, both felt important, he in his way and I in mine.

It's just possible that we both were right, that both companies *would have* floundered without us. I know for sure that mine would have.

I used to brag {never complain} that I knew of every loose bolt or missing screw or problem that needed a serviceman's attention in every mobile home I sold

I tried {and still do} to never waste *other people's* time.

There's nothing worse than to be retired and have nothing to do but wander aimlessly around, using up your minutes and hours to take {waste} other people's *productive* time, having no objective yourself other then using up time. There ought to be a law prohibiting wasting time.

Doctors are among the top offenders by scheduling several or more office appointments, for what seems to be, the very same time slot. They seem to put no value *on our time* whatever. How I abhorred inconsideration by others, in valuing my time *as worthless,* and as I grow older I still cannot seem to get over such callous thinking.

We have far more areas now than we need, where we *voluntarily* waste time; from waiting *in line* for a coffee to having deal with entire bridges and roadways clogged with traffic, because of either "standard" procedures or incompetence, you can be the judge.

"Time is precious; use it wisely, it is the most precious commodity you have"

Unpaid Board of Director

All major companies have *by necessity* a board of directors, meeting together as often as deemed necessary to exchange ideas, give advice and provide insight to the betterment of the company they represent.

Some individuals are directors in several or even dozens of companies.

In today's world *there is a startling few people* who have attained the plateau of having *enough of* both intelligence *and* common sense to be invited to serve as a director in many organizations.

My *fledgling* company was tiny *in comparison to even small companies,* representing only eight "at the most" employees.

The original name of the company was Bluenose Homes Company Ltd, later it was changed to Bluenose RV Centre.

We sold and serviced recreational vehicles {RV's} and associated products.

The name Bluenose came from a local fishing schooner that became Internationally famous for winning *all but one race* during twenty years of fierce competition against our American friends. They {the fishing boats and crews} first tangled on the high seas while travelling *to and from* the rich fishing areas located off Sable Island or Brown's Bank in the North Atlantic.

International schooner racing was a product of those original antics.

Bluenose RV Centre was an unlikely candidate for acquiring a Board of Directors.

But I wanted and needed my company to grow, where it counts most, in the eyes of the public.

It takes good product, good people, good management and a receptive marketplace to build, maintain *and grow any successful company.* I had some of the basic tools but I was *woefully short on experience.*

That is why and when I decided to acquire a board of directors; but I had no stipend to reward them.

I sought out and found several individuals *who* were known and trusted by me, *who were successful* in their own lives and were persons who didn't mind sharing with me *their thoughts and their ideas* on how my company might improve and grow.

Having only several small towns located in my company's business radius I choose my directors from within that area.

When approached for this novel venture, not one friend scoffed, and all agreed to make *their advice* available to *me*.

In retrospect it was a rewarding initiative both for my company and me.

I acquired as many as five directors. Not one received a dime for their services.

At every opportunity I would seek advice by asking them business related questions. Examples of my questions were; what are you hearing about my company?

What is the public perception of my products?

What are you hearing or know about other similar related businesses?

What products to you see your friends needing and buying elsewhere?

What do you see as my company's weakness, what am I doing right, any ideas on increasing market-share, what am I doing that I shouldn't be doing?

Would you purchase a product from my company and if so what type of product and why?

Does my company products have a future? etc etc.

Needless to say my unpaid Board of Directors was anxious to be asked information-seeking questions and in return, replied positively to those and other business related questions. We established a bond of mutual trust, confidentiality, and respect for each other.

My Board of Directors responded in kind with the same "sage advice" that they had gleaned from others or else, had acquired it over time, from successes and failures in building their own businesses.

Nothing creates success faster *then appearing to be* successful.

Today Bluenose RV Centre employs over twenty *well-paid* individuals and has sales in excess of ten million dollars.

I mentioned this unusual concept *of having an unpaid board of directors or advisory board available for my company* to a management consulting firm's representative from the United States. He thought it to be a novel idea, one *that his Company might consider worthy* for inclusion in their future portfolio of business related ideas for crafting other successful businesses

If, from a single acorn comes a mighty oak, then, from one simple idea, expect *unimagined* growth"

Survival Instincts

"Survival of the fittest" was a common slogan for countless generations. It is still used today in conversations usually relating to some persons or individual "over achieving" or coming out *on top of the pack* when the odds or obstacles of succeeding appeared to be insurmountable at the worst and doubtful at best.

For fish it's easy; the big ones simply eat the little ones.

Wild animals kill other species of animals and eat them; I doubt that either they or the fish have any qualms about doing it or even give it a thought on why they do it.

Both have what we call, *killer* instincts.

To have a *killer instinct* is *a colourful term* used by many sportscasters to describe the behaviour of a fighter inside the "squared circle"

The one having the "instinct" abandons all caution of self-defence and seeks to pummel opponents into submission even when their opponent is *in an indefensible* position.

We gave up physically *beating our adversaries into submission* a long time ago, now we just want or need to gain submission over them by using *social* or *corporate power, as that is an acceptable behaviour.*

Killer instinct is also a term used by law enforcement officers and news writers in explaining why many murderers behave the way they do. *It is not a pleasant term.*

Somewhere between the two terms of thought is the "why" many people behave the way they do.

Some humans, much like animals, fight for every inch of turf they can gain and control but unlike animals, which, in fact need *sufficient* territorial range to provide enough food supply to survive, humans go much further then just having *adequate or sufficient* space or assets.

We humans want more than just *standard survival.*

For thousands of years the human trait was for the strong to maintain power over the weak, first to conquer the people, control *all* their land and the food supply, steal away and hoard *all* the bounty and either slaughter or effectively humble the conquered masses.

In modern times we have softened that approach. We take only as much as we can get away with, knowing *now* that it international unacceptable to take it all

Remember Hitler?

How did we become so callous and uncaring about other humans, birds, animals, fishes, the oceans, the heavens, the earth, and all things, in, under, and upon?

The reality of the present is, that we are again living in "out of control" times, with multiple wars, continental crime, universal political corruption, continent wide social breakdown, worldwide financial chaos, accelerating environmental destruction, where individuals and families are torn asunder from *loss of personal power* to control the providing of *modern day* necessities for their families, while any escape routes are becoming increasingly unreachable.

There is no turning the clock back; our wants, our needs and our expectations have now reached the lofty peaks of Mount Everest, which only the fortunate few can attain.

We say we are concerned about our environment, about crime, about political inequities; that we hate wars, that we love all people, that we wouldn't hurt a flea, but in truth, is it not already *survival of the fittest* time, again, where we must, not out of want, but out of need, revive our "ancestral" survival instincts?

As children, at home on the farm, we were unwittingly subjected regularly *to life and death* experiences, witnessing events that made impressionable images that were difficult, *if not impossible,* to erase from many a young mind.

We learned about the survival of the fittest long before we should have.

To explain;

When there was need of food, the chickens were likely *the first to go*. With axe held high in one hand, the chicken was held *in the other*. And *beheaded*, without having any conscious thought of *doing or not doing what was right and natural*.

When autumn came and the pork barrel was empty, it was again time to refill it, in order to provide and ensure for at least a portion of the food supply needed for the family during another long winter.

A pig, weighing a few hundred pounds *or more* was the provider

The pigs were usually killed with a single gunshot to the head delivered by a twenty two-calibre rifle. It was *then that their throats were cut* to finish the job.

The larger beef animals *were usually hit on the head*, below and between their horns, *with a heavy iron hammer*, rendering them unconscious. They too had their throats cut and were bled dry before they could regain consciousness.

Butchering day was a big day on the farm as it meant a lot of preparation and labour for those involved, before the chickens, the pork or the beef was made ready for preservation or storage.

Our elders deemed the killing of farm animals as necessary, and we children accepted it as a part of life.

Chickens, running helter skelter around the yard, with no heads, pigs squealing when the first bullet failed and before the second shot could be fired, or kittens, being put in a burlap *feed bag* and then drowned, usually in the barn well. We kids weren't supposed to be around but we were and we witnessed far more then our share.

The one thing that still puzzles me was the silence *in which the beef animals died*, without nary a whimper.

The farm animals died then as they still do today; *that we humans might live*; nothing different about that *is there*?

Humans must have food to live, and along with the planting and the harvesting of grains and other *soil* produced foodstuff we humans have refined our palates *for the taste of flesh*. After all, "We humans do *hold dominion over the fish, the birds and the animals*; don't we"?

Close Calls

"Experience is the best teacher"

The saying, close calls, is a term used often today when refereeing sporting events, but long before becoming a catch phase in games and races, it was used daily in the work places of the country.

Today, most *close calls* are attributed to near misses while driving bicycles, motorcycles, ATV's snowmobiles, automobiles or commercial truckers.

Before the mechanization of the farms all heavy work had to be done manually, by hand. Hardly a day passed by without someone on the farm having a *close call or two.*

A *close c*all may have *almost happened* when an animal got loose from its stall, where it had been tied to, in the barn, and wandered away, only to retrieved before it did any damage to someone or someone else's property.

Or a *close c*all was when one of the children started to choke over a piece of an apple that was lodged in his / her throat, with the most common means of dislodging it, was to smack the child over the back with a bare hand, using enough force to dislodge the morsel of food.

If that didn't work, we were then *turned upside down* and subjected to more of the same whacking procedure.

Other *close calls* may have happened while working in the woods and having a tree fall in a different direction then it was intended to land.

Or, a close call might originate from a mundane chore like the removal of a large boulder from rough terrain when *clearing the land* where ploughing and planting was planned.

To start and complete the removal of a large boulder, the soil first had to be cleared away from one side of the stone. Then it had to be lifted by hand or lever and tilted toward the area of least resistance. Sometimes a few sticks of dynamite were available and placed in the space under the rock. Once the fuse was lit, everyone close by had to scramble to get out of the way of flying rocks and soil when the dynamite went off.

This blast served to lift the bolder up and out of its initial location. If the nitro didn't do the job you had to quickly *manhandle* the stone, before it fell back into its original place. If the original manoeuvre failed, this highly dangerous chore had to be started all over again. Yes, farm living dealt with a variety of *close calls* daily and *sometimes* hourly. *They were considered normal,* a way of life and living, in this new frontier.

Tool and contraptions

Rural living meant having to exist on your own initiative and energy.

Back then you did not have the luxury, *today's necessities*, of milk delivery, or pre-packaged store supplied butter, preserves, pickled beans and pork, apples, turnips, potatoes, factory made clothes and mitten, sock and hankies, as all were *in home* productions. Plough's, harrow's, mowing machines, churns, cream separators, spinning wheels, winnowing, pulping, picks, probe bars, shovels, sleighs and wagons were not luxuries, they were necessities, and they were only a portion of the vast array of simple, but effective hand-operated *production* tools, that every farmer needed.

Give me a Lever

"You can take the boy out of the country but you cannot take the country out of the boy"

Speaking of levers, no farm was complete without a "**crow**" **bar**

These, straight iron bars, were used for a whole range of farm projects, from lifting rocks and buildings to making fence post holes. No farmer could function efficiently without a good "crowbar"

The correct name was probably "probe" bar, but somewhere in the pronunciation, in the local dialect, it became crow bar, and every farm family had one or two in various sizes. Crowbars are still available in most hardware stores, as they are still needed today. They come in either grey or black colour, are approximately four feet long and are of varied thickness with a tapered lower portion.

How these bars retained their great strength, *I do not know,* as they have been around long before tempered steel was invented. They are primarily designed for one person, but two strong men can lift, using one bar, and not break it. I saw very few crowbars that bent under pressure, and not spring back to their original form, especially the heavier two inch ones. I never heard of one breaking.

At seventy -three years of age and living in town, *"I still retain a crowbar.* You just never know when you might need one"

Peaveys

No one I asked seems to know where the name peavey originated or why this tool was ever labelled *a peavey.*

A peavey is a lever with a difference. They are made with a three -foot length of *straight-grained hard wood* for the handle, or stock. The stock was then inserted into a round metal base. An *iron pick- or point* several inches long was then inserted at the bottom end of the wooden stock. To make the peavey an effective tool, a curved swinging hook was then attached to the upper end of the metal base.

The peavey was useful in lifting and turning large logs in the woodlots to enable the removing the limbs *from the downed trees.* No woodsman would think of entering his woodlot without having a peavey with him.

I also have a peavey in my basement, a gift from my brother Arthur. I have used it many times.

Pulping Machine

Our barn had a large metal grinding machine called a pulper. It was used for cutting up turnips into bite-sized pieces for the cows, and mangles for the pigs.

It had a large drum on top, which was filled with the produce. The drum encompassed a large wide cutting wheel with dozens of teeth. The drum was connected to a wheel on the exterior with a hand-sized handle that, when turned fast enough, would cut up or pulp, the produce.

It was hard work turning the pulping wheel but every-one of the boys wanted a turn or two at doing it.

If you slacked off and let the momentum of the wheel slow down, you then had to force it hard forward to get up to speed again and if you stopped after coming up against a hard or large turnip, you then often had to reverse the wheel in order to get started once again.

The *pulper* still sits where it did for over sixty years, in the ox-stable of the Young barn.

Hay Cutter

Our farm also had a *hay or straw* cutting machine.

It stood about three feet off of the floor and had a wide flat top where the hay or straw was placed. The top narrowed towards the one end compressing the hay or straw and assisting the blade to cut through the compressed hay with ease as *it* was being pushed forward towards the risen cutting blade.

It was a dangerous machine *if you weren't careful* and watched where your one hand, the one that was doing the pushing, was, as the other hand was busy raising and lowering the arm of the cutting blade.

As dangerous as this cutting board was, particularly for us kids, I cannot recall of even one accident happening while using it over the years.

Winnowing Machine / Hand Threshing

This machine was built to be a tiny version of a large commercial harvester. It was not used often.

But *to turn* small amounts of dry *grain into oats,* the stalk of grain was first fed into the top section of the machine called a hopper. The hopper vibrated back and forth and *hopped around* by the forces initiated by the turning of the machines *hand operated apparatus,* beating the grain out of its protecting pod. The grain or oats would then drop into a container located below the machine, while the husk or chaff that was beaten off the dry head of grain was then blown away through an outlet in the machine. This action was caused by the *force of wind* created by the rapidly rotating wheel, leaving nothing but pure grain for your efforts.

Hand threshers were a complicated piece of machinery; I am not sure of what fate the Young's *machine* deserved, or arrived at. It may still be around.

Sod Rollers

Sod rollers were used for smoothing out the soil after a planting of grain seeds.

Without a roller being used to press down the freshly sown field, the seeds may wash away in a heavy rain or been blown away by the wind.

The weight of the roller pressed the grain sees deeper into the ground, thus facilitating faster sprouting, giving the germinated seed firmer roots and improved soil stability.

Rollers were made from a large, heavy, and smooth, round log.

The *roller* was pulled forward over the field by using either a horse or a team of oxen.

A single pole or a pair of shafts, were attached to the roller by two iron pins protruding out from the centre of the ends of the log.

Today's *Rollers* are made of metal, are filled with water for weight, and are usually pulled by a tractor.

Cultivators

Cultivators or tillers had a configuration similar to that of a plough, only much lighter, with several soil cutting discs on the bottom. The cultivator was then pulled through the rows of plants, usually by a horse, removing weeds and softening up the soil, providing for speedier growth.

Cultivating the crops was usually a two-man operation, but if the pulling animal was steady and the teamster could maintain control of both horse and machine, then, one person was known to be able to do a two-man job.

Ploughs

The *rough terrain* that the settlers faced would never have evolved *by itself* into food producing soil without the use of a plough. Most *budding* farmers of the time used wooden ploughs, as they were the only type available. These ploughs had wooden handles and a wooden beam onto which a wooden *or metal* cutting edge was attached. According to my elder brother Arthur, he can remember when the Young farm fields were *broken up* with this rudimentary but effective plough.

The plough that I remember seeing was one that had a heavy steel shear blade and wooden handles It had a trip lever to permit the furrows to be turned up in either direction.

Ploughing the rough, rocky and rooted land was a two-man job, as the ploughs were heavy and the strength needed to keep them steady and straight was more than one man could muster.

As the plough-shear cut deep into the young but hard soil, enormous strength was needed to pull it forward over a prolonged period of time. A pair of oxen was the most popular mode for ploughing power on our farm, as they not only had great strength but endurance over the lengthy time period it took to plough a field. The oxen were slow and steady and didn't cost much to run.

It is safe to say, that because of the rough terrain found in Branch LaHave and almost every other areas of the Province, that without ploughs and oxen changing the landscape, it would have been decades later before any self-sustaining farms or villages could have been settled and maintained.

Seeders

Before seeders, the grain crop seeds were sown entirely by hand. I witnessed my father and grandfather, do this labour intensive and time consuming work more than once.

Once a hand held spreader was purchased, the seeding of a large field of grain was a relatively simple chore. The hand seed spreader had a pouch where a pail of seeds were poured. The pouch rested on the chest of the person doing the sowing.

The weight of the seeds and spreader was held up on the chest of the sower and was supported by a cloth strap that hung around the sowers neck.

A small metal fan located inside the pouch had a handle attached to it, which was then turned and operated by one hand, usually the right hand, turning the handle, spinning the fan and the seeds out of the seeder, spreading the seeds in all directions in front of the slowly walking sower, at a uniform rate. The end result was a near perfectly proportioned field of grain once the spouts took root.

As with every other ancient farming tool, seeders have been replaced by gas or diesel powered machines, while the simple practice of using a hand operated sowing machine, is today relegated mostly to lawn seeding procedures

Cream Separators

Our cream separator sat in the porch section of the house and was used almost daily.

The raw milk was first poured into the top of the machine and as the easy turning handle rotated discs inside the body of the machine, two spouts would *magically* deliver milk from one spout and cream from the other.

I do not know how this machine worked but I always enjoyed my turn at cranking the handle as the soft humming sound of the spinning discs was pleasant to hear *and better yet* was to see the separated milk and cream being delivered from those two spouts day after day without it ever being wrong, had me baffled, and still has.

Cleaning the disks and the spouts of the separator, after each use, was a labour intensive job, that was always done by the women of the house *and it was always done immediately after* the milk was separated from the cream.

The milk and cream was then placed in containers and hung in the well where it was cool, to keep it from going sour.

Churning Butter

This was a job I had to do, more than I wanted to do it.

It meant standing in one spot for what seemed like hours pumping the handle of that old faded oak coloured, *wooden staved* churn, *up and down* and *up and down* without stopping, until finally the texture of the cream started to change; it was thickening, slowly the cream *was turning into butter.*

Once the cream had jelled enough, Grammy would add some salt and put approximately a one-pound portion of it into a small hand operated butter press and then squeeze it in, until *like magic* a well-formed pat of beautiful yellow butter would emerge.

The butter and the milk was usually stored in a pail that was lowered into the depths of the well closest to the house, where it was kept safe, cool and handy, until needed.

As you can see, *deep cool water wells,* or *rocked walled cellars* served to keep our milk and other *sensitive* food products stored safely long before electricity and refrigerators came on the country scene.

Spinning Wheel

No farm was complete without having sufficient sheep to produce enough wool to make a stock of socks, sweaters and mittens to keep a family warm through a long cold winter.

As troublesome as keeping a flock of sheep can be, they were acknowledged to be worth the bother. Even on those occasions when several of them wandered away, going through the wired fences, out and into someone else's field, and had to be retrieved. To the adult Young family members, sheep were deemed necessary; to the children *they were deemed a damn nuisance.*

Our dad and grandfather would put large lightweight wooden yokes *on the ones that were suspected to be the ring leaders* in the escape plan, but even that didn't stop them from finding ways to get through *the dividing property line fence* and onto a neighbours property. *The phase, "the grass seems to be greener on the other side of the fence"* must have been penned by an owner of sheep.

Once the sheep were caught and sheared of their heavy wool covering, {which was preformed by hand-operated clippers}, it then became Grammy's job *to change the wool into yarn.*

She did this by first washing and drying the wool and once that was done the big spinning wheel was brought into the picture .By patiently feeding the cleaned and dried wool into a hole in the wheel where a bobbin would then catch it and spin it around and around twisting and turning the wool into yarn. The yarn was then made into usable sized bundles called skeins. {Skeins is pronounced *skanes}.*

The yarn was then dyed a grey or a blue colour and Grammy would then proceed to use it to knit woollen socks and mittens for everyone in the family.

I remember some of the mittens having a nice red *stripe or band* knit into and around the cuff area. I guess she must have either purchased some red wool or else she dyed a small amount of wool red for her decorating detail.

There is nothing warmer on a cold winter's day, even when they are soaking wet, than to be wearing home knit woollen mittens and socks.

When Grammy was sitting around the house on the rocking chair she was always knitting. She never seemed to pay much attention to her work as the two silver needles in her hands moved swiftly and efficiently producing her countless works of art.

I never appreciated all that she was doing for us back then to keep the feet and hands of the family warm every winter. I do now, and I say a belated "thanks Grammy"

Hay Pitcher

You might think a hay pitcher is "*a picture of hay*" or an individual that throws or pitches hay around, something like a baseball pitcher. If so, you haven't quite got the picture; read on.

Loading hay by hand, with *a pitch-fork,* up onto a high laddered hay wagon and then having it hauled by a team of oxen or horses to the barn, where it was stowed away in a barns hay mow {hayloft} took a minimum of two weeks in the summer. It took longer if any rain fell during those two weeks of haying. If that happened, the hay had to be re-handled and re-dried before storage.

Dad and Papa paid careful attention in making sure that all the hay that was stowed up into the lofts of the barn was thoroughly dried by the wind and sun.

Hay done right, has a special *sweet smell* to it.

Putting *wet* hay in storage *into a loft or a haymow* creates heat, which upon reaching a high enough degree causes *spontaneous combustion*, thus igniting into a fire. More then one barn and animals was lost by fire because of storing wet or damp hay.

Sprinkling a small amount of *course salt* over the hay after every load or two was stowed away was done *as a precaution*. It served as a deterrent *to any possible* over heating.

Mowing Machines

Mowing the hay was usually done by horsepower as horses moved faster than oxen and a single animal pulling the mowing machine was more efficient in speed and in preventing the *unnecessary* tramping down of un-mown grass along the mowers path of travel.

The sounds of the bright red, black trimmed, McCormick Dearing's large steel wheels doing their clank clank clank, as it was pulled forward and sideways in a turning mode, was an enjoyable sound of summer that most people today have never or will ever hear.

Before the day that our first hay pitcher arrived and was installed, all the hay had to be removed from the wagons the same way as it was put on, by hand.

The only thing worse then forking the hay onto the wagon was the fact that it had to be pulled loose from the load and then lifted high above the head of the man on the wagon and then pushed even higher up with a long handled pitch fork into the loft {or mow} of the barn.

The confines of the thrashing floor of the barn allowed little room for a much appreciated breeze to draw through and past the loaded hay wagon, a breeze that was needed to cool the over heated workers on many a hot August day.

Loading and unloading hay was back breaking work from start to finish, work that was mostly performed by dad, until Arthur grew older and stronger and was able enough to take his turn at forking off the loaded wagons.

We younger children were stationed up in the hayloft and were useful in stowing {moving} the hay and placing it into every available crevice.

After the *hay pitcher* was purchased and installed, unloading the wagons seemed like eating a piece of cake.

The *pitcher* came with a large two-pronged fork that was then pushed down into the hay on the wagon. The two prongs had mechanical operated hooks that held the hay in place in large bundles. The fork of the pitcher was attached to a long heavy rope that was again attached to a pulley located in the peak of the bar. The rope was connected to the *swivel tree, traces*, and harness, of a horse waiting outside to pull the fully loaded pitcher up onto the loft area of the barn.

A full load of hay could be unloaded by five to seven fully loaded pitcher pulls, in about twenty minutes, as compared to up to an hour of unloading the wagons by hand.

The only individuals that had to work any harder with the installation of the mechanical pitcher was the horse on the outside of the barn and the *stowers* {the people working up in the lofts of the barn} where there was hardly ever a breeze or a cool moment.

I, along with several other *sweat-hogs*, did the stowing.

Scythes and Wet-horns

Most persons reading this know what a scythe is. If not, you can see one in a caption of the Grim Reaper, usually seen in movies or books dealing with death or destruction. He {the Reaper} always holds a menacing looking scythe that causes the hair on the back of your neck stand up.

For those few that have not seen or do not know, a scythe is a hand held grass cutting devise that is used by one person and is utilized by swinging it back and forth in a side to side motion as it cuts the grass, or wheat or bushes, or in the case of the Grim Reaper, the heads off of people.

In my grandfathers, and even in my father's time, it was used daily during haying to cut any grass that was missed by the horse powered mower. A hand scythe was used exclusively for mowing the grain, as a machine was not allowed on the grain field because of tramping down and destroying too much of the valuable crop.

A hand held scythe has a steel blade about two inches deep and two and one half feet long that is attached to a curved, usually wooden, handle, about four feet long. The long curved handle has two short handles {about 4 inches long each} on it, that are grasped, one by each hand, to support and control the scythe blade when it is being used.

To keep the blade *razor sharp,* it had to be honed often, that's where a wet-horn comes in.

A wet-horn is just what it says it is, it is a horn off of a butchered animal, and contains water. A slim honing stone, about nine or ten inches long, tapered on both ends, is then placed inside the horn where it is carried on the belt of the person using the scythe.

Sometimes the horns leaked water or were two narrow at the lower end to accommodate the stone, it was then that the horn had to be cut off and a wooden plug was inserted to keep the water from leaking out.

I watched many times as my grandfather mowed grain with a scythe. The motion of both using the scythe and honing the blade was a work of art. When the wetted stone was being used it was moved back and forth over the blade, first one side and then the other, with a motion and speed that the eye could not follow.

The symmetry of sound and motion of the stone against metal was a summer ritual that few if any of my children will ever know.

Barrels from the States

Every year *or two* the Young family received a large barrel of used clothing *from our relation* who lived in the USA.

In the beginning the barrels were delivered to my dad's sisters home {Beulah's}

It came from our Grandmother's sister's {Edith} family, whose home was in Worchester, Massachusetts.

Edith had married a local boy, Stuart Hirtle, and together they moved to Worchester in the 1920's, reason being that there was little or no employment for Stuart in his native Nova Scotia.

Stuart found employment in the U. S. at the Norton Emery Company, a manufacturer of stones that were used to sharpen knives and grind cutting blades.

The Hirtles had four girls and one boy. Stuart and E-de {as we called her} They visited our home every year or so by driving *all the way* from Worchester to Nova Scotia, in a new or almost new {late 1940's, early 1950's} six cylinder Chevrolet four door sedan.

I can remember one little eccentricity {we thought} about Stuart; he never failed to wash his feet in a basin of warm water *every night.* Around our home you had to have an awfully good reason to wash your feet every day; more like once a week.

Whenever a member of the family would rib Stuart about washing his feet *every day* Stuart had a ready reply. "I only have one pair of feet and I am going to take *good* care of them".

When *the barrel* arrived it was a big day, especially for the girls. Dad's sister {Beulah} had a family including four girls. They made sure they were around for *the opening* of the barrel *and they had good reasons to.*

The barrel was stuffed to the brim with skirts, dresses, shoes and handbags, but little for us boys.

Mom reminds me that both Arthur and I did each receive a coat in one of the barrels. I cannot remember receiving it, *or anything else.*

As boys we shouldn't have expected much as the Hirtle family, who sent the barrel, only had one boy while being outnumbered by four sisters; but we still hoped *for something.*

We boys, like the girls, were excited for the arrival and opening of those barrels, but *our male enthusiasm dwindled rather quickly* as its contents were announced and removed.

The barrels stopped coming around 1950.

The Plane; The Plane

One summer's day around 1948 when my brother Arthur and I were working at the back extremities of our farm repairing some fences, when we noticed a small one engine plane attempting to land on a neighbours field quite close *to where we were* working.

As we had never seen an airplane of any kind up *this close* before, we dropped everything and ran as fast as we could towards the field. We arrived just in time to see the plane bump to a landing.

To our pleasant surprise out stepped two men who were members of the Hirtle family from Massachusetts *and they were looking for the Young farm.*

It was a relative named Bob Morse who had married Betty, one of the Hirtle girls. He was in the plumbing business and had become quite wealthy in his home city of Worchester. He also had a friend with him.

How the two managed to find that field on Walter Meisner's land, *so close* to our farm I never did find out; it would have taken both a good navigator and a competent pilot, with both courage and skill, to attempt such a feat as landing on a bumpy hay field. I am not sure which one of the two men was the pilot but I believe that it was Bob.

In thinking *recently* about that exciting moment, so long ago, when that plane landed, I bet that back in those days that Bob Morse never even needed *to advise either the U.S. or Canadian authorities* that he was coming to Canada by way of his own private plane.

Try that today and see how far you get. Those sure were simpler times to live.

In 1967 my wife Dolly and I made a car trip {vacation} to Massachusetts to visit the Hirtle family.

With *the exception of Stuart and Edith and one daughter Opal*, who had married the ambitious pilot, plane, and successful plumbing business owner, Bob Morse, it soon became apparent to Dolly and me *that it was their families who were now in need* of the same kind of assistance as they once provided to us. *They appeared* to have fallen on difficult times financially, but in the American tradition, they remained *too proud to ask anyone for assistanc*e, and thoughtlessly, we never offered them any.

Since the passing away of both Stuart and Edith and older relatives from both sides of *our* families, our Canadian-American interactions and personal visits have become few, if any. *"So very sad"*.

Wooden Toys

We had our share of *boughten* toys, like plastic pistols and the occasional ball but when it came to having larger toys *we made our own*.

Trucks and wagons were made out of spare boards, and for wheels dad would cut off four pieces of wood from a *round* piece of firewood.

For making *play cars* we would cut branches from either a young maple or birch tree and then cut the branches off to suit our needs. One branch might serve as a brake pedal while other branches would suffice as a *make-believe* horn or accelerator.

Pontiac play cars were the most popular as they were designed out of a V shaped branch with *the same pruning* of limbs for accessories.

Wooden oxen were the most popular toys on a farm. Dad would make them for us when we were too small to make them on our own. They were made out of two small trees about two feet long. Fir was generally used because of the colour, the markings of the bark, and the curvature of the limbs. Two long limbs attached at the one end to representing the head and horns.

A yoke was then nailed onto the heads of the two wooden oxen, making a pair. The pair of oxen was then attached to a miniature wagon that we could load with rocks or wood.

Play oxen were so popular *that they became a part of the culture of the area* and the local museum in Bridgewater has a pair as one of their art exhibits.

They were made and donated to the DesBrisay Museum in Bridgewater by my dad.

Personal values

I believe, that
I was rich long before I had money.

Mind over matter, matters.

Ignorance, is not bliss, it is what it is.

If life is worth living, it is worth writing about.

If I live longer, I will be dead shorter.

All of us are ageing at the same speed and travelling in the same direction, it's only the sojourns on the journey, which differs.
One smile precipitates another.

Yawning is contagious, so is yarning.

Friends need and deserve admiration and respect.

Pretence usually stumbles before pride finally falls.

In the beginning was God.

Talking to God isn't always about praying.

That God is neither male nor female.

That God is all intelligence, energy and power.

That God permeates every scintilla of space in the universe.

That God is within us.

That the universe never ends.

Negatives, are sin, positives, are Godly.

Whoever said that, cleanliness is next to Godliness, must have prayed standing up

Beauty is not only in the eye, but also, in the heart and mind, of the beholder.

Adrenalin is fuel for the mind.

There has to be a better way to settle disputes between countries, than going to war.

Giving, feels better than receiving.

Giving anonymously rewards the giver ten-fold.

Having a family, with children, is life's greatest rationale.

Many people know that their lives have no reason, beyond existing, dying.

I have feared no man, and only a few women.

I refuse to argue with fools.

I have never opened an Internet porn site on my computer, nor do I intend too.

I never pre-check the "whose calling" feature, on my telephone, before answering it.

I refuse to interrupt a phone conversation while receiving another incoming call.

I refuse to take my life too seriously; there are plenty of others doing that for me.

Never think that you are indispensable as there is always someone to take your place.

To most northerners, winter days are like taking bitter pills; *whether you like them or not*, you still have to take them, one at a time.

To me; sunshine is like penicillin for the soul.

===

Country *jargon*

It is remarkable how many "old sayings" survived over the generations. Here are a few contemporary sayings and also a number of *not so common* words and phrases that were used around the farm and the workplaces of the era and area.

Combobalation = Means, an assortment of things or events: "that's a *real* combobalation"

Discombobulating = *Confusion* {of things, events, or actions}

Didcombobulated = *personally*, when everything goes wrong with everything.

Looking a gift horse in the mouth. Meaning = not knowing a bargain when you see one.

That's the way the ball bounces. Meaning, = that no matter how much you plan, or how long and hard you work, you sometimes fail.

Dressed to kill = a man dressed up in his Sunday best but may or may not be going to church.

A bad trip meant having some trouble with the wagon or the weather on the way to town or to the thrasher.

A back stabber was someone you trusted, only to turn you in, to save his own neck.

Making a mess of something. Usually meant making a large meal of beans or sauerkraut.

Eating humble pie meant apologizing to a friend, when they were right and you were not.

Chasing the dog's tail = going around in circles, never getting anywhere's.

What goes around, comes around = be very careful at what mischief you might plan, or do, to someone, as it may come back to bite you.

The acorns do not fall far from the tree and neither do the nuts; meaning that we tend to behave in much the same way as our parents did, doing either good, or bad, deeds.

It's time to cough up = It's time to show all, and tell all that you know about something.

Time to fess up = is time to confess that you did the deed.

Don't bite the hand that feeds you =Be careful how you treat people who have only your best interests at heart.

Don't bite off more than you can chew = Taking on more tasks and responsibilities then you can handle and not doing justice to any.

The more things change the more they stay the same = History tends to repeat itself.

You never miss the water until the well runs dry = abandonment of good sense, and ill-using people or resources, until they too are gone

Needing to be taken down a peg or two = A person, *usually a male,* who is *smart talking* or using aggressive behaviour.

All that meat and no potatoes = A girl without a fellow.

A new broom sweeps clean = the newest employee is always the most productive.

Going on a wild goose chase= not expecting to find what you are looking for.

If you don't stand for something you are bound to fall for anything = Being resolute, not wishy-washy, in your personal position on issues.

All that glitters is not gold = Just because something including people, look great, it, and they, may not be true.

Standing on your head and wondering with your feet = seeing or hearing about something that is difficult to comprehend.

Jack-of-all-trades = good at everything but master of none.

***Being* as patience as Job** = calm and quiet, taking difficulties in stride

Cool as a cucumber = someone who does not get excited easily.

Going hell bent for leather = driving too fast.

Going like a bat out of hell = travelling fast.

Dead as a doornail = someone or something that is truly dead.

It's an ill wind that doesn't blow someone some good = self-explanatory.

Tempest in a teapot = usually about a mad woman.

Bald as an eagle = not a hair to be seen.

Light as a feather = a good dancer.

Proud as a peacock = A lady strutting, or a man satisfied with a purchase.

Put your money where your mouth is = If it's such a good deal, buy it yourself.

You have a yellow streak down your back = refusing to fight.

Black as pitch = describing a dark night.

Low as a snakes heel = being told that you were a no good untrustworthy scoundrel.

An ounce of prevention is worth a lb. of cure = Fix it, at the earliest opportunity.

Seeing, is, believing = show me, as you could be lying.

You can lead a horse to water but you cannot make it drink = You can only encourage a person *to go so far* and *no further,* to do something you want done.

Self praise stinks = It's okay for me to say something complimentary about you, but its not okay for you to say it about yourself.

As rare as a pork chop in a synagogue = something tangible found in an unusual place.

Going to hell in a hand basket = Continuing to do something that is personally disastrous.

Rotten to the core = nothing good, bad, through and through.

Scrooge = a tightwad.

Shooting the bull = men talking.

Sly as a fox = might just steal your chickens too.

Still waters run deep = A quiet person is a quality individual.

Tight as a clam = refusing to spend money even though you have it.

To curse like a Trooper = using socially forbidden cuss words with gusto.

Like peas in a pod = two people emulating each other.

Full of hot air = bragging.

Being on the wagon = not drinking alcohol for a period of time.

Walking on glass = being careful what you say

Walking on water = someone doing what appears to most, to be impossible.

Hungry as a pig = ready to eat anything offered, or, served on the kitchen table.

A snake in the grass = a verbal description of someone who was not to be trusted.

Johnny come lately = a new person on the scene.

Diamond in the rough = a child or a young person showing great potential

Chasing your tail = always busy but never getting anything done.

Leave it to Sweeney = a Doctors mistake's, Sweeney was the local undertaker.

Limp as a rag = a weak person.

Stiff as a poker = a person who passed out after drinking too much alcohol.

Tough as nails = describing someone who is sick but refuses to die.

Lower then a snakes heel = about a low as you could go in committing a foul deed.

Looks is only skin deep = a person looking good on the outside but is bad on the inside.

Black as a storm cloud =to not receive a cheerful welcome.

High as a kite = intoxicated, but not quite drunk.

Working like a beaver = never taking a work break.

The road to hell is paved with good intentions. =. It's not what you say you intend to do, but what you actually do, that counts.

A stitch in time saves nine = Fix it now or fix it later, at nine times the present cost.

Being afraid of your shadow = Afraid of everything and anything.

Looks is only skin deep = it's what underneath the skin that counts.

You can hang your hat on it = Saying or hearing something that is accurate or true.

That'll put hair on the dog = after drinking a stiff drink of liquor.

Mind your P's and Q's = keep quiet and do the right thing. {P means pint & Q, quart}

Hodge Podge = a number of different vegetables cooked together in one container. Was also used in reference to a mix of assets or events that were lumped together.

Banging Heads = Two people *not* in agreement.

Shithouse Luck = can be either - unexpected good fortune or bad *mis*fortune.

Having long nose = someone who is always probing in another persons business.

Read-em and weep = Being deal a dreadful hand of cards.

Life is no cup of tea = living or working with difficult people.

It's no bed of roses = Doing difficult work.

He/ or/ she, is acting shifty = suspected of being guilty of something.

Long as a month of Sunday's = A period of time that seem to never end.

Looking a gift horse in the mouth = Failing to know the quality of a job or an offer.

Tighten up your bootstraps = meaning you had better get back to work.

Having a silver tongue = Saying what people want to hear.

Having no sand = meant having no guts *or fight* in you.

Being two faced = Telling people two quite different stories of the same incident.

Crooked as a corkscrew = being dishonest more than once.

==

The following list is of *names and words,* also referred to as *country jargon*; used daily in conversations with their meanings.

Addled = someone who was not quite right in the head.

Blabbermouth = one who told secrets

Blockhead = a person that you couldn't make understand simple things.

Blooming fool = an out of control person

Blowhard = someone who owned little or nothing, but bragged mightily about it.

Blubber head = A name you called someone when you wanted to make them mad

Buffaloed = to be fooled or stumped by someone else's actions or speech

Bullshit = exaggerating during conversation.

Deadbeat = a man who hardly worked a day in his life.

Chucklehead = figure it out for yourself.

Dead eye = a person who never missed when shooting at squirrels or a deer.

Devilish = a comical person, one who could make you laugh.

Dribbler = a person that talked continually about nothing.

Drugs = were only sold by a pharmacy and used only to cure body aliments.

Dry = needing a drink; usually a beer.

Frigging around = a term you used to explain your frustration with yourself when trying to do a task that wasn't going too well, and not wanting to swear.

Frigging frig = showing frustrated, in words, about your own or someone else's actions.

Foxy = a person who usually got the best of you in a deal

A Green horse = a horse that was not *broken {trained}* to do farm related chores.

High stepper = a woman who dressed well and walked faster then your wife.

Holy frig = being surprised or startled at hearing or seeing something.

Holy roller = an ardent religious, person.

Loaded = a team of oxen or horses attempting to pull more weight then they could.

Loose = a woman with an enhanced sexual appetite, but not always around home.

Long headed = a smart person

A Nincompoop = sometimes, what you called your best friend, to his face.

Paralysed = being as drunk as a skunk.

Parched = thirsty, dry as a burnt boot.

Peddler = a door-to door salesman.

Rattled = a crazy person, in your opinion.

Raving crazy = acting erratic and saying things, none that made any sense.

Rubberneck = someone you could not make understand. Just short of being a blockhead.

Scatterbrain = one who converses foolishly without substance.

Shifty = Not to be trusted.

Skunk = a person you could never trust.

Slaphappy = not having a care in the world.

Sliver-cat = a slang name, usually for a female, who had a bad temper and a mouth to match.

Smart-ass = one who thinks he know everything but doesn't.

Snit = similar to having a tirade, only this time, being much quieter about it

Starvation cook = a woman that couldn't boil water without burning it.

Stuck up = a person who thought he was better than you and everyone else.

Stumped = having no answer to a problem.

Tattler = a person who told a true story about you without your consent.

Trafficker = a man who came to the farm with the purpose of buying or selling oxen.

T-Totaller = never takes a drink of alcohol.

Penuche = a woman who was *stuck up.*

Prissy = a girl refined in body movements and wearing smart clothing.

Knocked up = to be pregnant.

Whiner = one who complained a lot.

Whippersnapper = a young person, usually a boy, who acted clever in a witty way.

Wine-o = a habitual drunkard

Chapter Five

Adventure Section

The Awakening

The time: The first week of July 1990
The place: Jubilee Lake, Newfoundland, Canada

"Jesus Christ" the name – the sound- delivered with a volume of voice that of a military drill sergeants reverberated off the walls of our small wooden shelter located somewhere in the wilderness of the Canadian Province of Newfoundland, Canada.

It was 10 o'clock at night, it was dark, all were tired and it was time to sleep.

It was no mistaking the source, or the reason, for the outburst.

The source was Garnet Burns, a six foot plus, sixty years plus retired air force officer who was one of a foursome of trout fishermen who had traversed from the comfort s of warm, safe, comfortable homes located on Nova Scotia's South Shore to travel to and find ourselves in this God forsaken one room cabin on the shore of a lake called Jubilee in the wilderness of Newfoundland.

Frustration was showing its ugly head and we had been away from home for less than two days.

But that is what the lack of sleep will do to some people, especially those who are retired, being used to the good things of life, having traveled the world in comfort, accustomed to upscale motels, automobiles, and RV's, and willing and able to pay the price for life's pleasantries and peacefulness.

Such was not to be, in this cabin, on this lake and at this time of year.

To go without sleeping for one or two nights is difficult for most well conditioned youthful humans. To look forward or to even consider going a third night without sleep bordered on the unthinkable, hence the verbal outburst.

There were two reasons why we were unable to sleep.

First, let me tell you the second reason.

Steven the eighteen year old son of our journey's coordinator and initiator of this fishing expedition had a problem; none that bothered him, only others and only when he slept.
You see Steven snored. No, that is incorrect- Steven SNORZZZZED. His ZZZZZ were nothing easily described, only experienced.

Have you ever stood close to a steam locomotive when it struggled to pull a line of loaded rail cars behind it, or stood close to a 747 jumbo jet as it accelerates during take off? Well now, we are getting close to this experience but we're not quite there yet. To come as close as accuracy will allow I would say that Steven's snoring equalled or exceeded the decibels of a D8 bulldozer with its engine running, parked inside a small one room cabin, and remember this was in the middle of the night.

When I think back to that eventful week that has to be the most accurate assessment that I have made so far. Few will disagree. Garnet Burns, Steven's great uncle is among them.

Steven's bunk was directly across from where I bunked, not slept, and directly above Garnet's bunk, where he too lay, not slept, in our twelve by sixteen foot cabin.

Knowing that he was causing an insomnia problem for his fishing buddies, Steven did the most honourable thing that he could do under the tension filled circumstances. He would give his Uncle Garnet, his dad, Reid, and me a fifteen-minute head start before he went into his noisy sleep pattern.

Have you ever tried to sleep after someone threatened you? It cannot be done. Oh yes, the first fifteen minutes were heavenly, but then… Oh God, Steven opened all the portals of both heaven and hell with sounds that only he could generate.

That is what inspired Garnet's outburst!

I started laughing loud and long. It was sort of surreal, out of our control, and gaining momentum.

I could not sleep even though I too knew that morning would soon arrive.

Early was 5 am, late was 5:30 am and I, like Garnet, would have to endure another day without having slept for several nights and hope that maybe on the fourth night that I would finally collapse from sheer exhaustion.

I still shed tears of laughter whenever I think of this particular night and the events that had preceded this night.

Now I will tell you about the first reason for Garnet's outburst.

Our foursome had arrived at Jubilee Lake at about 3pm, 3:30 Nfld. time and during the flight in we were alerted by our pilot Gene Ploughman to the fact that bears were known to habit certain areas of Newfoundland, including the area around Jubilee Lake.

You would have to be a masochist or a fool not to have some concern when you were visiting, not hunting, in an area that could place you in danger, especially hungry bears.

After hearing all this bear talk, Garnet seemed much more anxious acting than usual. Certainly he was by far the most concerned of our foursome. To be accurate he seemed downright fearful of bears. He talked about nothing but bears, bears, bears. Reid and I were not overly concerned; after all, our chances of running into a bear might be considered a highlight of the trip.

We almost looked forward to seeing a bear.

Were we too cavalier and was Garnet the more responsible member of our group? Or was Garnet's unusual behaviour an act, was he telling us the truth or was his fear of bears all a big act?

Garnet went as far as to say that he had no plans of using the outdoor privy as no bear was going to corner him between the outhouse and the safety of getting back to the cabin.

"Do you think that Garnet really is that afraid of bears?" was just about the first question Reid posed to me as we motored away from the dock, out towards a large rock that seemed to attract us and our boat and has done so ever since.

This, our very first trip was not to be our last, as for over 10 years the magnetic waters of Jubilee kept pulling us back to ever new and exciting adventures.

"He cannot be that afraid of bears", I replied but the subject kept popping up during the rest of the day's conversation as neither of us could get Garnet and his fear of bears out of our minds.

After several hours of getting acquainted with the waters and near shoreline of Jubilee Lake, all four of us looked forward to getting ashore and having a great supper of trout and beans, capped off with a night of rest in the warm friendly confines of our cabin home in anticipation for tomorrow and our first full day fishing.

We planned to be fully charged for whatever Jubilee was prepared to dish out. We bunked down early, about 9pm, for the night.

We had no sooner settled back in our bunks than Reid remembered that our worms, thousands of them, along with several coolers full of foodstuffs had been placed under the front step of the cabin earlier that day. We determined that by keeping our aromatic necessities close to the cabin would discourage raccoons or other wild things from sampling them.

He decided to bring them inside.

By this time it was very dark and a flashlight had to be used to move around safely *inside and out* of our new and unfamiliar surroundings.

"I guess someone should give you a hand to lift those heavy coolers," said Garnet, knowing that Steven and I were now settling down in the top bunks and it would take more time and effort getting out and down from our lofty perch and climbing back up and into them again.

Reid, dressed only in shorts, flashlight in hand, headed for the cabin door.

"I think I hear something," said Reid, as he stepped out into the night, anxious to start and finish the anticipated five-minute chore.

We did not know it then, but in less then two minutes all hell was about to break loose!

By this time Garnet, dressed also in his shorts had arrived to share the lifting of the coolers and said, "I think I see something moving!"
"Where, where? ... "Over there"….. It's a coon …yes it's a coon…. it's not a coon …"
"Jesus, it looks like…. it's a bear!…no… no it must be a coon"
"Yes…yes …put the light higher …where? … higher…. over there towards the woods….further"…..
"See that black thing?…. There. …It's a bear!!….It's coming towards us!!"
…Crash …scrunch…grunt…...as someone or something, probably a cooler, was thrown inside the cabin.

"It's coming towards us!.....throw something at it!" (Someone threw a stick)

"It's still coming...It's stopping...I can't see it....Yes...it's still standing there! ....See it!'"?

"Get a piece of firewood .... Take that you......."

"Boy, that was close......I think you hit it.......got anymore wood?"

"It's moving , moving away........Jesus .....GET, GET, GET .....Yes, it ran up that way."

"Man, did you see that thing go through that brush?.....whew... "Let's get the hell back in the cabin before it comes back."

By the time the first alarm of "something black" was stated Steven had leaped from his bunk dressed only in his shorts of course and was peering out the cabin door with a flashlight in hand. Meanwhile I stayed safely up in my bunk listening and viewing, as best I could, the action that was taking place outside, below and around me. The event seemed surreal; this could not be happening.

I did manage to find a camera. I cannot recall if it was mine or someone else's, but I did manage to get off a shot or two of this real life adventure that was taking place in the battlefield below.

"It's going towards the woods," Reid exclaimed. "Either that bear never saw humans before or it's been around here an awful lot."

Reid was using common sense judgement earned and learned about the behaviour of bears while he worked as a teenager with his Grandfather Ralph for the Mersey Paper Company.

Bear experiences seem to be remembered long after many other eventful things in life are long forgotten.

"Do you think it will come back?" Garnet asked.

His concern came from knowing that he had the closest bunk to a not too sturdy cabin door, having only a *flimsy* turn button to keep it closed, should Mr. Bruin return and decide he wanted to eat one of us.

Garnet appeared to be the most intellectual one of us. We could kid him about the funny side of the situation but we really could not fool him. He knew full well that, where he bunked, was the first place setting at the bear's cafeteria. To put it frankly, should the bear attack the cabin, Garnet would die first.

"Not likely," someone answered.
It was Garnet.

"I'll fight to the death," says adrenalin hyped and fear-filled Garnet as he tried to settle back for some rest.

Alas, he did not have a chance.

About fifteen minutes later, we all heard it at the same time.
"He's back!" More than one muttered or should I say whispered, as no one wanted to talk too loudly as the bear might hear us and come to investigate what goodies might lay inside the cabin.

My bunk, being a top bunk, was located at an angle providing me with an excellent view through one of the cabin's side windows. It was above and looking directly downward at the bear's original objective, a garbage container. The container was about three feet high, about two feet across at the top and tapered down to about fourteen inches at the bottom. It had two handles and a top. It was hard to believe that a real garbage can could be found away back here in this wilderness. Somebody must have brought it in to the lake to carry out moose or caribou meat and found that it had more value as a garbage container instead.

It appeared as if it had been sitting outside the cabin for a number of years and was found to be more useful by both fishermen and hunters to stash empty bean and bully beef cans as well as the odd Jack Daniels bottle, empty of course.

It was situated just around the corner from the front and only door to the cabin.

There would be no more going for *a leak* by anyone this night.

"I can see him," I whispered, ... "He's eating the garbage!"

"God damn" Garnet moaned, "What stupid son of a bitch would leave garbage lying around a place like this!"

Garnet had forgotten for the moment where he was. We were in the wilds of Newfoundland and the garbage trucks did not have Jubilee Lake on their list of stops. Up here the bears do the garbage pick-up.

Everybody rushed over to my window to take a peek. Sure enough there was Mr. Bruin, who had the garbage barrel tipped over on its side, scratching and biting at bits and pieces of whatever the last fishing party decided not to take back with them or did not take time to burn. To start a fire and burn any leftovers would have been the most responsible thing to do, but it was too late for that.

What a sight! What a story, and all this was happening on our very first night!

Now, all we have to do is stay alive until morning and then survive a few more days of wilderness living before heading back home to tell our friends and families all about it.

After about half an hour, most of us realized that the bear was content on eating only the garbage as it showed no other interest like attacking the cabin. So Garnet, Reid and Steven settled back in their bunks and I from my better vantage point, delivered commentary on what the bear was doing.

"He's got a white tip on his nose", I murmured, not so loud as to disturb the bear.

"The only bear with a white tip on its nose is a Panda bear," growled Garnet, in a voice while low was still quite commanding. Well I wasn't in any position to argue with Garnet. After all he was six foot two and he looked like six foot eight to me. He was much better read and more traveled than was I. Who was I to argue with Garnet that this bear had a white nose when he said it did not?

Now the moon that night was the brightest I have ever seen it, seeing it for the first time from the perspective of another half a time zone north of my native Nova Scotia.

If I wasn't looking down at a white nosed bear, I was blind.

All I can say to my sleepy listeners is that, "I am sure it has a white nose".

It was as plain as the nose on my face; white is white, and with the brightness of the moon it appeared even whiter than snow.

Because of all the excitement Steven, who had not as yet entered into his dominant snooze pattern, had crawled quietly down from his bunk and crept quietly up onto a bench near my window so that he too could see what I saw. Once seeing the bear, he too confirmed, "Yes sir, its nose is definitely white."

That only enraged Garnet more, but he stayed in his bunk.

Steven and I watched until even the sight of a bear eating garbage got humdrum. He crawled back into his bunk and I continued watching until I was about to drop over from fatigue. Finally I let my head fall into one of my fishing jackets that was subbing for the pillow I now needed but didn't bring along on the trip. After all we were only going to be out here for three nights and how much comfort can one fisherman stand?

Count this as night #1 with little or no sleep for everybody except Reid. I never knew it until several years later when I finally found out that he slept like a big dog. Why? Because *he* had heard these sounds before and *he came prepared* and Garnet and I weren't. He never heard a damn thing. Nothing was going to keep him awake. He slept like a baby. How you ask? Simply by bringing along and wearing earplugs, that's how! Now, how's that for a friend? Some friend.

Dawn had not yet broken when we heard a loud shout coming from outside the cabin, "Jesus Christ the bear's still here!"

Garnet had just gone out for a "leak" and during his leaking, his mind wondered as he pondered if the bear was still there. Garnet told us this next part sometime later. That he, not believing for one in a millionth minute that it could be, but as soon as he finished watering the sod in front of the cabin step, he started walking around the corner of the cabin, a distance of some twelve to fifteen feet at most.

Sure enough the bear had also camped down for the night on a smooth spot of earth located at the upper corner of the cabin right under my bunk and immediately adjacent to Reid's lower bunk which was only two or three feet from where he slept peacefully, earplugs and all.

To Garnet, Reid and the rest of us, not knowing that danger in the shape of a wild black bear lurked so close by for several hours, again proves the old adage "that ignorance can be and certainly was bliss" of a sort.

"I looked death in the eye and I won!" shouted an almost jubilant Garnet. It was a comment that we heard repeated many times over the next few days as Garnet and his newfound confidence was made apparent to us, as well as to any bear. No more fears of going to the toilet, "bring on them bears" was the challenge that Garnet made to anyone that cared or did not care to listen. Garnet had truly faced his physical death, a death that up to then was only in his mind and he emerged victorious. Hurray for Garnet!

Garnet was given the Survivor's Award of a miniature black bear for his amazing victory and would you believe that it too had a white nose? The white tip on the bear's nose had to be hand painted on with white enamel paint. Garnet knew right from the very beginning, black bears do not have white noses. So why did both Steven and I insist that we had seen the bear that fateful night and agreed that it most certainly did have a white nose?

It seems that the fishing party prior to ours had left without burning or burying what remaining flour they had left over from frying fish and placed it into the garbage container next to the cabin.

The bear using his great sense of smell sniffed it out. Knowing full well that Robin Hood makes good flour he ran his nose deep into the bag in an effort to recover every last morsel, so every time his head appeared out from the garbage container to chew on a mouthful of the flour, both Steven and I could see nothing but brilliant white!

How were we to know that it was white flour and not a mutation of nature that caused the apparition? After all, it just might have been a Panda Bear back there that night.

On the second and third night it was not the bear that kept us awake with excitement. This time it would be our very own Steven to introduce and entertain us to the most amazing snoring event that this world has ever heard.

I am confident that if Garnet and I had to choose between Steven and the bear as a sleeping partner the bear would get a vote or two. We later found out that the bear's name was Yogi and that he only visited the cabin area occasionally. We have not seen him since. Steven left shortly after this trip to go out to Alberta and British Columbia and has not returned to Jubilee Lake. Perhaps Yogi went to visit Stephen; after all they did have a lot in common.

I'm still smiling as I relate this story of our first night and first trip to Jubilee Lake to you, it is only one of a great many memories and larger than life images that are retained by all who have ever fished the dark and wild waters of Lake Jubilee, Newfoundland, Canada.

Postscript.

Yogi did return. It was several years later and he was now much larger and potentially more dangerous.

For our safety our outfitter supplied us with a rifle.

But this was Yogi's home turf and we wanted only to share this amazing wilderness with him for a short time. We have since left the shores and waters of Lake Jubilee to him alone.

There were times that Yogi behaved like a bear, like the time he raked the side of our tent with his claws tearing a large piece of canvas away or another time when he ate a large radio battery plus some other camping equipment. But my friends and I left Jubilee content that we had left the region as good as or better than when we first set foot there and that includes leaving a live Yogi behind.

Chapter Six

Windigo

This adventure also took place in the wilds of Newfoundland Canada.

It did not happen while fishing the deep and dangerous water of Lake Jubilee, but inside an old, weather beaten, rarely used cabin, built by and for the use of the native people of the area. It was located near the shore and waters of a lake known as Kaegudeck.

Because of recently enforced Provincial environmental regulations, we were no longer, after ten years of fishing Jubilee, permitted to have a dock, to land, unload and reload our floatplane, nor were we, or anyone else, permitted to construct a permanent type shelter, near the water of our beloved Lake Jubilee. It was not a happy arrangement but was necessitated when our outfitter was given short notice to vacate Lake Jubilee in order to accommodate our group of four to this new location. We always booked our fishing expeditions one year in advance.

It was the night of June 11th, 2003, our second sleep at our new lake.

Or so we thought.

"It may have been a Windigo," I blurted, as all four of us were momentarily and simultaneously stunned.

Just what was it that happened a few moments ago?

"What's a Windigo?" Reid, or was it Allan asked. Allan was our youngest and newest fishing partner and usually spoke with a highly excited voice.

According to what my brother Arthur had told me many years previous, learned from his engrossment in reading and digesting dozens of Zane Grey novels, all about the old West, a Windigo was an Indian Spirit that visited old deserted Indian cabins, and if I remembered anything else other than the name, it was that a Windigo was not known to be a friendly sort of visitor.

"You're kidding aren't you?" Allan asked, this time with a voice that was almost pleading, sounding like he needed that explanation to satisfy himself, as well as convince all of us that he was not having a nightmare or experiencing some wild figment of his imagination.

Starting from the beginning.
It was night, pitch dark inside the cabin, with only a pale light emitting from the world outside the cabin, by a moon that barely penetrated a lightly cloud covered sky.

We had just bunked down for our second night of rest, after a supper of trout, beans, pickles and brown bread, for what was to be a five night stay, on a six day fishing trip. The old worn down cabin was to be our home for the remaining four days and nights.
Located under the shadow of mount Sylvester, the cabin had seen better days but still provided warmth and security from the cold nights and the Newfoundland elements.

The cabin had been originally built by and for the use of local Indians. It was conveniently located closest to where the securing of needed foodstuffs like fish and caribou were abundant.

Reid and I slept alongside the base of one wall while Rog and Allan's bunks were located against the opposite wall. All bunks were elevated about eighteen inches off the floor.
There were three windows in the cabin, one over the sink and two others, one of which was located above where Allan and Roger faced, on the same wall as where I lay. The window was installed about seven feet up from the ground in order to discourage any prowling black bears from entering.

The cabin grew quiet as we individually and collectively drifted towards a peaceful sleep.

I thought I heard it first!
Roger said later that he heard it too.
Reid was a sound sleeper and he was probably well on his way to being asleep.
As Allan being the newest and youngest, he was not about to fall asleep as quick as were his elders, and he was the one that had the best view of the window.

Then it happened!
Out of the silence and the darkness of the cabin came a shout that none will forget.
If it had been a woman's voice you would have called it a scream.
"There's something out there, and it's big!" It was Allan who shouted. His loud alarm brought everyone including the near asleep Reid to attention.
The cabin was soon filled with questions, like, "What did you see'? "Was it a bear" "Was it a moose or a caribou"?
"I don't know what it was, but it was big" Allan said, " Big enough to block out any light from the window"
"I heard something shortly before you shouted," I said, "but I didn't think much about it".
"I heard a loud noise but I thought it was either you or Rog hitting your arm or fist against the cabin wall," I said to Allan.

Reid said that he too had heard it, but we never knew for sure, as Reid was a quick sleeper, if you know what I mean.

Then Roger spoke. "I saw it too; I heard it before it appeared at the window".
Well that was good enough for Reid and me, and before you could take a breath, Reid was up and about and showed great concern for our safety. After all, we had never before heard or seen anything that

big or that close to where we slept. Even the bear down on Jubilee wasn't seven feet tall.

We had no firearms and were no match for anything that size, in the dark. A brace to hold the door shut was our only defence. This far from civilization anything could be lurking outside our old cabin.

That's about the time I came up with the word, Windigo.

I still wonder today how I came up with that name. I had only heard it a few times, and so many years ago.

It could have been a moose or a caribou or it needed to be a very large bear, to block out a window some seven feet high.

General consensus was that it must have been a moose, as the noises we had heard were similar to what their antlers might sound like if they had been racked against the outside boards of the cabin as they were passing by.

After agreeing on a moose as the prowler, we all settled down to get some sleep in what remained of the night.

Early the next morning everyone was quick to get outside and examine the soil around that side of the cabin to see just how large the footprints of a moose that big might be. Not a hoof-print to be found.

There were some wires strung up outside about the height of the window. They were intended to catch any elusive radio signals that might reach that far back from civilization, they too were intact. Our deduction was that a moose had not been the intruder, as it would have torn down the wires with its antlers and it surely would have left some footprints.

"Maybe it was a Windigo?"

I was beginning to sound like a stuck record, and it wasn't too long before I had the rest of the boys suspecting it just might have been something supernatural.

It definitely was something out of the ordinary.

The incident made for some interesting conversation for the reminder of the trip and it was not until we returned home did we gain any real insight on what the incident might have meant.

Roger made an Internet inquiry and came up with some startling information on Windigos.

According to recorded information there have been numerous visitations worldwide by Windigos.

The article confirmed our fears. We had provided excellent conditions for a Windigo's visit.

According to folklore they only visit old abandoned Indian cabins, located in the deepest of the deep woods.

If this folklore was to be believed, we were ripe for the picking.

One thing we do know for sure. There could not have been anything human in an area this remote.

So, what did happen that night in the wilds of Newfoundland in that old Indian cabin on the shores of Lake Kaegudeck? We four remain stumped to come up with a logical answer and we have been around the wilds and the woods for more than a few years.

Taking no chances the following and subsequent years, Reid's wife Eleanor supplied all four with a *protective* package containing herbs, spices, feathers, a clove of garlic and a cross.

No evil Spirits or Windigos were going to get us.

In a recent conversation with Allan, he still carries his Windigo warder-off with him. He hangs it on the wall above his bunk every night. "No good to take chances", he says.

I too can report that after several years of going back to the same cabin, on the same lake, with the same dark nights and the same wild habitat, we have never had a like experience.

Maybe *there is something* about cloves of garlic, crosses, etc. that evil spirits cannot tolerate.

Chapter Seven

Bad Deeds

Before the age of acumen, the realm for getting into trouble is endless.

I once caught *a rabbit* in a *jump* trap.

A *jump trap* is made of steel, having either one or two springs intended to hold the prey.

When the springs are forced down and *set,* compressed, it allows the jaws to remain open until an unsuspecting mink, beaver or muskrat steps inside the opening of the springs, thus tripping the lever that controls the trap's gripping mechanism.

Professional trappers need them to catch such fur bearing water animals to support their livelihood.

The trap is then attached by a steel tether and fastened to a tree or other stationary object, holding both the trap and the trapped animal secure until the hunter arrives to remove his catch.

While snaring is the usual method of catching rabbits, I had an idea that using a small jump trap might work just as well.

It didn't.

The rabbit I *trapped* was held fast by only one front leg and when I arrived to check my trap it was very much alive. By this time the bones of the seized leg were broken, either from the force of the trap springing shut and breaking the leg, or it was broken from the twisting and struggling of the rabbit to free its trapped leg.

The rabbit was probably seized by the trap hours earlier and by the time I arrived on the scene it was only attached to the trap by a thin sliver of twisted and torn skin. The rabbit had frantically fought to free itself from the jaws of the trap by pulling and twisting in a valiant but hopeless effort in trying to escape.

Had I been a half hour later in checking my trap, the rabbit would have probably torn itself free.

It had struggled to free itself so valiantly that I didn't have the heart to kill it, so I decided that I would remove it alive from the trap. This wasn't the smartest thing I ever attempted either.

The rabbit, not knowing that I was trying to help by freeing it, kicked and scratched at me with fury, the likes that I would never have previously believed, had I not *seen and felt* its strength. Rabbits can be powerful little animals, especially under these conditions. But I was determined to take my rabbit home and show the family what a great trapper I was. The still trapped and badly injured rabbit continued fighting to escape but after a few *difficult* minutes, with no help from the rabbit, I finally succeeded in removing its shattered leg from the jaws of the trap.

After all this, I was bloodied up pretty well, I was not about to let my prized catch get away, so holding it firmly against my chest to prevent it from kicking free and escaping, I hurried but *hesitantly* proceeded towards home.

The rabbit's valiant efforts in trying to free itself skinned my hands and arms up to such a degree that the open welts stung in the cold air. I still felt perversely *good* that I was man enough to be able to hang on to it until I finally reached the house.

Upon entering the kitchen, my grandmother was horrified at seeing me all scratched up and bleeding, holding a rabbit, its one leg dangling loosely and nearly falling off, or else, she was *shockingly disappointed in me* for what I had just done.

She immediately offered me fifty cents to release it.

That was a lot of money back then.

I gladly accepted the offer of fifty cents and was really relieved to have a sensible and profitable reason to let the rabbit go free. If Grammy had not come up with her offer and a good solution for me to release it, I don't know what I would have done. I would like to think that I would not have killed it, not after all we had been through together, and the only other option was to release it.

So, I was fifty cents better off and the rabbit was freed. As it ran or hopped away from me, its recent captor and tormenter, on its three remaining legs, I felt *more than a twinge of guilt* for what I had done.

Sixty plus years later I can still see and feel that rabbit struggling to escape *my trap* and me, and finally running away, as best it could, to freedom, when I released it.

Nature being what it is, the rabbit probably survived. I hope it did, and if it did survive, I take little credit.

My grandmother was the one that paid the rabbit's ransom - to me.

I still feel the quilt.

Shooting my first, *and last*, Deer

This deed happened out in one of the grassy fields that lay in back of our barn, a field nearby to where my dad and my granddad were engrossed in cultivating a field of turnips or mangles. They were using the horse drawn hand held machine.

I was supposed to be assisting them by following after the cultivator, picking up and removing some of the countless rocks that surfaced *every year, on this, and every other ploughed field* of the farm.

It was early in the afternoon and I was walking after the men, horse and cultivator with my head down, doing my allotted job when I was alerted by an unusual sound, like that of a fence wire *being* snapped.

Glancing up and in the direction of the "twanging" sound, I saw a small deer bounding over the wire fence and into the field. It was not far away, perhaps two hundred feet from the edge of the ploughed field where we were working.

The men did not hear the *twang*, as the noise produced from the cultivator being pulled through the soil made it impossible for them to hear what I heard.

The *wire snapping sound* was caused by one of the legs of the deer hitting the top wire of the fence as it leaped from inside the cow pasture, out into the adjacent and grass covered field.

It was planning to enjoy a meal of freshly grown *green* grass sprouts, a much improved and better tasting snack then the already munched over remains of the terrain found in the cow pasture.

Opportunity looked me straight in the face and it got the best of me.

A *new adventure* lay awaiting.

Now remember that I had never fired any kind of a rifle before. U*sing the rifle* was my older brother's domain, as he was the sole owner of the only gun to be found in the Young's household.

Without hesitating I quickly left the field *and my work* responsibilities behind me. I started running as fast I could go. Upon reaching the house I quickly grabbed *my brother's 22* and a few shells, *and just as quickly* gave the women {my mom and grandmother} some sort of "there's a deer in the field" reason, that I needed the rifle, and disappeared from the house.

As I stated previously, I had never shot at anything ever before, *that was always the forte of my brother*, he's the one who shot all the squirrels, I only did all the skinning.

Just maybe it was *the challenge,* and *not* the opportunity, that took hold of me.

Whatever the reason, Arthur was not around to use *his* gun to shoot the deer and I was the next best thing to providing some fresh venison for the family.

How good would that be?

It may have been my primeval instincts *taking control of me,* rather than any good sense.

It was a simple procedure, to load the single chambered gun, and everyone knew how to aim one, and that's about all that was required.

But I had no experience with *first shot j*itters. I heard about them, but that was about all.

I figured that I couldn't return to the field where the deer had been standing only five minutes before by using the same route that I had left the field, as *the deer would see me* and that would be the last I would see *of it.* My only return route, to not be seen by the deer, was to travel back through the cow pasture from where the deer had first been. There I could hide, concealed by some small trees and bushes *and hopefully,* not be detected by the deer which should still be grazing contentedly in the adjacent field.

I ran as fast as my legs would carry me, *both ways,* and I reached the location at the fence where the deer had earlier jumped over the fence into the field. Low and behold, it was still there and it did not appear to either hear *or* see me.

I lay down on the sod behind a medium sized cradle hill and took aim at the deer's head. "My," I thought, "its head looks so small." At that, my body started shaking worse than a bowl of cold Jello. I had heard of buck fever but I never knew just what it was, *until that moment* – God, was I shaking.

I aimed and pulled the trigger.

The deer was still standing.

Not only was it standing, now, it had heard the exploding shell and was looking directly in my direction.

I hadn't hit anything but air, but the sound of the guns firing alerted the deer *that all is not well.*

It still couldn't see me, as I was crouched down *really* low. I quickly ejected the spent casing and put in another cartridge.

By now I was not shaking quite as badly as I was earlier, as I again pointed the *single shot* rifle barrel at the deer and aligned the sights. This time I aimed at the neck of the deer, instead of the head, and pulled the trigger.

The deer fell down and never moved.
I jumped over the fence and ran out onto the field.
By the time I had reached the deer, which was obviously dead, my father and grandfather came running down over the field towards me.
"What are you doing?" one of them said, "we just heard a bullet whiz over our heads".
"I shot a deer," I said.

Now *as this was out of season,* the penalty for shooting a *deer* was steep, and the embarrassment *that went along with being caught and fined* would have been even worse.

"We'll have *to dress it,"* my grandfather said, not wanting good fresh venison to go to waste. "Run out and get some clean linen to wrap the meat in," he said .to me
So off I went again, running just as fast as the first time, out and into the house, telling the women what happened, asking them for some cloth to wrap the deer meat in.

Returning *to the scene of my crime,* the small deer was quickly skinned, cut up, bagged, and taken out to the coolness of the house basement.
The *remains* of the deer was carried into the underbrush and hid.
I cannot remember much if any discussion that followed about this *incident* and I don't suppose that anyone else remembers much about it either.

By killing this deer *I did everything illegal* that was possible to do.
I *was not of legal* gun carrying age.
It was not legal to kill a deer out of season.

A license is required even during deer season.
A single shot 22-calibre rifle is not a legal size calibre for hunting deer.

To my knowledge, it was the first deer ever shot by a Young on the family farm.

I have not shot a gun at a deer since.

Killing, for the fun of it

Another malevolent moment during my youthful years was the time I shot and killed a very rare bird.

It was a large red headed woodpecker.

I had seen pictures of such beautiful birds in nature books and the rare live one, while trekking around the woods.

What made this sighting different from those previous was the fact that this time I was carrying my brother's single shot 22-calibre rifle with me.

I had finally reached the legal age to carry a rifle.

My cousin Earle and I were out hunting something, maybe rabbits, maybe squirrels, maybe partridge, when we emerged from the forest and found ourselves walking out and into what was then known in the Branch as the Little Cemetery.

We both saw the large colourful bird at the same time.

It seemed *almost* like a competition; who could bag this *trophy-sized* woodpecker, first?

I remember bringing my rifle up, fast, with a portion of the barrel protruding out and past my cousin's head and shoulder, as he too was raising his 22-calibre rifle with the same intentions.

I probably would have *missed it* if I had taken more time to make the usual *careful* aim. But getting off the first shot *seemed important,* and lo and behold the gun came up, and without so much as a body quiver, the sights of the barrel immediately fell upon this unsuspecting bird, and I, in almost one motion, pulled the trigger.

My cousin Earl didn't get off his volley as the bird fell from the tree in front of him, dead.

I think he was surprised, or shocked, that I had aimed and shot so quickly. More likely it was because of my rifle barrel *being too close to him for comfort.* The detonation of my gun exploded no more than a foot away and parallel to his right ear.

A 22 is about as light a calibre rifle as there is, but when discharged that close to your ear, it probably sounded like a cannon.

I know I too was surprise to have shot it so quickly and easily.

But there was little jubilation in picking this once live and beautiful bird up and examining it.

Earle *may have felt* cheated or outgunned; I may have *felt superior* for the moment.

We have lived over fifty -five years since that incident and we never speak about it.

I know *that I am not proud* of that one thoughtless moment; I also wish that *I hadn't been the first* to pull the trigger.

There are so few of these beautiful *large red headed woodpeckers* left around our area.

I never look at a picture or see a live red headed woodpecker that I do not feel ashamed of what I once did.

If I could only erase one of my life's *"not so great" moments,* this is the one that I would choose.

Graduation runs amuck.

The last *negative* behavioural incident that I was involved in as an adolescent was the *trashing* of the community shingle mill.

The old mill had served our community for many years prior to my being born. It was needed to cut pine or spruce logs into shingle sized length blocks and then to saw the blocks into shingles. As all homes, barns and outbuildings were made of wood and covered with wooden shingles, shingle mills were a vital component for filling those needs.

Today there are only a handful of these mills *remaining in operating condition* in the county, still serving a diminishing but basic community need.

On several occasions I had assisted my father in packing the finished shingles and at times I even packed a few bundles myself.

But that was years prior to this fateful June day, where with the combination of youth and released exuberance of never having to go to school again, two of my schoolmates and I knowing that the old mill was no longer in use as it hadn't been run for a number of years, would *probably* never run again, therefore it must have no value.

That rationale was all the initiative we needed to justify and begin our demolition process.

It is hard to remember just who or what triggered the initial negative action.

It may have been the challenge to see if we were strong enough to lift some of the heavy machinery that filled the working section of the mill. This machinery was located on the top section of the building, above the waterwheel and stream below.

The lower section of the mill encompassed the large water wheel that once the dam gates were opened to provide water pressure, turned a combination of wheels, giving life and power to the belts, pulleys and saws above.

There was only one regular sized window in the top section area without a frame or pane of glass in it.

It overlooked the milldam.

That window would be the target for everything and anything that followed.

First to be thrown out through that window and into the water below were the smaller and lighter articles, like wood and shingles. When we ran out of small, loose items, we used our hand and our strong youthful muscles in our arms and legs, not our brains, to pull sections of the infrastructure of the mill apart, and dispose of the now smaller sections by throwing them out the window and into the water.

Once we ran out of machinery and wooden structures too large or too difficult to dismantle, we stopped our destructive actions.

We left the mill site and went our separate ways toward our homes.

I can only guess that the other two boys, now young men as we were all sixteen years old, left with the same apprehensive thoughts as I, what we had just done was not proper. Even though the mill was old and may never be used again, it was still not ours to destroy, but now it was too late.

I guess we hoped that no one would ever find out about our destructive actions.

We were dead wrong.

Families living within hearing distance must have reported unusual sounds coming from inside the old mill and told the owner, a Mr. Freeman Meisner.

It was later on in the evening when my father or grandfather returned from a visit at the community store, which was owned by the mill owner's son. It was then that the shit hit the fan.

I was asked if I had been one of the fellows that did this dastardly act. I confessed that I was. I was reminded that someone would have to pay for wrecking the shingle mill.

As I had no money it meant that the cost of restitution would have to be paid by my family.

The Meisners must have been forgiving people as nothing ever came of it.

What causes three otherwise normal boys to act in such an abnormal way?

There are answers, none acceptable.

The incident did occur on our last day of ever having to go back to school again. We were on a *once in a lifetime*, emotional high.

My two *friends* and I had, only minutes before, graduated from the little yellow community school, which we would never have to return to *ever* again. How much better could anything be than that?

I am not sure of my other two friends and cohorts, but I had just passed from grade ten into grade eleven and in our country school, the teacher could not teach beyond that plateau. I was through with school forever; hooray, I finally made it. I guess that my two compatriots felt the same high as I.

As the new rural high school planned for New Germany, about 20 miles away, was only in the construction stages, the completion date would arrive too late for my friends and me to expand our learning skills.

Too bad, as we three still had much to learn, even though at the time we thought that we knew all there was to know.

Life's *real lessons* were about to begin, and we three *potential criminals* hadn't started out so well.

Chapter Eight

Character Section

Characters

"All the world's a stage. And all the men and women are merely player's" Shakespeare.

If what the Bard wrote is true, that the entire world is filled with players *or actors*, then I am here to suggest to you that the finest and most colourful of all may have resided in the county of Lunenburg in the Province of Nova Scotia, Canada.

While our landscape is dotted with hundreds of similar colourful stories, I will limit my relating to several of *those characters* that I knew best, several coming from right here in my home village of Branch LaHave. It would encompass an entire book o cover the exploits and idiosyncrasies of all those who merit *character* status; perhaps that is fodder for another book.

All but a few of those included here are now deceased.

Wilbert William Whynot Sr.

"A bad man if there ever was one" according to family, neighbours and the police.

Shades of William Tell, as neighbours living near to the Whynot home, told of times when he {Wilbert} would stand one or more of his several sons up against a wall and practice shooting at them, coming as close to them as possible without hitting them, using a 22calibre rifle. He must have been an excellent marksman as no one can recall any incidents related to his mad activity.

If "character is the result of our conduct" as, stated by Aristotle 384-322 BC, Wilbert Whynot Sr. certainly lived up to its meaning in every *negative* figment of his being

For more intimate details on Wilbert William Whynot Sr. and his family, please read the section of this book entitled, **Dysfunctional.**

Lawrence Grace.

Lawrence must have been born with the Midas touch.

Amongst his many attributes, he had a penchant for purchasing land.

Every parcel or acreage that he attained, he paid for by using cash or by trading a used car or a truck of equal value. All of his acquisitions were in or near the then, sleepy little town, of Bridgewater. As real estate in any stagnant growth area is worth very little, all of these properties were purchased at bargain prices.

They soon grew in value, for within a few short years the town experienced a mild growth surge and with that surge came wealth and opportunities for anyone lucky enough to own any prime pieces of land.

Alas, Lawrence, in spite of all his uncanny ability or good luck, having once owned these choice parcels of real estate he was not destined to be amongst the wealthy or fortunate.

Lawrence was what we call, always behind the eight ball. He never was able to hold on to any of these *potential gold mines* of land long enough to receive any of the *real gold himself,* as that was now being realized by the new land owners.

When the *land rush* arrived and with it the opportunity to sell or resell many choice sections of land within the town's boundaries, most at inflated prices, it was too late for Lawrence, he had already got rid of his holdings. The question is why?

Lawrence was continually harassed by the local banks and loan institutions to make monthly, or agreed upon payments for his purchases, always just before their value increased. He seemed destined or forced, at every transaction, to sell his potential gold mines of land, for a pittance of their potential value. He did these innumerable times, all in order to keep his indifferent credit rating as honourable as possible.

He was continually caught up in a need to borrow from Peter, to pay Paul, syndrome, and a spinning financial wheel that he could never escape.

Lawrence once owned *individual* lots of land which automobile dealers, service stations, electrical repair shops and super sized retail stores now occupy.

His largest acquisition was a section of land, also within the town's boundaries that he purchased for around $3500.00. He too soon had to sell it for around $6500.00, a good profit one might say, but, that one parcel of land now contains hundreds of modern homes with a single lot now fetching as much as $50,000.00.

Lawrence was a physical, dynamic individual but he was no manager of either his land purchases or himself.

Lawrence's tale of *almost riches* is a sad one, sort of like the story of Ali Hafed in the book by Russell Conwell, entitled Acre of Diamonds. One major difference was that Lawrence not only found and purchased these plots of land, but he knew their potential value; he just could not afford to hold on to his gems long enough for them to develop into their new and true value.

There was another side to Lawrence, a baffling behavioural side.

Lawrence had what some people call, a Jeckle and Hyde personality.

During the day he was a very successful car salesman, at nightfall, things changed. With the assistance of a 40ounce bottle, or more, of rum he became a force to be reckoned with. When Lawrence couldn't find time during his sober and busy day, to purchase his off hour's necessities, the local bootleggers were always available and anxious in the after hours to earn some extra non-taxable cash.

Lawrence's problem was that when he consumed even a small amount of alcohol, he was not able to think or converse rationally with anyone who disagreed with him. Unlike most drinkers Lawrence became verbally and physically belligerent and lost all reason and common sense. His conversing was more often than not with his fists.

He once told me that when he was drinking he had no fear or respect for anyone, and that included his family. "I would punch my grandmother out if she were to annoy me".

Lawrence was by far his own worst enemy, but like most *bingers* he failed to realize it. To him, his life and what he did with it after working hours, was his, and it was nobody else's business.

He felt that his evening and nighttime hours was his to do with what he pleased, and if the rest of the world, including his friends and family didn't like him or his actions, "they could go to hell".

Lawrence had more bare-knuckle brawls than anyone else in the area, and that included some pretty active pugilists. Lawrence was a fighter in every sense of the word.

Twenty, or more, of Lawrence's fights, were of the organized variety, where he performed with excellence and was highly regarded inside every boxing ring. At that time boxing rings were somewhat of a necessity in almost every town in the Province, as boxing was very popular, attended by thousands monthly. All of these fight cards were organized and sanctioned by the Provincial Boxing Authority; they included approved referees and adhered to all governing rules. Lawrence won most of his fights by knocking out his opponent.

But a great majority of Lawrence's fights took place outside the ring. Those were street fights; real knock- down, drag out affairs, often taking place outside *or inside* dance halls, on the street, or at his, other people's homes, or places of business.

Lawrence wasn't particular where he fought and he came out on top of just about every fight he instigated.

Of all the colourful characters that came out of the Branch, Lawrence had to be ranked near the top. An out of town businessman, Mr. Victor Rodney from Yarmouth, after learning about the experiences and exploits of Lawrence, suggested to me, there should be a book written detailing the life and exploits of Lawrence. Lawrence had created countless golden opportunities, all by his own initiative time and talent, but because of his anti sociable after hour behaviour; he allowed those golden opportunities to slip away as if they were quicksand.

This gentleman also said to me, that, "Lawrence needed a manager". The problem with his theory was that Lawrence, being a rebel, was unmanageable.

Many who knew Lawrence Grace will agree.

Earle Wentzell

Earl was the typical, none character. He was the status quo regular Joe, a *salt of the earth* individual, the type that never receives their fifteen minutes of fame. I consider it an honour to merit Earl worthy to be included in the halls of the hailed and mighty, and most certainly, worthy to be on my list of characters.

Earle was little different from dozens of other men from our community.

He was happily married with a sizable family, and like most, he had an inherited sense of accountability in supporting them, no matter the personal cost or consequences.

For example, in the early winter, usually a day or two after Christmas, Earle would pack his clothes in a knapsack and start walking. His direction and destination were towards his employer, the Mersey Paper Company, now known as Bowater Mersey.

The Mersey's woods operation was located some 30 miles away from his family and home in the Branch, reached only by traversing through a maze of dirt back-roads.

Three months later Earle would return to his home in the Branch, by the same method as he had left there…. walking. Today that sort of dedication to family responsibilities and personal behaviour might be considered obtuse, back then it was called responsibility.

Archibald Hebb

Archie, *as he was called*, was my grandfather on my mother's side. Archie was a hard working farmer for all his life but he was also something more, a rarity at the time, he was a businessman. Archie was fortunate enough to have acquired revenue to purchase and stockpile fertilizer for the crops and fields, which he in turn sold to his neighbouring farmers. Archie knew the importance of maintaining good relations with his bankers and bank employees and became quite infamous for delivering packages of fruit, vegetables, or chocolates to the pretty girl tellers at the Royal Bank of Canada on King Street whenever he went to Bridgewater. This annoyed his wife; my grandmother to no end, so much that one-day when a visitor to the Hebb farmhouse asked to see Archie, she told him that Archie was out in the pigpen.

Pointing her arm and finger towards where the pigpen was located, she detailed the following message to him; "Archie's the one with the hat on".

Like hundreds of others in the county, Archie was also a brewer of homemade beer.

His wife and the girls were away from the house one morning when one of his beer brews was coming to a head. The pressure of the hops and yeast and sugar and whatever else he had in it, had been working for days while sitting in the warmth behind the large iron kitchen stove. The fermenting juices had built up rapidly in the keg with a pressure that became too much for the wooden bung in the barrel to hold back. Archie either forgot or was too busy to remove his brew from its location behind the kitchen stove.

The keg of brew blew up!

When the inside pressure of the keg had finished spewing its contents over the entire kitchen floor it was several inches deep.

Archie was home alone at the time of the keg's eruption.

As this was not something that had ever happened before, Archie was not sure how to handle the situation. But knowing that something had to be done before his wife walked in and came upon this mess or all hell would surely break loose.

Doing what he thought was the quickest and best method to clean up his mess he wheeled sawdust and shavings into the kitchen from a pile that was stored near the barn. The pile of shavings and sawdust was intended for use in providing bedding for the animals during the winter. A good portion of them now laid spread unevenly over the floor of the Hebb's kitchen.

After the sawdust and shavings had absorbed the stench filled liquid, Archie was then able to shovel the beer soaked material into a wheelbarrow and carry it out of the kitchen.

The stench lasted long after the beer-laden sawdust and shavings were removed.

Archie continued to make his home brew his way, but because of this smelly incident he had to find a new location. From that day on all his brewing took place in the cool, rock walled, ground covered floor of the cellar.

I can remember visiting Archie's cellar as a child and being offered a taste of Archie's brew by my dad.

The taste was something that I won't easily forget.

Merle {Bull} Cook

Merle passed away only a few days ago. Over fifty family friends gathered to pay their respects to his family. A small vase contained his ashes. The burial scene took place at Hillside Cemetery, which is located near the upper end of the Branch community.

It was a number far greater than many would have expected.

Merle was once a huge man physically. Because of his acquiring only a limited amount of education, his physical prowess was his only means of supporting his lifestyle, mundane as it was.

Either from his own initiative or from necessity he rapidly acquired a street fighting mentality. With his size and roughhouse fighting ability Merle soon gained the nickname of Bull.

My brother Arthur performed the lay ministerial funeral service. He reminded those in attendance of the rough and tough lifestyle that Merle chose. He also reminded us about an accident that changed Merle's life. The accident happened some twenty years prior to this day and was so severe that it would have, without doubt, taken the life of a mere mortal. But being a big and strong man, Merle survived.

The accident was an unusual one. It happened during the unloading of saw logs from a truck. One of the larger logs hit the end of another log while it was rolling downward from off the loaded truck. The weight of the heavy log hit another log causing one end of the dropping log to pivot upwards, hitting Bull with catapult force. It impacted with Merles head squarely under his jaw.

His jaw and face were shattered and his eye was dislodged from its socket.

Bull was not expected to live and those that had visited him in the hospital, said, that if he did live he would be nothing more than a vegetable.

He survived, but barely, but his forceful fighting days ended abruptly.

From that moment on, he was only a shell of the man he once was.

Merle was much like the old Western gunfighters, the faster you were on the draw, the more times you had to prove it.

In Bulls case, his size was such that many locals needed to find out if they could lick {beat} him in a fight. Being big and strong he was always willing to accommodate and prove that he could take on the best. Sometimes he won, sometimes he lost, but as Arthur said, "he lived his life, his way".

Max Rafuse

Max came from a neighbouring farming community called Maplewood, located about twenty miles north of Branch LaHave.

Max was a tall, lanky, raw-boned fellow with muscles like steel, hardened from years of trucking, handling lumber and logs.

Max drank a lot of rum and he didn't like his brother-in-law too much, so after years of squabbling and fighting each other with their fists, this rowdy family situation finally escalated into a real live gun battle.

Max, unhappy, and wanting to settle a festering old score, took his truck and drove over to his relation's home. He began firing rifle shots, not to miss, but to shoot directly at and into his rival's house.

His brother in law obliged by returning the gunfire, and, eventually during the exchange of several shots, one of his rival's heavy gauge rifle slugs hit Max and Max went down with his leg blown apart and barely left dangling above his knee.

At the hospital the doctors advised Max that the leg needed to be removed to save his life.

"You may as well kill me now, if you plan to take my leg Do anything else, but do-not remove my leg".

The doctors complied and the leg eventually healed.

Max's soiled reputation soared even more from a threat he made and carried out while imbibing too much rum one evening at his favourite watering hole, the Bridgewater Elk's Club.

"I am going to hit the next son of a bitch that walks through that door", Max told his listeners, and eventually, a man, a small man, unwittingly opened the door that fateful evening, planning to enjoy a beverage or two with his friends, when unexpectedly, Max's hard fist hit him squarely on the side of the head.

The defenceless man never fully recovered from the blow and walked around the remainder of his life with the aid of a cane.

Max had a reputation of *playing chicken* when he was behind the wheel of big log truck out on the highway. He may have seen the chicken act preformed in a James Dean movie or maybe it was his own idea.

When he met a familiar looking car, driven by someone he didn't like, it was either the ditch or death for his car-driving foe.

Max had a highly publicized fight, performing before a highly publicized jam- packed crowd of over twelve hundred fight fans at the local Bridgewater Memorial Arena. This bout was the highpoint of Max's fighting career. His opponent was also a local celebrity that went by the name of Two Gun-Tex.

The fight lasted less than one round and Max was declared the winner, as Two-Gun Tex wilted before the long flailing arm swings of Max. Tex gave up without much of a fight.

It was the one and only professionally managed and sanctioned fight for either of them.

This overly supercharged Max bit off a bit more than he could chew when he picked a fight with a local professional fighter by the name of Bob Grace. Bob was much smaller and lighter than Max and Max figured that if he could lay a beating on the popular Grace his reputation would be even greater. He needed to prove to all his doubters that he could lay a whipping on a professional fighter.

Max was cunning and he chose what he thought to be the best location to attempt his coup.

The site he chose was in a local farm feed warehouse owned by Canada Packers.

Max figured that the narrow rows between the highly stacked piles of feed would not give the smaller but faster Grace any opportunity to move or escape his physical size and excess power.

Witnesses said it was one hell of a fight but Max finally came out on the short end of the brawl, as the smaller but quicker and more experienced Grace proved to be a lot more than Max had bargained for.

Grace believed that the bigger they came the harder they fell, and for this occasion he once again proved it.

Size counts but speed kills.

Bonnie and Clyde

Not that many years ago, maybe twenty-five, a Hatfield's and McCoy kind of wedding celebration took place at the local Branch LaHave Hall

"Rough and tumble" was how one attendant described it.
"It was a real hullabaloo", said another.

One would have had to be there, in person, to see it, as hearing about it second hand could never do it justice.

I missed seeing the action too as I had left the Branch many years prior, so I, like you, had to go by the memory and verbal accounts of others, in this case, my mom and my sister in law Elizabeth, {everyone calls her Betty,} who, because of her physical stature and bold nature, became a central figure in this seriously hilarious wedding celebration.

The event was to celebrate their union in matrimony with their family and friends from the Branch and from other near-by communities.

Getting together with family and friends at times like this was the in-thing to do then, as it is now. The result is what differs.

Folklore; being what it was and is, *this* incident was not too dissimilar to some of the 1960ish drive-in movie plots that most of us were accustomed to seeing at the drive in theatre over in Northfield.

The Lutheran minister in the Parish was Reverend Gustafson, who had earlier performed the Holy part of the wedding ceremony in the local church, St James Lutheran, which is located just up the road a stones throw, or two, from the village hall where the celebrations were to take place. Reverend Gus also attended the celebration as he was one who not only did God's work but he also liked food.

There had been some earlier dissent expressed by a brother of the bride, who was unhappy with her selection of a husband, so with a couple of like minded friends, he decided to see what could be done to undo the union between his sister and his disliked friend.

They gathered outside the closed and locked door of the hall, cussing and shouting and pushing against the heavy door causing it to move in and out from the force against it.

When the door could no longer hold back the pressure, it exploded open with the trio or more of rowdy fellows falling or stampeding into the one room hall.

Because of the upheaval and aftermath of the wedding party, the quietly married, but wildly celebrated couple soon became known locally as Bonnie and Clyde.

My mom described the event this way. "The bride and the groom had arrived and were happy and busy mingling with family members and the friends they had invited". "The wedding cake had been placed on a table near the hall's stage, and the couple had just left the reception area to go up on the stage area of the hall, where the groom was about to acknowledge their happiness and thanks, when all hell broke loose"

"The main doors to the hall flew open and several rowdy type males came rushing into the hall, like a pack of wolves from out of the hills"

Knowing that this unannounced and uninvited pack of hoodlums meant nothing but trouble, someone slipped out a side door and ran next door and called the RCMP.

Meanwhile back at the hall, Mom was conscious of the fact that there were no men amongst the guests physically fit to take on these intruders. That's when my sister in law stepped forward to confront the one who appeared to be the ringleader.

She gambled that they would not punch out a woman, even one as bold as she.

The two squared off face to face with their noses just about touching. "His fist was up in Betty's face but he did not hit her," Mom said.

"You're nothing but a whore," he shouted at the bride, as he sidestepped Betty, smashing the wedding cake with his fist as he continued on with his objective of disrupting the wedding and the wedding party.

As the noisy, intoxicated and fist swinging gang spread out to cause timidity and fear to the gathered quests, the groom, not liking what he was hearing and seeing, charged the leader from his advantage of being up on the stage above his invader.

"He came flying through the air," both my mom and my sister in law said, "and landed with a flying tackle on top of the mouthy chap".

Down on the floor and all around the hall bodies and wedding decorations went flying.

Trying to help the groom overcome his opponent, one guest swung a heavy wooden chair down over the lead hooligan's head with such force that it separated the seat of the chair from its legs and backrest.

"It looked just like a horse collar around his neck," my mother said, as the enraged attacker startled and wild eyed and still with the remains of the chair hanging around his neck, looked around for someone else to pummel.

The RCMP {Royal Canadian Mounted Police} who had been called immediately upon the invasion arrived in time to see that they had a real countrified riot to contend with.

In a loud and authoritive sounding voice, "You have thirty minutes to clean out this place". the lead constable advised all those in the hall. Every last person had to leave, as it was difficult if not impossible for the police to tell the invited guest s from the uninvited ones.

The armed RCMP officers waited around long enough to see that their instructions were adhered to before leaving the vicinity of the hall.

As rowdy as dances and parties can get, even in the country, nothing of this nature had ever happened before in the Branch, especially at a wedding reception.

It was just one more negative example on what can happen when alcohol and bad intentions get mixed together.

M B.K Anonymous.

Cowards die many times before their deaths, the valiant never taste death but once. Shakespeare

MBK came from this area and is a bit younger in age than I am.

I wasn't there when this incident took place but as MBK has never told me an untruth at anytime; I am including it "as the whole truth and nothing but the truth".

MBK had a good paying job; locals would refer to his job as an elite position.

His responsibilities to his employer required him to travel to many cities in Canada and the United States.

This incident happened in a place called New York City.

No one in the world, who can read or hear, doubts the magnitude of NYC.

It's The Big Apple

All dressed up in his best suit, shirt and tie and strutting along Fifth Avenue, anxious to get the job at hand done and move on to the next, when out of the blue MBK comes upon a scene that most of us have only seen on TV.

One man was apparently killing another man, this in full view of dozens or hundreds of other people who were also using the same sidewalk as MBK

I repeat the verbal term *killing* as MBK told me, "one man was stabbing another man with a large knife".

What would you do under these circumstances?

Would you be like countless others, who had just passed by the scene in their hurry to put the, "none of my business incident" behind you as soon as possible, to not get involved?

To New Yorkers it might seem commonplace. To MBK it was not.

But how commonplace can a scene as awful as this, be, even for crime hardened New Yorkers?

MBK didn't hesitate.

Without concern for his expensive dress clothes or for personal safety he jumped on the assailant wielding the knife, grabbed him from behind and wrestled him down and away from his intended victim.

This is not your common every day heroic act, it may not be even called a *sensible act* by anyone anywhere to attempt save a total stranger in a strange city?

Unheard of!!

MBK was required to make a statement to the city police but he urged them not to publicize any of his actions. It would make mighty good press and sound heroic to many, as it was, but it also might jeopardize his job.

That he would put his job, his personal safety, along with his family's future, in jeopardy in one unnecessary and thoughtless moment was not consistent with responsible decision-making or could it be accepted as prudent social behaviour.

Neither his family nor his employer knows of his, either dumb or courageous act, and that's the way MBK wants to keep it

Many times I have considered this incident and what decision I might have made under similar circumstances. I can only hope that I never meet with an altercation of this magnitude and be called upon to make a decision that MBK felt he had to make.

Chapter Nine

Pandora's Box

According to Greek mythology, to punish mankind for having learned the use of fire, the gods created the first woman, Pandora. Curiosity led her to open a box and thus let out all sorts of ills into the world, only hope remained.

When I began writing this book I had little thought of adding a character section. That just happened. But as my thoughts developed about individuals I knew that were different from the norm, I thought about several that lived in and around my home of Branch LaHave. Wilbert William Whynot Senior was one of them. He was a local man that definitely filled my bill for being a character.

What I failed to contemplate at the time was the fact that as I investigated deeper into his family history another story containing troubling information *emerged. Answers to my probing questions were getting disturbing answers in return.* I needed to know more *but in doing so was I about to open a Pandora's box.*

"There's some bad in all of us, there's some good in all of us" cwy

If verbal records have any credibility Wilbert William Whynot Sr. was a man abhorred by all that knew him. He was a fulcrum of all things bad and there was nothing of good character *that you could possibly think or say about him.*

Negative things, that Wilbert was accused of doing or being.

He was repulsive.
He refused to work, unless he could be the boss.

He was a source of annoyance and aggravation to all that walked near his dwelling.

He drank far more than he could afford.

Much of his subsistence came from his parents.

He blare-guarded, {a local term for swearing and blaspheming} in every conversation.

He fought physically with several of his neighbours.

He had no friends that anyone knew about.

No employer would hire him.

There were rumours of continual ill-use to his children and his wife.

The local detachment of the RCMP {Royal Canadian Mounted Police} detested him.

The local Bridgewater police hated him.

Just about everyone in the Branch feared him.

It appeared that even God wanted no part *of this family.*

Wilbert was an outcast from every local social event. He was the one person whom you did not want to associate with in public

When someone from the Branch *married, it was customary after the wedding to invite everyone from the community to a reception or celebration, to share their special day.*

When I married in 1956, I too wanted to invite everyone I knew to come to *my post wedding celebration, which my wife and I had both agreed would be held in the local community hall. But my wife Dolly said "no way" as she had heard about Wilbert previously, while living and growing up in Bridgewater, some seven miles away from Branch LaHave.*

It was evident that Wilbert's reputation had reach beyond the borders of the Branch.

She insisted that he not be invited. I relented. I didn't want to, but Wilbert's was the only person from the community excluded from receiving an invitation to attending my wedding celebration.

At the time of my being married, my personal experiences with Wilbert were not all that bad.

Years earlier, as a boy, I too was deathly afraid of him.

This had precipitated from the countless stories I had been told about his penchant for drinking, fighting and bad language.

It was well known that he drank the cheapest wine and whether that affected his mind or not, he would fight with has neighbours at the drop of a hat.

Just about everyone in the Branch considered Wilbert a threat and avoided him like the plague and that, I believe, *was the way he liked it.*

I attended school at the same time-period, as did several of the youngest Whynot boys, Glen, Lee and Wilbert Junior. The oldest child and only girl, Dora, and the two other sons, Douglas and Delbert had left school before my entering it.

As children we saw no difference in either their dress or behaviour from that of any of the other children attending school from the Branch. We were all kids, non-judgemental, doing what kids do together, playing and studying. It's a matter of fact that most of the bad behavioural problems while I attended school were not instigated by the Whynot boys, but by others.

It was only as I grew older and gained more confidence that I lost all of my physical fear of Wilbert. It was also the time I realize just how good I had it as a child.

The Whynot children had become an integral part of my life, from childhood to man, I guess that's why I feel strangely obligated to try and tell the story of their lives, a story that they were and are unable to tell.

It seemed, everyone knew; but nobody cared.

Was writing their story *a chance worth taking, or* was I about to open the proverbial Pandora's box, where nothing but bad would be found?

So, after nearly a lifetime *of conversations, of listening to opinions and here-say, of speaking to the remaining family members, by contacting and using local sources and information providers; even being told,* not to go there *by some who believed that the past should remain past and it would not be pleasant accounting for surviving family members to account or rehash an unpleasant collection of activities* long ago buried *deep in ageing and fading memories; here is what I found.*

*This portion of "**You should have been with me when I was alone**" is dedicated to the two surviving children and relatives of Wilbert William Whynot Sr.*

The word dysfunctional was not one used back in the days of my youth.

Had we known what it meant, we would have applied it to this family.

The family *of eleven, in total,* was made up of nine children: seven boys, one girl, their father and mother.

It's a tale of unimaginable abuse *and the untimely death of all but two of the entire family.*

Only the eldest daughter and the youngest son survived this nightmarish ordeal.

Here then, is more of their story, a story that is not easy to tell.

It is not easy for several reasons, one, being that there are few survivors left to relate the full and accurate account of how this family managed to survive without receiving any social intervention, assistance from the community, their extended family, or, from friends, *if they had any friends.*

The mother of all nine children died long before her normal span of years. *Her death certificate report said her demise was caused from birthing complications.*

It is from her sons, *the boys* that I once knew and went to school with that I have garnered my interpretation of the life and events of the Wilbert William Whynot Sr.family; events that I have seen, heard and known personally.

As stated earlier, the father, Wilbert Sr., was known as a *reprobate; that was the name the people of the area used for describing a very unsavoury individual.*

In Branch LaHave language, Wilbert was an out and out, no good person.

He never ceased in his use of profane language and he drank far more than he could afford or was good for him. He incited fights with neighbours and with people he barely knew... He never worked at any job that I know of, and he kept mostly to himself, the reason being, that just about every person living in the community considered him dangerous.

Strangely, of all the bad things that must be said about Wilbert's behaviour *and there were many,* I never heard anyone say that he had ever been accused of stealing anything from anybody and there had to be countless times when a crime of stealing foodstuff *may have been justified* in order to feed himself and his family.

Living *on a shoestring* wasn't unusual for many families in the Branch, but Wilbert's family's standard of living was far below that.

Perhaps the family allowance, an amount paid directly to the mother of the family, by the Canadian Federal government, along with whatever help was available from his parents, Amos and Clara, and was sufficient to render them a meagre existence.

The youngest boy, Wilbert Jr. is presently the lone surviving male of the family and he survived only by the compassion and actions of his aunt Mildred, sister of their father, who removed him from the family home when he was only a baby, and even with her good intentions and rapid removal from the home, Junior did not escape the stigmatism *that had been branded* upon the family by the people of the community.

We were told that he, Wilbert, the father, would *on occasion* stand *one or more* of the boys up by their garage and using a 22-calibre rifle would then see how close he could shoot at them without hitting them
Could it be true?
After *all the other things* that were seen and heard by neighbours *and others,* this extreme type of behaviour might be considered *normal for Wilbert.*
Maybe Wilbert Sr. had read about William Tell and *his* antics, but used a gun and his children instead of a bow, arrow, and apple, for an ancient but similar endeavour.

Physically, Wilbert was a tall skinny man with a razor thin face and he had big bony fists. I can personally attest to the size of his fists as he rubbed them under my nose several times on trips to town on Saturday nights while travelling on the back of Calvin Snyder's converted log truck.
On those trips to town, a distance of about seven miles, few *if any* adults would associate or converse with Wilbert, so he would come over and stand or sit by me, and then continue to relate to me stories about how he *beat people up.* He then proceeded to show me his large bony fists just to illustrate his point.
I was only about ten years old back then and even though I was uncomfortable sitting or standing beside him, listening to his bad language, seeing those large knuckled fists and hearing his threats about others, I personally cannot remember ever being *really* afraid of him.

It may sound crazy, but I think he liked me.
I found out the reason he sought me out, only years later.

The Young family, especially my grandfather Elvin, allowed Wilbert, who was vilified by all others, to come unto our property and cut small trees for firewood. This endeavour was to secure wood fuel for his stove and subsequent household warmth when there were no others that he could *turn to, to* ask or expect any help.

My older brother Arthur told me that he believed that Papa even hauled some wood out to Wilbert's house as there was no other means of getting the firewood to his home other than by carrying it out on his back.

Perhaps that is the reason he appeared to like me and as I grew older and was trusted with the family car, I would never pass by him without stopping and picking him up.

A strange but true thought. My grandfather being Wilbert's benefactor during his times of need was returned by a strange act of kindness to the grandson, his conversations with me. I didn't know it at the time but Wilbert was no threat to me.

But his family members had a far different story than mine.

The atrocities that his family lived with and experienced *every day,* from the day they were born until the day they died, was everything but friendly.

Family Members

Wilbert William Whynot Senior was born on October 15th 1895.
He married Evaline Jesse Wilkie in 1923. Evaline was 17 years old.

The **first child** born to Evaline and Wilbert was named Willis.
A small family Bible records that he was born August 31ST 1924.
Little is known about Willis except that he died as a young child, who, *is thought to be* buried, in the cemetery at LaHave, Lunenburg County. That's about twenty miles east of Branch LaHave.

The **second child**, a girl, was named Dora.

Dora was born March 13th 1926.She is now Dora Murphy.

Dora survived the family violence and at the age of eighty-three is the one person most qualified in providing me with accurate information on the shenanigans and abuse she was a principal and witness, both *during and after* the earlier years of her life.

The **third child, second son,** was named Douglas.

Douglas was born on May 11th 1928.

Being the oldest living son, Douglas had a better chance than succeeding siblings by finding a girl and getting married and moving away.

He married the former Irene Lohnes and consequently moved to Upper Northfield, the community home of his wife. Douglas and Irene had three boys, Chester, Milford and Mitchell. Mitchell died from injuries received after being hit by an automobile in 1971. He was sixteen years old.

Douglas was acknowledged by his friends and associates to be *a fine young man and was not* categorized by having any of the violent tendencies of his father.

In spite of getting away from the atrocities of his original home-place, he died of a gunshot wound while living at his new residence in Upper Northfield. His death took place early one morning where he was found dead still sitting on a chair at his kitchen table. He was dressed and his lunch box was packed. He *appeared to be* having an after breakfast cigarette and ready to go to work.

Douglas died in 1971 at the age of 43 years.

The RCMP called it a suicide.

Douglas is buried alongside his son Mitchell in the Upper Northfield cemetery

His younger brother Glen told me that *in his opinion* his older brother's death was not a suicide. After listening to his version of what he thought happened, I tended to believe him.

He said to me, *"No one* gets up in the morning and packs his lunch pail planning to go to work, then sits down to eat his breakfast and then all of a sudden, decides to kill himself, while still sitting at the breakfast table".

He also told me whom he thought did it.

The **forth child, third son** Dawson died at home, by fire, when his clothing was ignited from a spark *shooting out* from the kitchen stove. Dawson and Douglas were apparently playing around the stove and *were thought to be* poking a stick through the draft opening to the firebox, when, somehow, his clothing became ignited. Douglas was the only other person with Dawson in the kitchen at the time of the accident; their mother Evaline was upstairs.

A blanket was wrapped around Dawson in a vain attempt to save him.

Dawson was born April 10th. 1930, he died May 23rd. 1933 at the age of 3 years.

The **fifth** child, **forth son** Delbert, was born November 5th 1931.

Delbert was *a quiet, stay at home* type, having been blessed with a strong muscular body and a quiet disposition. Delbert had a reason for staying close to home. People from the community called him *cross-*eyed, as he had one eye that was not focused properly. Today, such a defect would be identified as a muscular problem and medically repairable if attended to in time. Without receiving any medical assistance he was doomed to a lifetime of disfigurement and visual impairment.

Back then you needed cash to pay for any medical services and many families had barely enough money to provide food, much less any extra money to pay for a doctor's services. Delbert's family was amongst them.

It was unofficially reported that Delbert died of choking while eating some food, a particle lodged in his throat cutting off his air supply. The word around the Branch was that he fell on his knife while eating dinner. A neighbour, who was delivering a meal {it was around Christmas time} to the home, had a far different opinion of what happened.

He said that while he was at the Whynot home he saw several police {RCMP} cars at the home when he arrived, he did not see Delbert, but he did see *a lot of blood* at the scene. If his account "of seeing *a lot of blood*" is true and I tend to believe that it is, would that not rule out the choking scenario? As *anything and everything bad* happening within this family unit was considered believable, meaning that someone else may have been involved in Delbert's death. The community wanted to believe the worst and possibly the wrong reason. But, then again, they may have been right.

I could attain no records confirming the date or the official reason for his death.

The **sixth** child, **fifth son** was named Glen Hugh Whynot.
Glen was born in 1934.
Glen carried with him many of the same characteristics, as did his vilified father.
He was physically lean and agile, and never one who walked away from a good fight.
Confronted daily, by the opinion of most people with whom he associated, that his father was *no good*, that he too was no good, he soon formed the same opinion of himself.

And so he lived emulating the same negative behaviour, as did his dad. He was lightening fast with his hands and had a beautiful long left hand jab that rivalled the legendary world champion boxer Sugar Ray Robinson.

He carried that very same artistry into his vocation of repairing shoes. Blessed with strong hands and agile fingers he could be considered a master repairman. Too bad that he could not manage himself as the owner of the repair shop where Glen worked told me once that he intended to turn the business over to his only employee, meaning Glen, upon his retirement.

But Glen failed to grasp this elusive truth, that he was better than good, he was great.

His employer knew it and on those occasions that I spoke with him, he also told me of the wayward side of his talented employee and of the many days Glen stayed away because he was too intoxicated to come into work.

Glen could never find the willpower to change what had been his long accepted destiny.

Glen's death came January 6th 1992 at the age of 57. He died from drowning in a well at the home of his daughter Doreen, either by accident or design.

According to the official death certificate {I did not see it} ruled his death a suicide.

On the evening of his death, Glen had apparently left the house, "going for a walk," according to his daughter Doreen. When Glen did not return to the house, one of the grandchildren aroused the adult members of the house that Papa was missing.

Searchers found him minutes later in the family well.

The RCMP was soon called and came to the home.

Glen's death was certified a suicide.

I visited the scene of where the family well once was some eighteen years after this incident. The well was covered over and its exact location had to be pointed out to me by Doreen.

In conversation with Wayne, Doreen's brother and son of Glen, Wayne throws a different light on *what might have happened* on the evening of his dad's death.

To counter the official report that Glen had *jumped* or *even fallen* into the well, Wayne told me; "At the time of dad's death there was a wooden box over the well with an opening hardly big enough for a man to pass through. The well was approximately six feet deep and was only three feet wide. The sidewalls were lined with *field type* stones and there was not a lot of water in the well. I heard the ambulance attendant report on the police radio, that dad was not dead but *in cardiac arrest*, meaning that dad was still alive while being transported from the well area to the Bridgewater hospital. When I visited my dad's body at the hospital the first thing I noticed was that there were no injury marks on his body other than a lump on his head. I found no scars on his hands that might have occurred in his falling *or jumping* into the well and thought it strange that if he was alive why he did not try to save himself. The well was narrow enough that he should have had some scars on his fingers because of trying to escape in the narrow well. I have my own thoughts on what happened that night".

Wayne also confided in me, that, "Dad was not liked by many people that knew him, he had some enemies. The RCMP had no love for dad as he gave them reasons *not to*, many times."

Another version of both Wilbert's and Glen's lives and their subsequent deaths come from Glen's estranged wife Evelyn.

It is a very negative one.

I garnered the following text and tale while searching for further information on the Wilbert William Whynot Sr. family story.

In doing so I was asked to contact Evelyn Keddy. Evelyn, who was once married to Wilbert's son Glen, had lived with Glen inside the Wilbert Whynot household for a number of years before moving away from the Branch.

If I and the residents of the community of Branch LaHave thought we knew the limits of Wilbert's treachery, of the family abuse, what having fear of another person really meant, we were wrong. This is a tale that can only be, in the words of Evelyn, hell on earth.

As difficult as it was for her to tell me about her sordid memories, here, in her own words, is what Evelyn told me.

"Glen and Wilbert were of the same mould. Both were God-awful.

Wilbert used to shoot his 22calibre rifle off inside the small two-story house.

He would shoot at anything. He once fired several shots up into and through the ceiling of the upstairs where I and another family member had fled. I don't know what saved us, as there were only a couple of straw filled mattresses up there that we used to sleep on.

The cops were afraid to come, when called there, because they were afraid that he would shoot them. He used to beat his wife and the children with the weights he found and then removed from the bottom of the pant legs of the army cadet uniform. These weights were metal balls interconnected by a wire that was placed there and sewn in by the manufacturer of the trousers. The metal weights were placed inside the bottom cuff of the pants to help them keep a highly sharp and visible press, maintaining a perpetual well-dressed look for every cadet. He, {Wilbert Sr.} was terribly abusive to his wife and children. He beat his wife Evaline shortly before she died, at about the time that she was near to giving birth to their ninth child. The baby died along with Evaline. He tried to commit suicide once and he was planning to blame his death on me. He had it all planned and prepared. He went upstairs and stood on a chair with a rope tied around his neck. He ran the rope down through the upstairs floor and the kitchen ceiling and attached it to a beam in the upstairs ceiling. He did it in a way, that when I opened the front door to enter the house, the chair would be dislodged out from under him, and he would be left hanging by his neck, upstairs. He even had a note written blaming his death on me, saying that I killed him. When I entered the house, dislodging the chair out from beneath him, I almost immediately found him hanging by his neck from the ceiling upstairs, I could not save him by lifting him myself, so I ran next door and got Jesse, the wife of Onie Whynot, to come over and help me. Between the two of us we were able to lift his body up, unhook him from the ceiling and save his life.

Wilbert tried to get me to go to bed with him, I would tell Glen about his actions, but he would put me off by telling me, *the old man's* only fooling around.

Glen stabbed me in the shoulder once with a knife, and I ended up in the hospital. The police came, took him, and locked him up, but I knew that throwing him in jail would only make him worse. I was in a coma for a week.

After being beaten black and blue once too often, I left him. The welfare took me in."

In speaking about Wilbert's behaviour, Evelyn said, "People thought that it was the wine that Wilbert drank that made him get crazy, actually it was potato beer, and he made it often".

Speaking again about her ex husband Glen, "I once started to make some notes on the abuse that I went through, but I never finished it. I was going to entitle it, Hell on Earth, as that was what I and the others in the whole family went through, *both they and I from Wilbert*, and *I alone* from Glen".

Glen's demise was not expected, nor was the way he died.

Even after all their troubles together, Glen would often call her by telephone.

He did so in the early evening on the day of his death. "He was sober when I spoke to him," she said. "I went to play Bingo, and when I returned home I heard that he had drowned".

"Both the Bridgewater police and the RCMP were all afraid of both Wilbert and Glen. The RCMP probably said, good riddance," she said.

You should have been there, with this family, when they were alone.

The **seventh** child, **sixth son**, Lee, was born April 23 1936.

Lee was about my age as I was born September 25th of the same year.

Lee was *a likable lad with the same inclinations* as any other boy his age. He was quiet, polite and *good-looking.*

He, like me, started to learn the art of boxing and he became quite proficient at it.

I was scheduled to meet him as an opponent in a *three round bout* at the local exhibition, which was held in September in Bridgewater.

It was his first fight before a large crowd. It was my second.

After the bout was over I was awarded the decision. I was happy to have received the winning nod but in retrospect the fight was close enough that it could have been called a draw. Even though the judges may have agreed that I had a slight edge in points it would not have hurt me and it would have given Lee a giant ego boost if the bout had been called equal with no winner or loser. After all, it was only his first public fight; why not give the kid a break.

I believe today, that the negative family history that he carried with him back then, through no fault of his, most likely was the reason I was given the winning decision.

He left home when he was young and joined the Canadian army.

According to a member of his family, Lee drank too much. I was told that Lee died of stomach cancer.

The family think that Lee died around the age of 50 at his home near Petawawa, Ontario, Canada.

The stress of being born into a home of abuse and poverty, of never ending family turmoil and strife collectively may have led to the premature ending of his life.

The eighth child; seventh son.

Wilbert William Whynot Jr. was not only the youngest and only surviving son, he also carried with him the heaviest burden of all the children, that of having the namesake of his father. Junior as he was called was born on February 19th 1838. He is still alive today at age 71 and resides in a local nursing home. He was married twice, his first marriage lasted 20 years, and his second marriage lasted only one year. He has one child, now 18 years old that he never sees and he has no knowledge of where he is. Both his wives are deceased.

Wilbert Jr. was the one and only child that had been removed from the original *hellhole* home by a concerned aunt Mildred, but even with the removal Junior never found total acceptance by society either.

On one of my visits to see Wilbert Jr. at the Mahone nursing home he told me that *had he not been removed* from the original home he would not have survived.

"It was Lee that took the brunt of my father's abuse. He would beat Lee with a limb off of an apple tree that grew out back of the house. He did this often; I don't know why he beat Lee so much" Wilbert Junior.

I asked him if he had any family pictures. "I used to have a picture of my mother but someone else has it now," he said. He could not tell me who had the picture.

The caring Aunt Mildred who rescued and isolated Wilbert Junior from the home of his abusive father when he was only a baby *over* protected him. Consequently, during his juvenile years Junior was never given freedom or ample opportunity to develop any self-reliance, thus failing in normal social growth and remained unable to participate in life's many positive endeavours. In his adult years Wilbert Jr. physical attacked and abused his aunt. Doctor Rowter of Bridgewater along with the Bridgewater town police was called to their residents numerous times to contend with and avert more serious situations.

Junior was a humorous fellow to talk with and he appeared to be totally harmless, but one day, with his past still gnawing and haunting him, he, *without malice* and without having the mental tools to differentiate between right and wrong, took a gun and shot an acquaintance in the stomach. "He taunted me and I shot him," he said.

Luckily for Junior, the wounded man did not die.

Junior never really seemed to understand that what he did was wrong. He had seen and heard too many family tales about abuse, to him there was no comprehension for either right or wrong, just surviving, the only way he knew how.

"I was sentenced two years in the Nova Scotia Hospital's schizophrenic section. It was better than going to the pen {meaning Penitentiary} I have never been crazy and I wasn't crazy when I shot him, but they had to do something with me," he said.

When did this litany of behaviour and abuse start and was it ever to stop?
Apparently, *it was not to be* during the lifetime of this family

The **mother** of these seven boys and one girl finally found escape and peace when both she and her baby succumbed during the birth of her **ninth and final child**.
Her death certificate records the cause of her death in March of 1939 as pulmonary oedema. Evaline was 31 years 3 months and 20 days old. There are no records to indicate the sex or a name for the baby.
"Wilbert beat her shortly before she died in the local hospital while attempting to give birth" A member of the family.

GOD; can **You**, *being a God of love,* ever forgive those of us who were there, were aware, knew *and stood by,* while the devil *and hell* was alive and active these many years in our home community of Branch LaHave, a devil disguised as a man concealed as a husband and father, in the person of Wilbert William Whynot Sr.? Can You?

Other information.
No pictures are available of family members or their home.
No official, on line, information could be found regarding the reasons for the family deaths other than the death of the mother Evaline.
A small black Bible was the only tangible article available for reference.

Additional family commentary.

"Wilbert would not work unless he could be boss He was cruel, we never had a good day, I never liked him very much. He beat me too, lots of times. I hit him so hard once with an ironing board that I broke a couple of his ribs, he never picked on me much after that.

When he had money he would go into town and return with as much as a gallon of wine.

He would place the bottle on a mat in the centre of the kitchen floor and drink until he got drunk. He sometimes made his own brew by using molasses. I am not sure what he put into it." Dora.

In checking with some friends who were more adept at making home brew than I was told me that home brew usually contained raisins and hops. Perhaps drinking too much of this unhealthy concoction was what caused Wilbert's violet behaviour.

"His second wife Frances left him fifteen times. She stayed with him for ten years and finally left him for good. I left home at the age of fifteen and went to work for Clyde Robar and his wife. I got paid five dollars a week" Dora.

"Wilbert was a doll; he would always give us a dollar when he visited us" Granddaughter Doreen.

"Amos and Clara supported Wilbert's family for the most part." Dora.

"We avoided him as much as we could." Sister-in-law Hazel.

"Delbert would have never have killed himself in that manner." Local citizens, after hearing the news that Delbert had fallen upon a knife cutting his throat while sitting at the kitchen table.

"It was horrible, I never would have survived if it had not been for my aunt and my grandparents taking me away." Wilbert Jr.

"My grandfather taught me a lesson once when I was drinking that I was not about to forget. I was supposed to milk the cows one evening when Amos was away. When he returned and found that I had not done so he took the ox whip and gave me several lashes over my back." Wilbert Junior.

Summary

After listening to these horrid stories from both neighbours and remaining family members I am more convinced than ever that Wilbert Whynot Sr. *was* the most detested man in Branch LaHave for all of his adult life.

If there is any good to be found in this story it is the sole comment by one of Wilbert's grandchildren, who said, "I still loved and adored him."

Except for the youngest son Wilbert Junior, who is now nearing the age of seventy, the original family of seven boys no longer exist.

Finding authentic documentation on their lives, and deaths, was almost impossible to secure. A search of the Provincial archives proved negative and the local funeral homes provide little information on either the father Wilbert Senior or on four of the deceased sons.

In my early quest for family information, the few remaining relatives had nothing tangible and little to offer other than from memory that would be helpful in my quest of establishing factual proof of family member's birth-dates, their ages and dates of death. I could find no family pictures or official written reasons for their demise.

Therefore, all qualifications to legitimacy, other than visiting the Provincial archives and finding records on two of the family members as well as being shown several notations that were hand written on two pages of a three by four inch family Bible, a Bible that is now in the possession of daughter Dora, I had no other resource. All other information is verbal.

An adjacent property owner has since purchased the house and narrow strip of land where the original Wilbert Sr. family once lived. He has removed the house.

The heirs, the grandchildren, have gone on to build constructive lives. They are to be congratulated. It must have been a difficult journey.

We are reminded of these words; "to really know why another person behaves the way he does, we must first walk a mile in his boots".

I do not pretend to have many answers on what caused the weird and inhuman behaviour that took place within the Whynot household, or why it was left to continue for so many years.

What I do know is this, *what happened to this family should not have happened.*

Today there are social agencies with governing laws formed to protect women and children against abusive husbands and father. Back then there were none.

The community of Branch LaHave did have what was known as a *local constable*, an ordinary untrained citizen that could, should an *incident* be reported to him, intercede when problems arose between local residents. Back then there were few rules and little intervention into divisive family matters, especially rumoured ones.

The local RCMP detachment, the local Bridgewater police along with a fledgling Social Service Department *must* have heard and seen enough telltale signs to have legitimate reason to intervene.

If so, this did not happen. There was no intervention from community individuals, from either Provincial or Federal Policing bodies, nor from any Social Agencies or authorities, or from the local church.

For that non-effort, everyone having knowledge of the situation should hang his or her head in shame.

I guess it was the same back then as it is now; it's easy to look the other way, to turn a blind eye to the problems of others.

In defence of the community of Branch LaHave it was made easy to turn away and present a blind eye to the plight of this hurting family because of the scorn *that was earned* by the husband and father Wilbert Sr.

The testimonies related here by the family survivors is without doubt only a small portion of the atrocities that were committed. The remaining victims can only remember *living through a hell* that was, by others, not recognized at the time,

The full measure of the daily pain and shame that comprised this family amounts to nothing less than an *unparalled* tragedy that *no one but they* can imagine.

I have always wondered what precipitated this father's negative behaviour. Why would Wilbert choose to subject himself and his family to such long-term abuse, and why did the citizens of the community and the county tolerate his behaviour for those too many years?

I said earlier, "Inside every bad person there is some good". This I discovered late in my prodding for bits and pieces of information that might assist me to complete this puzzle and help better understand the man, Wilbert William Whynot Sr...
It may surprise you, as it did me.

The small black Bible that is now in the possession of his only daughter Dora, was first given to her by her mother Evaline, Wilbert's wife, given to Evaline by Wilbert himself.
That inside, the front and back pages contained hand written memos, by Wilbert, of the birth dates of all his children and the times that they died, while he was still alive and able to keep such records.
One interesting finding was the spelling of his last name. Instead of the surname Whynot, Wilbert had written in Winett. Perhaps this simple misspelling was the reason I was unable to acquire proof that several of the family ever existed. Then again maybe Winett is the correct and original spelling. I never did find the time or opportunity to confirm this.

Also written inside, by hand was a line or two acknowledging the Bible as a gift from him to his wife Evaline. The Bible was probably given to her when they were married as it appeared to be in the family for many years, the cover and pages being well worn, indicating that it had been opened many times.

Who would have opened the Bible on so many occasions? I earlier told you that this home appeared to be abandoned by God. Perhaps I was wrong. My best guess is that it was Evaline, who in her moments of despair, of pleading and praying to God through His book for His mercy, for peace and love, for help that never came.

Was Wilbert driven by an unseen devil from his past to continue doing such evil and mischief?

Or, is it possible that Wilbert Sr. was also a victim of abuse himself? If the story, *as told to me*, by the only surviving son Wilbert Jr. has merit, and I believe it does, then there is strong indication that he, Wilbert Sr., may also have been dealt the same measure of corporal punishment *when he was a child* that he as a father, applied to his own children.

This story leaves little doubt that the heirs of this family were left holding an empty cup of inheritance.

But hope heals a wagon full of woes, and to those of this maligned family who have survived this **Pandora box** of hurt and rejection must be congratulated by evolving into a society that respects honest and upright citizens, thus assuring themselves a promising and positive future.

Perhaps this book will assure *that your perseverance for truth and justice* will not go unnoticed.

The dissecting of the *why* all this happened to one family would make for an interesting debate amongst *societal do-gooders* and possibly be subject matter for an interesting but controversial documentary.

I thank all those of the Whynot family who took the time to share their words and emotions with me.

I hope that I have done justice in telling their story.

YOU should have been there- *when they* were alone.

===

Chapter Ten

Faith Section

"Complexity is the enemy of simplicity"

As almost all Pastors or preachers expound upon the virtues or vices of the Holy Word {the Bible and the New Testament} with scholarly and trained minds, I have included what I think is an understandable sermon, one of several that I had the responsibility or opportunity to deliver to our church members, one each year, over a period of several years when our Pastor was on vacation I trust that this, my very first spiritual message, may enhance and enrich your life. I entitled I;

It's Just That Simple

May the words of my lips and the meditations of our hearts be acceptable to God our Heavenly Father; this we ask in the name of Jesus, A-men

As every one that attends this church can see, I am not your regular pastor, but for those who do not know me, my name is Caroll Young and as chairperson of our church council it became my responsibility to provide the message this morning.

To me it was an awesome task to attempt to fill our pastor's shoes at this lectern.

I have thought long and hard on what I would say; I trust that my message may be of some value to you.

Have you ever kept a secret, if so, for how long?

Keeping secrets is not easy, I found that out when I was preparing for what I would say here this morning.

First I started writing on the keyboard of my computer; the two handed, two-finger version, and after several days and probably three or four pages later I accidentally hit the wrong key and kaput there goes my sermon. I called in Kevin from KD Computer and after searching cyberspace and just about every other place, even Kevin could not find but two words of the several pages I had written. Was God sending me a message or was he giving you a blessing, sort of a reprieve?

Whatever the reason I got right back to my word processor and started a second time to prepare my text, my message, for today.

You see it was very important that word of what I was doing here today did not get out.
Many of you know me quite well. Some know that I play a lot of cards and do some fishing, mostly in Newfoundland. If my card playing and fishing friends along with a few others ever got wind that I was attempting to give a sermon, in church, every last one of them would be sitting here this morning, sitting right up here in the front pews, staring straight at me.

I have been told so many times that God will get me "really good" for some of the antics I pull, like doing just about anything short of cheating to win a card game or being accused of telling unbelievable Newfoundland fish tales, that, they say, God has finally caught up with me. God has got me.

Then again, for many of you who are here, had you known that our Pastor was away and left me to carry the message, you may have stayed home.

Kind of like a rock and a hard place.

So that is why I had to keep it a secret, so for better or worse, I am yours for the next 15 minutes, more or less.

For those listening in on radio, if you do not like what you are hearing, you have the power to turn me off.

I have prayed to God that I do not disappoint you who are here at St Paul's church or those who are listening in by way of radio.

Like that female handyman on TV says, my message today is entitled, *Its Just That Simple*.

I, like many of you, have occasions when we do not attend church for one reason or another, but for obvious reasons to me, I find that being in church on Sunday *morning is the place I need to be.*

It may have been a habit formed from our youth, it may be because we have married a church going spouse and come along to stop the hassle or just for the looks. It may be a ritual where we come and sit and be seen, while all the while we are quietly sitting here planning our next week's work or dreaming about some leisure activity we might like to be doing instead.

Some might even use church time as a time to catch up on a few lost winks when the preacher talks too long, on something in which you have little or no interest.

While we know that these scenarios are rare, they can and do happen. *While it has never happened to me* I can assure you that it has happened to others.

I miss attending church several times a year for one reason or another, like visiting a son who lives in another Province or other relatives who live in another town. Fishing takes me away a couple of Sundays and then there is always the unforeseen, like sickness or weather.

Did I mention fishing?

I always feel a bit guilty when I miss church. Perhaps you feel the same way.

I sincerely believe that going to church *is what God wants and expects* from all of His children.

Wasn't it a preacher who once said, *you need not do what I do; just do as I say. I guess we're all a bit like that.*

So why are you and I here in church today, and for those of you out there in radio land that are not, and are still listening in, *just why are you not in a church somewhere* today?

Remember the Sabbath Day and keep it Holy.

Were you too tired this morning to get out of bed? Is church going just a nuisance for you? Perhaps there are no churches that you feel comfortable attending? You say you do not like the minister or you do not like the way he preaches.

You're sure you cannot afford it and you do not have acceptable clothes to wear. Perhaps you are too busy catching up on other "just as important things" you never had chance to do during the week. You claim you do not have to be in a church to serve God, and that you are just as good or better than most of us hypocrites that do go to church on Sunday, then behave like the devil for the other 6 days. Or perhaps you went fishing.

You may think that you have a solid argument; but let's look at a few good reasons why church is not such a bad place for you and me and our family to be on every Sunday morning.

A hospital is for sick people, providing a place and opportunity to be healed when we have accidents or are sick, with doctors and nurses and specialized equipment, all there to help us get well again.

A church is much like a hospital.

It's a place to go for a sinner, to be healed and be made well again from sinfulness and according to the Bible, not one of us is without sin.

It's a place to go to experience the healing power of God through Christ.

Yes, we need physical healing that a hospital can provide but we also need to be spiritually healed, and in this church and other Christian churches, *Christ is the Doctor, Christ is the nurse, and Christ is on call 24 hours a day 7 days a week. He's here today, tomorrow and every day of every year of your life.*

Jesus said, *I am the good physician;* all that are laden with burdens too heavy to handle on your own, physical or spiritual, come unto me. If you are hurting, if you are sick, if you are tired and worn, I will give you rest. You, who feel helpless and hopeless, only come unto me, I will heal you, I will carry your burdens and I will give you peace.

Jesus does not care how you look, how you dress or how much or how little money you have.
Jesus wants you just as you are.

Come unto me and I will make you whole again. Sounds simple? Can anything be simpler?

Listen again to these words from Jesus.

Knock and the door shall be opened, seek and you will find. Sound simple? Too simple?

"I am the way the truth and the Life", says Christ. All you need to do is come.

When the winds of life blow you around and sometimes topple you, or when life's waves of loss and abandonment wash over you and you feel that you are going down for a third and final time, remember Jesus, remember what Jesus promised. *You always have me, I am your rock, and I will keep you safe. I will keep you secure. I was here in your beginning I am with you now.*

I will be with you until the end.

I will rescue you.

All you need do is ask.

Just how simple can it get?

Jesus is waiting. His door is always open.

Seek and you shall find.

Church doors are also open and you do not need to seek too hard. Just find one and walk in.

If you have not been to church for some time, now is as good a time as any to go to church. God has sent you invitations over the months and years. Perhaps you were too busy to notice.

He is sending you another invitation today. God will keep on inviting you as long as you have eyes to read and ears to listen to His calling.

So why are we in church today when we could be doing something else?

Every person on earth looks different, thinks differently, has different needs and desires and every last one of us acts and reacts, differently.

But as for many who come here to worship our God and Saviour, I come here to thank my God for my many blessings.

We come here to sing His praises through the hymns and psalms. We come to share our joys and each other's sorrows. We come here to pray and to share the Peace of Christ together. We come to listen and hear the living word that Christ died for us and to be reminded weekly why he died for you and me.

He chose to carry my sins, your sins, with him, and by the Grace of God, through Jesus Christ we have been set free of our sins.

My peace I give unto you, my peace I leave with you. Christ's promise to you and me. Do we need ask for anything more?

Through the Grace of Christ, from his dying and arising from the tomb_*gives me, and you, peace, courage, hope and power over sin and the grave.*

It's the greatest gift imaginable and it's free for everyone.

We churchgoers must never get too uppity-up or too smug about the promise of the Kingdom. It is not for us alone to claim, for the promise of Christ's Grace is available to everyone.

Christ reminds us that *the Kingdom of God is within us*, within every man, every woman and every child on this planet.

There is an old native saying that goes something like this_*never judge another person's behaviour until you have walked a mile in his or her moccasins.* That is still true today.

It is a reminder for all Christians to remain tolerant and thoughtful, not to be hasty to judge one another on *why we choose to go, or not to go to church.*

You and I have the same Grace given power over our own thoughts and actions.

We also have individual freedom of choice and freedom to different opinions.

For an example: I may like the earlier service, you may like the late service

I may prefer that stores be open on Sunday, you may prefer them to stay closed

Did you hear about so and so? Now how could he or she do such a thing, wear such things-say such a thing, even to think such a thing? Why I never could.

I always keep Sundays for sports and recreation, or I never watch sports on TV at anytime, especially on Sunday.

Some people want to remain single, while others want to remain married.

Dolly and I have 4 children; other couples may not want any children.

I said to my wife some years ago, "Wouldn't it be nice if we had 40 children?" She said, "That's ok by me, but why don't you have the next one?"

Enough said.

And so it goes. We have the God given ability to disagree and complain about others, *but we are wrong when we think we are right* about how God's other children must look, dress, behave, buy, sell, say or do, on Sunday or on any other day.

We seem quite aware of the sins and omissions of our brother and sisters, *but we fail to see the log in our own eye.*

In the first lesson today, we heard a story told by Nathan to David.

The story is told about a man who had been well blessed by the Lord. He had been given much prestige, power and riches. He was even made King.

Among his many riches was a great flock of sheep, but when it came to sharing one, just one of his lambs with a visitor, he used his great power and took the one and only lamb that a poor neighbour owned.

Now the story is a bit more complicated than that.

You see King David wanted Uriah's wife, the *only* wife of Uriah, whom Uriah dearly loved.

But David, who had many wives, coveted Uriah's wife and so to get Uriah out of the picture and to get Uriah's wife for himself, David sent Uriah off to war, to the front lines of the battle, where David was certain that Uriah would be killed, which he was.

He then took Uriah's wife, whom he had earlier made pregnant.

When Nathan told this story to King David he became enraged. "How could anyone do such an evil thing? *That man surely deserves to die*".

Are we like King David in the lesson today, who could not believe that Nathan was talking about him, when Nathan told him the story about the deceitful deeds that a man richly blessed by God had done to a poor man?

Are we like King David, never having quite enough, never being quite satisfied, always wanting a little more, when we are already richly blessed? In many ways *are we not like King David?*

If I leave you with any positive thoughts today, it would be for everyone who attend church regularly, to continue to do so, if not here at St Paul's in Bridgewater, try to attend a church of your choice.

If you do not attend a church regularly, or if you do not attend any church, anytime, that is your decision. If you have other places and other ways to thank and praise Christ and other ways serve God, continue to do so.

For those of us who do attend church regularly, it is not for you or me to judge our friends and neighbour who do not.

Let us first take a closer look at our own actions.

We are reminded of the teaching words of Jesus, who said, *He who is among you that is without sin, cast the first stone*, and again, *do not judge, that you be judged, and to love thy neighbour as thyself.*

We all have been allotted the same fate, to be born of woman, to be given a limited number of years to live and then to die.

But because of Jesus Christ, we, you and I, churchgoers, and non-churchgoers have been given a gift, a free gift from God, that gift being Christ and His Grace, and His promise of eternal life.

Christ said; my Grace is sufficient for you. Again; how simple can it be?

We have been baptized into Christ, believing in and accepting His saving Grace as the one simple act that forms the common bond of Christianity.
Loving our brothers and sisters in Christ is not that complicated.

The Kingdom of God is within you; seek and you shall find; knock and the door shall be opened.

It's just that simple.

A-men

Chapter Eleven

A letter to **God**

Without Malice

Dear God.

God, I need to speak with You.

I would like to have met You face to face, but I understand that no person shall look upon your face and live, so I thought the safest way to communicate with You would be to write you this letter instead.

I really need to know a few things and *I figured* that You were in a definitive position to know the correct answers.

I will try and be as respectful to You as I can possibly be, but God, it's hard to be nice and polite and courteous when you have so much on your mind, but I know You are quite forgiving and hope that You can *forgive me once again* if I stray too far over Your limitation of Godly tolerance.

To get to the point, just *what* in heavens name is going on in and around Your universe?

You must know what I mean? *You*'re supposed to know everything.

To say the least, I am getting kind of fed up with your *nonchalant* behaviour.

But first a more personal question, one that You might find quite trivial, You might call it *my* curiosity?

Over the course of my lifetime, my adult years at least, You have tried and tested me at least a dozen different times. What was Your purpose? What did You hope to accomplish?

You seemed to have it *in for me* more than usual.

Was I on Your most watched list, *were You* testing me, or, was I just someone *to toy around with* in Your spare time?

I am referring to those *mean things* you did to me *at least a dozen times or more*. You know what I'm talking about, those nasty incidents and accidents you sent my way. Why, *You* could have killed me.

If, You are upset at me over something I did, or didn't do, or said or didn't say, I am sincerely sorry? Isn't that good enough? And if You're still mad at me, *why* is your wrath so long-lasting?

It wouldn't be because You're getting older and more easily tired out and that You have less patience or a shorter tolerance fuse than when You were younger, *is it*?

Well let me remind You about a thing or two, like *if You forgot* or didn't already know?

My parents did their best they could with me, *mostly* to please *You*. The very first thing they did shortly after I was born, *they had me baptized*, next, to make sure I learned as much as I could about You, *they sent me off to Sunday school*. Then for *every sum*mer of my youth I was expected to go to vacation church school, *which I did*. On top of all that, *it was away to church every Sunday*, walking all the way, one mile there and back, *each way*.

When I entered my teen years I became one of Your *most loyal* members of Luther League. *That should have pleased You.*

As I grew older, got married, *in a church*, had children of my own, *all four being baptized*, and later they too were sent off to Sunday school. Why I even taught Sunday school for a couple of years. *That must have pleased You?*

And, like if that wasn't enough, I served You over these remaining years on several of Your Church councils.

I still speak well of You and continue to sing praises to You, *in*

Your choirs, as often and as best I can and I also do a variety of other related jobs in and around Your church. *Does that* not please You?

And if that still wasn't or isn't enough, I even joined and participated in just about every social betterment organization that was available to me in this area, every last one of them formed for the benefit and enhancement of *Your prized creation*, this earth and mankind.

Sure, I know that I'm still not even close to being perfect, and I do have some glaring weaknesses. It seems that I cannot seem to find legitimate excursuses, or the right time, or the proper words to say when I want or need to talk to You.

So, that's why I'm writing to You instead.

I have faith that You have received this letter and feel confident that I now have Your full attention, so I will continue.

I was taught that You are a jealous God and will not stand for any other God or God's *coming before You.*

Have I offended You in some way by putting You off in second or third place of importance from other aspects or activities in my life?

Sort of like keeping You on the back burner, using You only when You were needed, necessary or convenient?

I most certainly do not hold or bow down to any other God, but You, *as far as I know.*

Why I wouldn't even think of doing something like that.

I'm now near the end of my life's string, it's getting late and more difficult for me to find the energy *to change myself* or *other things*, just what else is it that I can do to please You? but please God, try and keep it simple.

I often feel like I'm a **yo-yo**, with You controlling the string.

Are You?

And, if You are, are You having fun.

To think that You are just *toying around* with me makes me disappointed and frustrated.

Only recently, I, as well as millions of other's, contributed, me, in my usual small way to help right a disastrous event, one so chaotic, that few humans, here on earth, can comprehend. We feel helpless to fix it. It's, so enormous that *only a God* can do anything worthwhile to make it better.

Again, You know what I am referring to. Its Haiti, that beautiful little God loving, God fearing country, containing millions of Your followers, which somehow and for some reason has suddenly and without warning, has been physically devastated.

I hope it wasn't anything You did to precipitate this awful catastrophe?"

I almost said God awful, forgive me"

I had the opportunity to visit Hatti once, some forty years ago. They, *Your people*, were poor and improvised back then, they are even worse off today. *Why are they still so poor*? *Where* have You been? *Do You not see* their sufferings and plight?

Or, are You too busy? Because if You are You can stop pulling on my string and get on with the *much more important tasks* at hand, like the business of averting disasters, like the works of saving souls, of healing wounds and easing suffering, of supporting the poor and feeding the hungry, and while Your there in Haiti why not start creating some much needed prosperity and happiness.

You have allowed *me to* live many times when I could have died – *Why*?

You have given *me* a great family, lots of friends, wealth and happiness beyond my expectations, Why *me*?

It was You who bestowed upon me the Grace of Christ and it is You who gives me *this freedom to express my innermost thoughts* and actions about You, to You.

So, if we still are friends, I now have several *really big* questions I'd like answered.

First, *Why have You spared me*, and second, *why have You taken the lives of so many innocent Haitians?*
And while You're doing that, why not start doing something substantial about ending war, crime, famine, fire, floods, earthquakes, hurricanes and tornados. And why 9 – 11, why Chile, why New Orleans's, why those tsunamis, and ...., well, *You* know? WHY?

This world, *Your* world, could use a bit more caring, sharing, tolerance, peace and love.
Is that too much to ask for?
There has to be a reason for Your malevolent behaviour.
I would like to know.
I feel I deserve a reply.
You must know that *You are needed here, now, right now, today* more than ever.

I must go now.
Anyways, I think I've asked enough questions for one letter.

Thank You for hearing me out.

I know that *I am no match for You* when it comes to playing **yo-yo.**

Hoping to hear from You soon.

I remain - Your servant.

Caroll Young

Chapter Twelve

SONGS & SONNET Section

Inspirational Songs

Try and visualize this scene; the sounds actions and reaction of Christ's second coming.

Hallelujah Day

When The Day has dawned, a New Jerusalem
Glory from on High, as the Heavens divide.
Every knee shall fall at the trumpets call.
Halleluiah to The King

Hallelujah, Hallelujah, Hallelujah, Hallelujah
Hallelujah, Hallelujah, Hallelujah to The King

Every voice shall sing, all creation ring
As the Saints arise joyous to the sky.
Joining Three in One, Father, Spirit, Son.
Life and love reborn, to reign.

Feel the Spirit soar, to Heaven's open door;
Life's vibrating wings rushing forth to cling
To the Saviour's Grace_Bonding Joy and Peace.
Hallelujah to The King.

Repeat Refrain

Every thought and deed, every footstep leads.
Every hurt is healed, every debt repealed.
Every pulse and beat hastening on to greet
Hallelujah to The King.

The Book of Life

Do you ever ponder long enough to think about what eternity means for you? Then, to say thanks, for the unparalleled and boundless power of God and infinite Grace of Jesus.

The Book of Life the Bible says
Records the name of all those saved.
Written down by a God of Grace
To endure through time and space
Of body, Spirit, man was formed
Was sent to earth, by woman born.

Refrain

Does the Book of Life contain your name?
Or are the lines obscured with sins dark stain.
God sent Christ with Grace for all
The Spirit only He recalls.
Does the Book of Life contain your name?

I had no right to grant my birth
I had no might to give me worth.
God's commandments tell it all
Too teach and guide me from the fall.
With mind and body, blood and soul;
to share His likeness with the world.
To make a temple for my God
The Spirit only He recalls.

From dust and breath mankind was made
Returns to dust in a mortal grave.
Burdens of my sins thus gone
My Spirit freed, returns to home
To find the page is filled with Grace,
The stains of sin have been erased.
The Book of Life can hold no blame,
The Book of Life contains my name.

Like seeds returned into the earth
Christ Jesus only gives rebirth.
God's promise truly is revealed.
For sin and death have been repealed.
Misdeed and debts have been removed
Christ's saving Grace will not exclude.
To live for God was pre ordained
The Book of life contains my name.

Jesus

Why, in God's plan, was it necessary to go to such extreme measures to convince mankind what immeasurable love means?

Jesus; Your birth announced by angel choirs.
Jesus; The Prophets named you as a child
Jesus; Your destiny was God approved
God loved this world and gave us you.

Refrain

Jesus; everlasting Friend
Jesus; defeated sin and death
Jesus; Saviour of us all
Jesus Christ, our Lord.

Jesus; God's promise true in human form
Jesus; Mary and Joseph's Promised Son
Jesus; you came to teach, to tell, to save
You are the Life, the Truth, and the Way.

Jesus; the generation's come and go
Jesus; two thousand years Your Glory grows
Jesus; Thy name sweet music to my soul
It helps and heals and makes me whole.

Jesus; was once a boy in Galilee
Jesus; was born to die, to set me free.
Messiah for the human race
To all who ask, receive God's Grace.

God Only knows

Stop, look and listen; then think; **behold the wonder of it all**.

God only knows how the earth and heavens were formed.
Why the baby Christ was born.
Sun and moon and stars and sky
Then gave His only Son to die
God Only knows.

What if there was no season called spring?
When earth awakens and songbirds sing.
What if the earth lay barren and bare?
In a world without love or laughter to share
No reason to smile, no reason to cry
No reason to live, no reason to die
No reason to work, no reason to play
No reason to hope, no reason to pray?
God Only knows

God Only knows
How the earth and heavens were made; why He gave His Son to save
Why He helps and heals and shows that love and life can be transposed.
God Only knows

Tell me your story-show me your way,
Give me your impulse that I do not stray.
Where is your rainbow, how shall I know
The lessons of life; what is the goal?
I need to know, I need to find, I need a reason, just give me a sign.
Where is your comfort, show me you care, a touch of your hand to know that you're near?
God Only knows.

God Only knows
The weakness of man, the lessons of sin,
of fallen angels, when Grace begins?
The reason for Christ, His Son justified
The reason for faith, the reason He died?
God Only knows

The promise was Christ for all man to share
The goodness of life, from a Father who cares.
A morning of glories never to cease
Grants life eternal for all that believes.
Just comes unto Christ, a Saviour for all, the promise of hope the promise of God.
The promise of life, the promise of love, the promise of Christ comes from above.
God Only knows.

God Only knows
Where and when and how and why, the earth and oceans, air and skies

Are here to share with us their might and with a Saviour Jesus Christ.

God Only knows, God Only knows.

Prince of Light

Be happy or sad, be humbled or awed, be thankful, be compassionate, and above all, believe in God, believe also in Christ, for He is the promise.

It started with a baby's birth
A saviour Christ was born on earth.
God loved so much the Bible says; the Chosen Son would light our way.
From boy to man the Word records God's saving Grace in human form.
Sent here that we could share and see His journey on to Calvary.

He taught us love He spoke of peace, to hurt no other, to turn our cheek.
He asked no glory He sought no fame; The cross He bore, our guilt and shame.
The sick He healed, the blind made see, the lame to run, the prisoner freed.
The weak made strong, the hungry filled, the tempest tamed, the waters stilled.

The course was set, it had to be. Jesus the Christ must die for me.
No other one, no other way; the Prophets and the Gospels say.
His blood was shed, the price was paid; our earthly sins have not enslaved.
The victor Christ, the risen Son, God's Grace complete for everyone.

Refrain

His name is Jesus, we call Him Love.
Sent here to guide us to heaven above.
We kneel before Thee Oh Prince of Might.
From Babe of Mary to Prince of Light

The Children of God

Sometimes we need to be reminded that it's not only the kids that are God's children.

When you read about
When you hear about
The children of God,
When you talk about
When you think about
The children of God,
Never lose sight that He's also your God
So let's all sing about
The friend we call Lord.

Jesus our Saviour,
Jesus our Friend,
You're here with us now,
You're here to the end.
We sing to Your Glory,
We cling to Your Grace,
That old-new love story,
We share in this place.

So, let's all read about
Let's all talk about,
The children of God,
Let us all think about
Let us all sing about

The children of God,
I will never lose sight that He's also my God
So join me and sing about The One I call Lord
Jesus my Saviour, Jesus my friend,
You're here with me now,
You're here to the end.
I sing to Your Glory,
I cling to Your Grace,
To that old-new love story
We share in this place.

Guardian Angel

Many of us want and need someone or something to protect us during our daily mundane activities, times when we think that God is too busy looking after more important tasks.

Guardian Angel, by my side
The times I fell, when fever swelled I could have died
You chose to save me, I know not why?
To share with me your heavenly gifts
Of life and love and tenderness.

Guardian Angel, Triune given
Silent Messenger from God
Gift of happiness from Heaven
My prayers are realized
For You have shared my life
To man from boy, a childlike joy
The blessing that You bring

Guardian Angel, gentle Friend
Always near to pick me up

Sooth my bruise and kiss my tears
What can I say or do
To show my thanks for You?
Once in a while this earthly child
Can be an Angel too.

Guardian Angel, Protector Being
Lending hand and welcome beacon
Guiding star that I was seeking.
You need to understand
I'm but a fragile man
So calm my breast and ease my breath
And slow my racing mind.

Guardian Angel, watch over me
From height and depth and cuts and scrapes
From deeds that harm and words of hate.
Grant me God's Peace and Love with grace to do.
Then set me free to go and be a Guardian Angel too.

Countrified Ballad Section

Every red-blooded country boy knows where ballads of this nature come from and exactly what they mean. "Nuff said"

Drinking Snow and Eating Crow

My life has been quite simple, the best in it, been free
But I'm not a fool, its natures rule; the birds, the bears, the bees
It's true that two together are as it's meant to be
So I'll drink snow and I'll eat crow if true love follows me.

Just once in every lifetime that one dream girl you find
She was so sweet I could not beat the hunger that was mine.

For this bit of heaven, the earth I'd move to have her notice me.
Yes, I'll drink snow and I'll eat crow if only she loved me.

The things I always wanted were things I could not have
Like candy as a baby and true love as a man.
Your love will make my life complete, for all the world to see.
Yes I'll drink snow and I'll eat crow as soon as you love me.

I will brave the coldest blizzard, walk on red-hot coals,
Go to jail; sleep on nails, to share this ring of gold.
On you its spell of magic will last eternally.
Yes I'll drink snow and I'll eat crow if you marry me.

I'll climb the highest mountain, swim the widest sea
The moon and stars, turn upside down, are offered you by me
To be in love forever as we were meant to be
Yes I'll drink snow and I'll eat crow now that you love me.

I have climbed the highest mountain; I have crossed the widest sea
The moon and stars that shine in your eyes were given you by me.
To share this love forever, together we will be.
Yes I've drunk snow and eaten crow, since you married me.
Yes true love followed me.

A Little While

A little while to hold your heart
A little smile to play the part
It's all I want, it's all I need
To fool myself, to just believe
That you're still mine, that there's still time
For just a little while your mine

Refrain

It's only make believe
I only am deceived – a little while

Sure I'm a fool to play the game
But aching hearts just love the pain
I've lots of time to hold you close
To fill my mind, then turn you loose.
No one will know heartaches don't show
A little while, that's all I loose.

You left for good, that's not all bad
There's other loves my thoughts have had.
I'll pick the one I'll choose the day
There's lots of time, you heard me say
My minds made up, why hesitate?
A little lifetime, that's all it takes.

A Working Man's Dream

He comes from the country on a Saturday night
To stroll along Main Street where the neon's are bright
Six days in the back hills a slugging it out
To slick shoes and a hair do for strutting about.

Refrain

It's a working man's dream just coming to town
Where hot lights and cold beer and foxes abound
It's a far different world in six miles he's seen
From old trucks and small bucks, to the working man's dream.

As a boy he was poor, but he didn't know it
As a man he had more but he didn't show it

The road that was his was long, hard and busy
The dream he still lives, never comes easy.

For fathers and sons and grandfathers before
A tradition of country the townies abhorred
With fierce pride and strong muscles
To prove he was right
For a girl with potential he was willing to fight.

Now most folk will tell you he's the salt of the land
His friends and his family are true to the man
He lives for the country
He'll die for it too
Please respect where he comes from, he's done it for you.

Two–Divided by Fools

When you're feeling lucky and right with the world
A man and a woman, a boy and a girl
As natural as nature, as true as the stars
As silly as putty we are.

Refrain

Two--divided by fools
Two-divided by me and you
Two-just pawns in life's game
Fools - Two of the same.

Remember as children going to school
We learned about life, the gold in the rule
Adding, subtraction, division and such
And two unto nothing doesn't leave much.

The choices we make and the promises we keep
The days that we long and the nights that we weep
When love hits the right spot we fall mighty hard
I know; I've been there before.

The odds are, were even, so who's there to say
We must have a reason for feeling this way?
If I had a chance for a change in my life,
Would I choose another man's wife?

Loves Lesson # 1

It's a story so old
To me it's brand new
It happened to me
It can happen to you
Of a drink and a quarrel
On a night with a moon
Left this guy on a barstool
With a glass full of gloom

Refrain

I glanced up; on the dance floor it's a dance that I longed for
And you're with another your eyes full of stars
My memory starts churning as your bodies keep turning
In time with the music, in rhythm with the night.

In your eyes there's a glow
You once had for me.
In your body motion that filled me with glee.
I turn my head and stop looking
My heart keeps on hurting

But this bar and this bottle
Will soon set me free.

So fellows and girls I've a message for you
When you're drinking and dancing
Stop playing the fool.
Pay attention to love
It's a mighty big scene
It can help you or hurt you, if you know what I mean.

Refrain

So pay attention to love,
It's a mighty big scene,
It can help you or hurt you,
It can heal you or steal you,
It can thrill you or kill you,
So please know what I mean.

Chapter Thirteen

Enlightenment

"Don't tell me there's no God" Don Cherry

*Were **You** there*, when I was alone?

Incident #1
Was it years of experience, skilfully honed driving ability, mental swiftness, definitive reasoning power, or, was it just plain old good luck, that guided me and that out of control, run-a-way, Diesel Motor Home to a safe stoppage, as, only by having perfect symmetry of mind-body and hand co-ordination working as a single entity, was a major accident averted.

"I swear to God, that I had never done anything like that before. So, the question arises, were **You** there, within me, guiding my every thought and action to the ideal solution"?

Incident #2
Why were those several *spindly* twigs protruding outward from the land bank of that swiftly flowing stream? Why were they located in the only place that I could reach them with my out-stretched arm with roots strong enough to hold my clutching hand and nearly floating body, giving me a chance to pull myself towards the safety of the shore?

Was all this in *your* preordained plan, made long before the earth and this riverbank was formed?

Incident #3
Where did that lonely pine branch come from, the one that served as my buoyancy and support when I was stranded alone, out on that lake of rotting ice?

Did *You* provide that limb for me to use in my time of need?

This one solitary limb must have broken free from some old large pine tree, falling down onto the ice covered lake, maybe weeks or even months before, then, by the force of wind was blown out over the ice covered lake, stopping at the exact place of my dilemma?

Hard to believe, isn't it?

Whatever, I know that I was very thankful to have been able to reach that one old pine limb. It served as my comforter and saving support in my time of peril.

Incident #4

What unseen force intervened to protect me from being hit with that errant bullet when it was accidentally discharged from the gun being carried by my companion?

It happened without forewarning as we walked alongside each other, the barrel of the gun carelessly pointed in my direction.

The bullet went whizzing directly across in front of me.

The saying, *an inch is as good as a mile* is true.

I will never forget what a big difference, a small distance can make.

Were You protecting me, my friend, or both of us?

Incident #5

What power stirred me from my sleep to suddenly being wide-awake and then to quickly move from the comfort of my mobile bed? The bed *or cot* was in the rear section of the Oldsmobile station wagon that we were driving. I had no sooner r seated myself alongside my youthful driver where I was able to alert him to an approaching and potentially perilous situation, one that he seemed oblivious to is difficult to understand.

Something alerted my subconscious, to suddenly awaken me.

Whatever it was, it had everything to do with me being in the right place at the right time to avert the loss of several lives.

Do You really have a universal plan, with power to fulfil it?

Incident #6

Was there an angel guarding over me that day on that dilapidated dock at Jubilee Lake in Newfoundland as I stumbled and tumbled down through those half sawn plank boards that once made up the docks supporting surface, my head hitting a large wooden log several feet below.

My loss of balance and subsequent fall happened so quickly that I was unable to react fast enough to save myself, my body landing amongst the timbers, my head hitting with a resounding thud.

Imbedded in that old weather-beaten timber was a long rusty spike, the pointed end protruding menacingly upwards.

After regaining my senses and my posture, I walked away from the dock with only a mild measure of embarrassment, but not before noticing that the distance between where my head had hit and the protruding spike was only four inches.

Four inches away from certain death.

I felt extremely lucky.

Maybe the word is *blessed.*

"Did I say thanks"?

Incident #7

How, in the name of heaven, did I survive that perilous automobile ride where I found myself sliding downhill with absolutely no control on an ice covered hill, moving at increasing speed, *backwards*, in the dark, avoiding being submerged in the deep and swift flowing waters at the base of the hill, then slide between two large steel entry supports of the bridge and sliding backwards another one hundred feet before finally stopping, and then, walking away from all this without so much as a scratch?

Saying "thanks" is getting repetitious.

It is also a pale repayment for delivering me *unharmed* from such an unbelievable journey.

Incident #8

Was it a miracle or good timing that saved me from being instantly crushed and killed by a large dark coloured sedan which suddenly without my seeing it, passed in front of me at a 90-degree angle, missing my vehicle by only inches, all because my truck and trailer were *also* indistinguishable to the driver of the sedan because of two-meter high snow banks and billowing snow obliterating the roadway.

I too was unable see the other vehicle as it sped along, coming in my direction.

The car swept past at considerable speed, missing me by inches, without the driver even seeing me.

The driver and passengers in the other vehicle will never know the difference that a split second made in their lives, and mine.

No explanation or apologies on my behalf for my lack of attention will suffice, nor can any reason be found to explain my confusion with Quebec's road system on that cold and windy winter morning. Had he/she hit me, it would have been one hundred percent my fault, but there is little consolation in admitting it.

In jest, I once wrote a letter to God {I never mailed it, but I am including it in this book} accusing God for using me as a yoyo. That last incident was about as close as I ever came to hitting bottom.

You made it a lot closer than I would have liked, in making me the author of my own demise, but again I emerged safely, without a scratch or a dent, only, a "My God" statement, an increased heartbeat and a deep breath or two of thankfulness.

"Please God, please, please don't try this one, ever again"

Incident #9

Miracles can and do happen, there can be no other explanation.

Without this incident, and the ensuing discovery of the silent killers that I carried around with me, there is no way on God's green earth that I or anyone else would have discovered and then followed up with a multiplicity of unbelievable events, starting with a major accident far from my home and ending with a multitude of angels ready and willing to save me.

"Sometimes it takes inexplicable events to understand the simplicity and perfection of God's plan for us".

But, was it really necessary to subject me to such a force-filled accident, such a myriad of complicated courses and subsequent events in order to alert others who would ultimately save my life?

Sometimes, some things, in life, are difficult to fathom out.

Or, maybe it's just that simple, all in a day's work, for God?

Incident #10

How did I walk away from this almost unbelievable and totally unimaginable incident with hardly a scratch?

This event *takes the cake* when we speak about surviving under the most bazaar circumstances.

Again, I emerged from this, once in *ten* lifetimes, accident, with no personal physical injuries other than a tiny scratch on my forehead. Events such as this can start you thinking seriously and eventually believing that some of us possess some *super human* survival power that in truth does not exist.

It also starts you thinking, when is this good luck or God's Grace going to run out?

Incident #11

Was it a flash of universal power or a beam of cosmic reasoning that enlighten my mind on that clear and sunny morning when I first became aware, and afterwards took such an unusual course of remedial action, thus averting a disaster of major proportions?

I do not know the question, much less the answer, all I know for sure, is that I, as well as others, could have been blown to smithereens?

Since the time that I was a young boy I was told, and believed, that, It is an *unforgivable sin* against God *to take away your own life*. Society calls such an action suicide.

That simple belief may have saved my life.

Confronted that morning with the mundane and usually simple act of removing a propane tank from a recreational vehicle, turned into *an everything but ordinary* event, when, upon arriving at my destination and discovering that one of the large thirty pound frontal tanks that had been located on the front framework of the RV I was towing, had fallen off. The friction of the tank been dragged along under the RV against the paved road surface had burned a gaping hole through the wall of the cylinder.

The highly explosive contents of the pressurized cylinder was now discharging a large and enveloping gas cloud that quickly surrounded the rear portion of my truck my trailer and me.

Because of the escalating danger, any controlling action had to be immediate, as the tiniest spark would have blown me and everything else in close proximity to kingdom come.

It was decision time.

It could have just as well been my doomsday.

I had to act fast.

One action was highly suicidal. Any alternative action results were unknown.

I was the only one that was near and cognisant of the mounting danger.

With the message "God will not forgive you" resounding in my heart and mind, I made one of the most important decisions in my life.

The whole truth and nothing but the truth; finally **revealed**.

The answer to my earlier question, "Were **You** there, *when* **I was alone**?" has to be a resounding, *yes*, because all other reasoning seems shallow at best.

To reinforce this statement;

A few months ago my wife Dolly and I were travelling *by car* on the Provincial 100 series highway going towards Halifax.

No conversation had passed between us for a minute or two, when suddenly, my wife alerted me by exclaiming, "Look what that car is doing"!

At about the same moment, I too had seen a vehicle pull out from the line of oncoming traffic, out into our lane. We were now headed on a collision course.

This section of the 103 is a *two-lane only* highway, and this vehicle had just crossed over into an oncoming traffic lane, my lane, with no indication of returning into its correct lane.

At the time, I was driving on cruise control at 100 kilometres per hour. The oncoming vehicle was probably travelling a like speed. We were only a few seconds away from a collision.

Instinctively, I steered my car to the right, but the oncoming vehicle, which now looked much larger than a standard sized car, was moving even further *toward his left, my right*, and appeared heading towards the shoulder and possibly off the road on my side of the highway.

As my wife and I were driving a smaller Toyota Camry and the oncoming vehicle was a much larger and heavier Ford Suburban, it looked like a no win, everybody looses situation, as it came ever nearer with no indication of altering speed or direction. It looked like as though a head on crash was evident.

I pulled the steering wheel of the Camry to my right while still travelling at 100 kilometres per hour, in cruise, attempting to move away from a direct frontal impact.

It looked like we might end up going off the road to avoid the Ford, but at 60 miles an hour that was also a difficult decision and possibly a disastrous manoeuvre, when out of nowhere an extra lane appeared before us, allowing enough road-space to steer the Camry further right. Even with this additional room and the speed we were moving, it did not appear that I was going fast enough to avoid getting hit by the oncoming car, it now seemed certain that we would either run off the road or be hit either head or side on.

As the large vehicle was now almost directly in front, our only chance of missing it, was to continue moving sideways, right, at about a 35-degree angle, and hope for the best.

As the massive looking vehicle passed by, we both thought that it was still going to impact the rear driver's side of our car.

It did not hit, missing us by inches.

Maintaining control of the Camry I was now able to slow my momentum.

Shocked at what nearly happened, but still in control, I returned to my lane of the 103.

I was and will remain eternally thankful for that extra lane of paved road surface that suddenly and un-expectantly appeared when it was needed most. The extra lane turned out to be an entrance onto the 103 from a secondary highway. It was constructed years previous in the exact location needed for our survival that day.

As the large red Ford passed by I watched its movements in my rear view mirror.

It travelled far enough along the wrong side of the highway behind me that its tires kicked up the dust and rocks on the roads shoulder, as the driver appeared to wake up, *or whatever*, and regained control of his errant vehicle.

"He's crossing the highway again," I stated, and as I watched, the red vehicle moved back across the highway, returning precariously back into its correct lane. The vehicle then pulled off the roadway and stopped.

"I'm going back" I said, "there's either something wrong with that vehicle, or else the driver needs help"

Turning around and going back less than a kilometre, I drove past and stopped in front of the Ford.

Walking up to the front passenger side I saw only one person, he was sitting *sober faced* behind the steering wheel. All four doors were locked.

I noticed that he was a man of senior years and that he appeared confused.

After knocking on the side window of his vehicle for a moment or two, he released the lock and I entered the late model vehicle and sat down on the passenger seat beside him.

He was sweating profusely, even though the air condition was running at maximum cold.

"Did you fall asleep back there?" I asked.

I received an unsure sounding "yes"

"What is that for?" I asked, looking at a white cloth that he was using to wipe away the large beads of sweat that were running down his face and neck. He then placed the cloth back inside a plastic bag. He did this several times as I was conversing with him.

"I use it to keep me awake," he said.

By this time my wife was also able to speak with him through an open driver's side window.

Dolly quickly assumed that he was having a diabetic attack and took the following action.

That morning I had done something that I rarely do; I had put a few small chocolate bars inside the car, just in case we got hungry with no place nearby to stop for a lunch.

Returning with one of the bars, she made sure that the gentleman ate some chocolate, because by now, she was certain that he was having a diabetic attack and he needed to get some sugar into his system to regain ample understanding.

It appeared to work.

Whether it was the sugar or the period of time that had elapsed since his misadventure, the man regained his composure and was able to answer several questions coherently.

I soon found out that he was driving a USA registered vehicle and that he had purchased and licensed it in the State of Florida.

His vocation had been with the Massachusetts State Hospital.

His new or temporary residence was somewhere in the Halifax Municipality and he was *driving down the shore* that morning to visit some friends.

As I started to relax and sit back in the leather seat of the Ford, I noticed directly above me a pewter medallion, attached to the Fords large sun-visor.

"Where did you get this?" I asked him.

"I *had* two of them, but one got lost," he answered.

The image engraved on the medallion was that of a cherub, *an angel with wings.* It contained the inscription, Guardian Angel.

"Well, you still have one left," I said to him, as I removed it from the visor and showed it to my wife.

After a phone call, friends of the gentleman agreed to come and meet him where he was parked along side the 103 Highway.

We left him in the protection of an RCMP officer.

What makes this story noteworthy?

Only moments before this incident, my wife Dolly and I had been conversing about the possibility and presence of angels, about out doubts an or our belief in them, to whether they existed or not, with the reality that back in Bridgewater, inside the town's cemetery, inscribed on our recently-purchased tombstone, you will find an engraved image of the very same cherubs, with the same words, Guardian Angel inscribed into the grey granite, *the very same words as those inscribed on this gentlemen's medallion.*

Go figure; "What are the chances, what are the implications of such a coincidence"

If I needed any further confirmation of a higher power watching over me, this was it.

By now you must think that I am either the biggest liar or the luckiest person hat you have ever read about.

I do have witnesses, after the fact, *in most cases,* that will confirm that "yes, it is true; all these incidents did take place". So, was it luck that I survived and able to tell you about them, or, was there something more involved? Consider this. While over the period of time that these series of life-threatening incidents were taking place, each one seemed to impact with a measure of danger greater than the one before. *My survival had to be more than luck.*

It was apparent that the level of my chance for survival diminished with each incident.

To exemplify:

Sliding down off the barn roof as a child in my first *close encounter* with disaster.

Consider the near miss of a bullet discharged from the rifle of a school chum. {Incident # 4}

How about that life saving twigs in incident # 2?

What element might have placed the large pine limb within my reach on that ice-covered lake? {Incident # 3}

Why did my *continuing dream* of *highways and truck's,* suddenly stop, never to return, after incident # 9?

How about the significance of the miraculous discovery of my melanoma moles? {Incident # 9}

What subconscious physical power was given me in incident # 1?

What caused me to awaken suddenly in incident #5?

Was it luck that saved me in incidents # 6 - 7 and 8?

It would be difficult replicating an incident like # 10?

Now try to imagine the deadly scenario of what could have happened, in # 11?

Why did I not only survive all of these *potentially fatal* incidents *but one* with hardly a scratch and the one incident that injured me was the impetus and reason for my being here today. Being saved from a serious physical condition that I carried within my body, one that remained undetected by doctors before the time of the incident?

Why me? I cannot answer. I suspect that there are others who are also *tested* in a myriad of ways, ways far different but no less significant than mine.

I cannot articulate for others having similar issues; I only know what happened to me has presented me with personal confusion and questions that have no answers.

===

As I mentioned earlier, some months ago I decided to write **a letter to God** *A first letter version* is exclusive to Chapter 11 As I did not hear from God, this is my second attempt at a similar but updated transmission.

Without Malice
Dear God;

Why did You not reply to my first letter I wrote to You? I waited around patiently and looked everywhere I could think of for a return message, but so far, no answer.

God, I still need to speak with You. As I stated in my first letter, I would liked to have met You face to face but after some sober second thought, *that* may not have been such a good idea, as I understand that *no person* has ever looked into your face and live to tell about it, so with discretion being the better part of valour, I thought the safest way to continue my communications with You would be to write this follow up letter instead.

I really do need to get those initial requests off my chest. I still need to find answers to my previous questions.

I will continue to be as respectful to You as I can possibly be, but God, it's hard to be nice and it's increasingly difficult to stay polite and courteous. Are you still busy, do You really have so much on your mind that You cannot answer one letter? That statement may seem a bit callous but I feel I know You well enough that I can be quite frank with You.

I hope that You remain forgiving and trust that You will grant me another blunder if I should happen to stray too far over Your limitation of Godly tolerance.

To reiterate the same points as in the first letter, what in heavens name is going on in and around Your universe?

You must know by now what I meant by my query as You had plenty of time to think it over; You're supposed to know everything.

To say the least I'm getting even more sick and tired, *and morally fed up* with such nonchalant and evasive behaviour.

Again I will repeat my original question, the one that You must have found it quite trivial as You never bothered to answer me. You probably credited it to *my* curiosity and hoped that I had forgotten about it or that I would just go away.

Not in a heartbeat

During the course of my lifetime, You have continually tried and tested me; first as a child, then into my adult years. What was the purpose of Your harassment, what exactly did You hope to accomplish?

You seemed to have it in for me *big time*.

Was I and am I on still on Your most watched list? Obviously, I must not be on Your *most wanted* list as You could have easily *done me in* at least a dozen times, You know very well what I am talking about, don't You.

Perhaps You needed someone to *just toy around* with in Your spare time.

I am referring to those nasty incidents and accidents that I have had, why, *You could have killed me* each and every time.

As I said in the previous letter, if it's something I did, or didn't do, that upset You, I am extremely sorry.

Isn't an apology good enough, and if You are still holding on to some kind of a God sized grudge against me, why, and why is Your wrath so long lasting?

I forgive You, now, how about You forgiving me?

Has Your *out of the ordinary* behaviour towards me grown even *more intense than before,* because of my previous letter, or, may-be You're finally running out of patience with me? I trust and hope that's not the case, is it?

If Your *tolerance fuse is* getting shorter I can understand that, You know, none of us are as young as we used to be.

Perhaps it's *the generation gap* we hear so much about that has grown wider between us. Remember, the times are continually changing and *we all must change* with them; *Oh, there I go again, I forgot,* God *never* changes.

Perhaps *it was* something my parents did or didn't do?

If so, let me again repeat and remind You, just to fill You in, like You didn't already know. My parents did the best they could with me, most of it to please You.

The very first thing they did, shortly after I was born was to have me baptized.

Next, they made sure I learned as much about You as possible *by sending me off* to Sunday school.

On top of that, during every summer of my youth, *it was off to vacation church school.*

Did I mention how far it was from our home to the church building, it meant walking *over* a mile, much of it *through the woods* and over a *sometimes* dangerous brook with dilapidated bridges. This happened *every* Sunday morning, both ways. Some days it rained, other days it was cold, wet and slippery, *but we had to be in church* no matter the weather conditions.

I would much rather have stayed in bed, or gone trout fishing, as I did read somewhere how You bonded well with fishermen.

As I grew older, I married a God fearing girl, *in a church*, fathered four great children; had all four of them baptized and as they grew older they *to were sent off* to attend Sunday school. Why I even taught Sunday school myself for a couple of years; that must have pleased You immensely.

And, like if all that wasn't enough, I even served Your church as a member of council for several terms.

That all took time and commitment and I was awfully busy back then, just trying to earn a living.

I still speak well of You and still sing Your praises in Your choir, and I still perform several other chores and activity *in and ar*ound Your church building, surely that pleases You.

And, as if that wasn't enough, I joined and participated in several local service organizations like the Jaycees, the Kinsmen and Luther League, every-one of them dedicated to the benefit and enhancement of Your most prized creation, *this earth* and mankind.

Sure, I know that I'm still far from perfect and I do have some glaring weaknesses. For starters, it seems that I cannot find *legitimate excuses*, or *the right time* or *the proper words* to use when I need to talk with You. I get so uptight when anyone asks me to speak about You. So that's why I'm writing You once again.

Our Pastor calls his conversations with You, praying, *and he's good at it.* I'm not such a good *pray-er*

I still have faith that You do receive my letters, that I still have Your attention and that You will eventually answer me, so I will continue.

I was taught and believe that You are a jealous God, a God that will not stand to have any other god coming *before You.* I am not to argue with You about that.

Than again, perhaps it's not me, but someone close to me that offended You. You know, You can't blame me for everything.

Or, am I still putting You off, keeping You in second or third place of importance to other aspects and activities in my life? Sort of *like keeping You there, just in case* I might need You. Yes, that seems more logical as a reason for our misunderstandings.

I most certainly do not bow down to any other gods, why would anyone do such a foolish thing?

I have now lived beyond *the allotted age* of three score and ten years and I realize that I must be getting near the end of my lifeline. I find it increasingly difficult to do the things I once did, *some of them* just to please You, so if there is anything left for me to do on Your behalf, *please* God, try and keep it simple.

When it comes to my ups and downs in life, including *my incidents,* I have often felt like a **yo-yo**, *with You controlling the string.*

Were you?

And if You were, or, are, *are You still having fun?*

Just thinking that about You makes me disappointed and frustrated.

Recently, I, as well as millions of others around the world contributed our hard earned dollars and energy towards helping right a disastrous event, one so chaotic, that few humans could comprehend. We felt so helpless trying to fix it. It was so enormous that only **a God** could do *anything worthwhile* to make it better.

Again, You know very well what I am referring to. It's Haiti, that beautiful little God loving, God fearing country, containing millions of Your followers. Why was it suddenly and without warning, socially and physically devastated?

I hope it wasn't anything You did to precipitate this awful catastrophe?

I almost said God awful, forgive me.

As I told You in my first letter, I had the opportunity to visit Haiti some forty years ago. They, *Your* people, were poor and improvised back then. They seem even worse off today. *Why* are they still so poor and neglected?

It appears to me that You are to busy to do anything to help them, because its been several months since that earthquake and flood hit Haiti an according to what I have read and heard since that time, nothing much has changed for the better. If You would only make a little extra time to helping Haiti by *stop playing **yo-y**o* with me, it would be appreciated.

After doing that, You might put Your attention to the business of averting disasters elsewhere. Try focusing more on saving lives, healing the sick and wounded, easing suffering, supporting the poor and feeding the hungry and eradicating the debilitating diseases of this world, and, if You ever decide to go to Haiti, why not create some much needed prosperity and happiness for those folk.

Earthquakes, volcanoes, wind and water are elements of Your creation, all of those forces *are beyond human control* and all are being used against men, woman, children, animals, birds and *yes*, destroying nature itself.

These violent storms have physically and emotionally laid to waste dozens of towns, cities and villages of this world, many containing Your followers; *what have they done* so awful that You had need of destroying their lives and their homeland?

Just *think of all the pain, sorrow and suffering* that has been wrought upon *Your* children

Do You have a reason or an excuse for such behaviour, such destruction?

May-be, with Your rationale You do not need one. *If that's the case* let me remind You of something else. Have You forgotten the reason why You created this earth *and all things in it*, in the first place?

Please, *I'm begging now, stop pulling on my string right now* and get back to doing what only God can do.

I sincerely believe that You can be much more effective by bringing some happiness and prosperity to bare; You might *even save a soul or two* by performing such good deeds.

Now comes that trivial question again, the one You haven't answered yet.

Why, on earth have you spared me when You had me so vulnerable, *right on Your fingertips*, so many times?

You allowed me to continue to live, to enjoy my life and my family. You gave me a host of true and trustworthy friends. You even blessed me by providing me with ample wealth and health. You have thrust upon me a measure of happiness far beyond my expectations.

What have I done to deserve such love?

I guess when all things are said and done, I should be thanking You, *not condemning* You

Was it not You who bestowed upon me the Grace of Christ and is it not You who gives me this freedom to express my innermost thoughts and actions *about You*, to You.

Maybe you are a God of compassion and love after all. And if that is true, this world, Your world, could use a bit more of Your caring, sharing, tolerance, peace *and love*. Is that too much to ask for or expect?

If You have the power *to make good things happen*, why not *start using that power* accordingly?

You know that good and positive actions are needed on earth, *here* and *now, right now, today*

You must have a good answer for all Your malevolent, and yes, Your nonchalant behaviour.

I think I *and everyone else* deserve an answer.

I hope I haven't taken too much of Your time and have not annoyed You further>

I know I am still no match for You when it comes to playing yo-yo.

Still hoping to hear from You.

I remain; *still,* You're patiently waiting servant
Caroll Young.

===

I cannot in all good consciousness continue to live or conclude my life with the belief that *our one and original God,* is a man, as many of earths faiths propose. My God is more likely to be, *a supreme universal power.* A *power that was here in the beginning* of time, *is here now,* and *will always be here, forever.*

As science delves into and explores further and deeper into the unknowns of our universe, it is obvious that there is *so much more* to discover in the *unlimitedness* of the sky above, around and beyond us. It will then *become apparent* that our universe goes on forever and ever, *just like we were told.*

We humans can merely imagine *on* the *wonder of it all.*

Perhaps, it's only the beginning.

I would like to conclude this book with the simplest of poems, one by Cecil Frances Alexander

All things bright and beautiful,
All creature's great and small,
All things wise and wonderful
The Lord God made them all.

Each little flower that opens,
Each little bird that sings,
He made their glowing colors,
He made their tiny wings.

He gave us eyes to see them,
And lips that we might tell
How great is God Almighty,
Who has made all things well.

In conclusion

I almost forgot - **my childhood prayer.**

Now I lay me down t sleep
I pray the Lord my soul to keep
If I should die before I wake
I pray the Lord my soul to take.
A-men

Finish every day and be done with it. You have done what you could. Some blunders and some absurdities no doubt crept in. *Tomorrow is a new day*; begin it well and serenely with too high a spirit to be cumbered with your old nonsense. *This day is all that is good and fair.* ***It is too dear, with all its hopes and invitations, to waste a moment on the yesterdays.*** {Ralph Waldo Emerson}

===================**CWY**===================

Would you like to see your manuscript become a book?

If you are interested in becoming a PublishAmerica author, please submit your manuscript for possible publication to us at:

acquisitions@publishamerica.com

You may also mail in your manuscript to:

PublishAmerica
PO Box 151
Frederick, MD 21705

We also offer free graphics for Children's Picture Books!

---

www.publishamerica.com

CPSIA information can be obtained at www.ICGtesting.com
Printed in the USA
BVOW07s1201040913

330215BV00002B/6/P

9 781456 066956